# THINKING PROTOCOLS for LEARNING

JANELLE WILLS

Solution Tree | Press

American version published in the United States by Solution Tree Press.

555 North Morton Street
Bloomington, IN 47404
800.733.6786 (toll free) / 812.336.7700
FAX: 812.336.7790

email: info@SolutionTree.com
SolutionTree.com

Printed in the United States of America

Library of Congress Cataloging-in-Publication Data

Names: Wills, Janelle, author.
Title: Thinking protocols for learning / Janelle Wills.
Description: Bloomington, IN : Solution Tree Press, 2021. | Includes bibliographical references and index.
Identifiers: LCCN 2020047348 (print) | LCCN 2020047349 (ebook) | ISBN 9781951075972 (paperback) | ISBN 9781951075989 (ebook)
Subjects: LCSH: Critical thinking--Study and teaching.
Classification: LCC LB1590.3 .W5425 2021 (print) | LCC LB1590.3 (ebook) | DDC 370.15/2--dc23
LC record available at https://lccn.loc.gov/2020047348
LC ebook record available at https://lccn.loc.gov/2020047349

---

**Solution Tree**
Jeffrey C. Jones, CEO
Edmund M. Ackerman, President

**Solution Tree Press**
*President and Publisher:* Douglas M. Rife
*Associate Publisher:* Sarah Payne-Mills
*Art Director:* Rian Anderson
*Managing Production Editor:* Kendra Slayton
*Copy Chief:* Jessi Finn
*Production Editor:* Alissa Voss
*Content Development Specialist:* Amy Rubenstein
*Copy Editor:* Jessi Finn
*Proofreader:* Mark Hain
*Text and Cover Designer:* Rian Anderson
*Editorial Assistants:* Sarah Ludwig and Elijah Oates

*Thinking Protocols for Learning* originally published in Australia by Hawker Brownlow Education

# ACKNOWLEDGMENTS

Just as it takes a village to raise a child, it seems that it takes a village to create a book. There are many people who have contributed to the final production of this book, and there are particular people who deserve special mention.

I would first like to thank my family and friends for their enduring love, patience, and moral support. Special thanks go to Nathan Wills, Valerie Wills, Hannah Wills, and Greg Hambrecht for providing so much encouragement along the way—they were my sounding board, a source of ideas, and even at times well-needed comic relief. My dear friend Barb Sinnamon never failed to be on hand to celebrate each milestone, push me on to the next, and laugh with me as I recounted my latest adventure or misadventure.

I would also like to acknowledge the team at Hawker Brownlow Education and the incredibly talented Olivia Tolich. Olivia was an absolute godsend—she kept me on track with schedules and provided exceptionally constructive feedback and advice. Writing isn't something that I particularly enjoy, but Olivia somehow made the process positive and—believe it or not—enjoyable.

This book is a compilation of many ideas and strategies that I have used or developed over a very long career. There are so many brilliant educators who have inspired my work—Robert Sternberg, Robin Fogarty, Eric Jensen, Robert Marzano, Tammy Heflebower, Bruce Wellman, Laura Lipton, and Art Costa, just to name a few. For many years, I have also been fortunate to work alongside inspiring Australian colleagues who have supported and encouraged me throughout the journey, including Tony Ryan, Gavin Grift, Colin Sloper, and Joanne Casey.

Finally, I would like to acknowledge the many educators who I have been able to work with from schools across Australia. As I have shared ideas and strategies, I have also learned so much from so many. Thank you to the dedicated teachers who have been open to trialing these ideas and willing to share their insights and practical application. Each and every one of you makes a difference every day!

This book is dedicated to my wonderful children,
Nathan and Hannah Wills, of whom I am very proud.

# TABLE OF CONTENTS

# ABOUT THE AUTHOR

**Dr. Janelle Wills** is the lead training associate for High Reliability Schools™, the New Art and Science of Teaching, and other Marzano Resources topics. She works extensively with schools, regions, and systems throughout Australia.

With over thirty years of teaching and leadership experience, Dr. Wills maintains a strong commitment to continued learning that enables her to remain both informed and innovative in her approach. Throughout her career, she has been adept at linking theory with practice, resulting in the development of significant initiatives both within schools and at a sector level. Dr. Wills firmly believes in the importance of teaching as a profession and fervently promotes the need for teachers to actively engage with research through action research and reflective practice.

Dr. Wills's PhD thesis focused on self-efficacy and contributed to multiple fields of knowledge, including special education, gifted education, assessment, and feedback.

To book Janelle Wills for professional development, contact pd@SolutionTree.com.

# INTRODUCTION

Why do we have schools? In these modern times, do we really need them?

In a world where access to information is readily available, where it is possible to watch YouTube clips to learn anything from basic mathematics to the complexity of changing a head gasket in a car, or listen to thought leaders via TED talks or take virtual field trips of art galleries and museums throughout the world, where learning opportunities are everywhere . . . are schools still needed? This question probably causes most educators to almost audibly gasp. But if the answer to the question is simply, "Of course we need schools. This is where students learn. It is where they learn all aspects of the curriculum and where they learn to socialize," we have fallen short.

In an evolving world, the notion that schools are purely places of learning is not enough. Rather, acclaimed theorist and thought provocateur Gert Biesta (in Nielsen, 2015) puts forward the case that "the point of education is not that children/young people learn, but that they learn something, that they learn this for a reason, and that they learn it from someone" (16:10). In other words, education is about three core elements: (1) content, (2) purpose, and (3) relationships. Purpose, according to Biesta, is multidimensional and has three domains: (1) qualification, (2) socialization, and (3) subjectification. The qualification domain encompasses knowledge, skills, and dispositions. The socialization domain involves teaching students about tradition, practices, and ways of doing things and engaging socially and culturally. In such a way, the process of education itself changes the person. Finally, subjectification is the formation of the person, producing people who can think and feel for themselves and take responsibility, in contrast to the creation of what Biesta refers to as obedient robots (Nielsen, 2015). A simplified version of the integration of the three domains is captured in figure I.1 (page 2).

Rupert Wegerif (2017) maintains that knowledge, or *subject matter* as Biesta refers to it in figure I.1, is only the dialogue so far. He suggests that knowledge as it is taught in schools consists only of answers that have been given to questions that have already been raised. Therefore:

> ***Teaching knowledge not as finished and final but as the story of this dialogue leaves a space for the learners to enter into knowledge as an ongoing dialogue in which they themselves are able to ask further questions and find further answers. In this way anything and everything can be taught as an invitation to join a dialogue and so as an invitation to think. (Wegerif, 2017)***

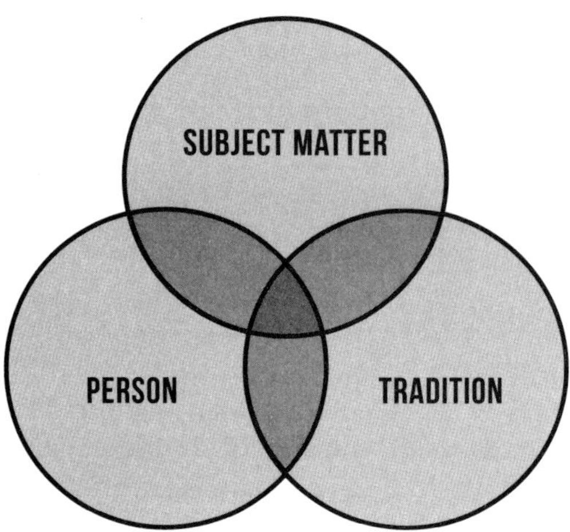


Source: Adapted from Nielsen, 2015.

**Figure I.1: Three purpose domains of education.**

Susan Brookhart (2011) takes a similar stance, pointing out that even simple knowledge rests on historical higher-order thinking, as our predecessors discussed and considered the reasonableness and plausibility of what counts as truth. She maintains that when we are engaging students in these thinking processes, we are not teaching skills for life in our 21st century but rather teaching students to be human!

So, the answer to the question of whether schools are still relevant is a resounding yes! And I would argue they are even more relevant today as students grapple with the complexities and challenges of an ever-changing world. But we need to really consider the full purpose of education within our schools. Education is about producing not sausage factory–like clones but thinking and feeling individuals who are able to adapt, interact, persevere, act ethically, and, most importantly, think! And by this, I don't mean students who "group think," which is often witnessed in a world of social media and instant connectivity, but instead students who can think and reason for themselves, ask questions, and find further answers. In other words, schools are still relevant if they are communities of learners thinking and wondering together, where everyone (teachers and students alike) learns from and with one another. Communities of learners where critical and creative thinking is promoted alongside dispositions such as commitment and perseverance, relational skills, and the development of ethical intelligence.

Thinking skills (such as creative and critical thinking and problem solving) and relational skills (such as teamwork and collaboration) are not innate. They must be explicitly taught. Extensive research clearly shows that simply exposing students to tasks that require thinking does not on its own have a significant impact on students' thinking abilities (Costa, 2001c). Rather, the skills must be taught through modeling, guided practice, and explicit instruction (Beyer, 2001b). The investment in time is well worth the effort. Steve Higgins, Elaine Hall, Viv Baumfield, David Moseley, and colleagues (2005) conducted a meta-analysis of thinking-skills interventions on student cognition, achievement, and attitudes. They specifically evaluated the impact of programs that required learners to articulate and evaluate specific learning approaches and instruction in specific cognitive, and related affective or conative, processes. The results showed effect sizes of:

- 0.62 on cognitive outcomes (for example, verbal and nonverbal reasoning tests; an effect size of this degree translates to a percentile gain of twenty-four points)
- 0.62 on achievement of curricular outcomes (for example, reading, mathematics, and science tests)
- 1.44 on affective outcomes (attitudes and motivation)

These findings are very similar to the overall figure reported by Robert Marzano (1998) of 0.65 for interventions across the knowledge, cognitive, metacognitive, and self-system domains. Marzano also found that metacognitive interventions have a relatively greater impact. The metacognitive system is sometimes referred to as being responsible for executive control. Its primary function is monitoring, evaluating, and regulating the functioning of all other types of thinking. Not surprisingly, given the findings of the meta-analysis, Higgins and his colleagues (2005) concluded that thinking-skills programs and approaches are likely to improve students' learning and that their use in schools should therefore be supported.

Clearly, the notion of explicitly teaching thinking skills is not a new concept. Indeed, the importance of explicitly teaching thinking, particularly critical- and creative-thinking skills, dates back to Plato and Aristotle. It is Aristotle who is regularly quoted as advising us that "the mark of an educated mind is to be able to entertain a thought without accepting it" (as cited in Bennion, 1959, p. 52). Later, Jean Piaget (as cited in Duckworth, 1964) asserted that:

> ***the principle goal of education in the schools should be creating men and women who are capable of doing new things, not simply repeating what other generations have done; men and women who are creative, inventive and discoverers, who can be critical and verify, and not accept, everything they are offered. (p. 499)***

In more recent times, however, the explicit teaching of thinking skills has been at risk of being overshadowed by an overemphasis on standardized test scores and the pursuit of evidence of learning outcomes and higher effect sizes. On top of those challenges and the pressure to perform, "the widespread, unquestioned acceptance of educational fads, coupled with the overcrowding of the primary curriculum through the unreasonable shifting of expanding social responsibilities to schools, has created an untenable situation" (Dinham, 2016, p. 61). With the pressure to raise test scores coupled with time constraints caused by the burden of covering the content of an overcrowded curriculum, time spent on explicitly teaching creative- and critical-thinking skills is at risk of becoming viewed as a luxury item rather than a necessity. Teachers continually lament that they don't have time to cover the curriculum let alone explicitly teach thinking skills. Yet, it is these very skills that students require to navigate the complexities of a rapidly changing world and maximize the opportunities presented by technological advancements.

The explicit teaching of thinking skills should be viewed not as something extra or an afterthought but as an integral part of the curriculum. Research suggests that the most effective approaches involve teachers designing lessons where thinking skills and curriculum content are taught simultaneously:

> ***In this approach students are introduced explicitly to strategies for more skillful thinking and then prompted to use these strategies to think about the content they are learning. By putting an emphasis on higher order thinking into content instruction, deeper understanding is reported along with higher levels of student engagement. (Swartz & McGuiness, 2014, p. 17)***

Fortunately, the Partnership for 21st Century Learning (2015) recognizes thinking skills such as problem solving, creativity, teamwork, and communication within its Framework for 21st Century Learning, specifically within the framework's learning and innovation skills (critical thinking, communication, collaboration, and creativity), and endorses an integrated approach in line with research. This framework helps teachers "integrate skills into the teaching of key academic subjects" so that students master the skills, content knowledge, expertise, and literacies they need to succeed in work and in life (Partnership for 21st Century Learning, 2015). Critical thinking and creative thinking in the Framework for 21st Century Learning are seen to involve students' reasoning effectively, using systems thinking, making judgments and decisions, solving problems, thinking creatively, working creatively with others, and implementing innovations in all subject areas at school and in their lives beyond school (Partnership for 21st Century Learning, 2015). The key is to highlight these skills and explicitly teach them within the context of the curriculum content—not as an added extra but as an integral part of the learning process (Swartz & McGuiness, 2014).

Apart from thinking skills being an expectation of the curriculum, it appears that employers are demanding thinking skills from employees entering the workforce. To understand the economic and social conditions affecting young Americans now and into the future, the McKinsey Global Institute (2019) produced a report confirming:

> ***Workforce skills have been a growing concern in the United States for many years. Now new and higher-level skills are in demand, including not only digital skills but also critical thinking, creativity, and socioemotional skills. The skills needed in fast-growing STEM roles, in particular, are continuously evolving. The old model of front-loading education early in life needs to give way to lifelong learning. Training and education can no longer end when workers are in their twenties and carry them through the decades. (p. 17)***

More specifically, the *Future of Work in America* report presents the skills that human resources professionals believe will grow in importance for entry-level jobs in the near-future workplace (McKinsey Global Institute, 2019). Among the surveyed professionals, "the top responses were adaptability (62 percent), initiative (49 percent), critical thinking (49 percent), and creativity/innovation (46 percent)" (McKinsey Global Institute, 2019, p. 43). Also, the National Association of Colleges and Employers' (2020) *Job Outlook 2020* survey states:

> ***Beyond a relevant major for the position and a strong GPA, problem-solving skills and the ability to work as part of a team are the attributes employers most want to see on résumés. Ninety-one percent of employer respondents are seeking signs of a candidate's problem-solving skills, and 86 percent want proof of a candidate's ability to work as part of a team.***

An ongoing rate of innovation and automation in the economy is predicted to persist. The Organisation for Economic Co-operation and Development argues that "the increased rate of innovation across economies requires the workforce to possess both technical competence and what are termed 'generic skills'—problem-solving, creativity, teamwork and communication skills" (Toner, 2011, p. 8). It is essential that we equip our students with these vital life skills so that they can successfully navigate the challenges ahead.

Thus far, we have established that explicitly teaching thinking skills is important, that it is a curriculum expectation, and that employers want employees who can think critically and creatively and collaborate, but this also raises another question. When employers are asking for skills such as problem solving, critical and creative thinking, and teamwork, are these simply buzzwords or are they really what employers want? Can employers recognize creativity, for example, especially if they are a product of a more traditional school environment where such thinking wasn't valued or fostered? A quick online search of "creativity in the workplace" generates 88,800,000 results at the time of writing, with the first seven articles discussing the benefits of creativity but also the challenges of fostering and promoting it. Further, Matthew Crawford (2009) also argues that many of our so-called middle-class workers are not dealing with complex problems at work but instead a great deal of their work has been reduced to standardized operations. Andy Hargreaves (2010) suggests that the way we view work also needs to be transformed.

Perhaps it is time that we no longer simply justify the teaching of thinking skills as a response to calls from employer groups and for the world of work in the 21st century. The teaching of thinking skills has a much higher purpose. As we encourage students to question, explore multiple answers, consider multiple perspectives, and interrogate the ethics of a situation or application, we must understand that these skills are not just for the world of work but for the world! Hargreaves (2010) poses the following questions:

> ***Where in the 21st century skills agenda do we make sure that future business leaders will practice corporate integrity?***
>
> ***How can we be sure that our teachers will teach that torture is always wrong, even in the name of democracy?***
>
> ***Will attending to diversity just mean learning to get along with a range of others in the workplace, or will it also address the right of and necessity for different ethnic and religious groups to learn to live together?***
>
> ***How can we be sure that 21st century skills will equip young people to fight for environmental sustainability, the eradication of poverty, and greater quality of life and social equality? (p. 337)***

Given the importance of teaching thinking skills, it is a moral imperative that in this era of accountability, standardized testing, and obsession with input and output, we create the time and opportunities for greater dialogue, for students to see knowledge as information known so far rather than final, and for students to think and wonder, wonder and think, and consider ethical responses. In an interview with *Forbes*, Sir Ken Robinson reminds us that "there's really a lot more room for innovation in schools than people suspect. A lot of what goes on isn't required by law; it's more a function of habit and tradition and routine than anything else" (Berger, 2017). It's time to break with tradition, break habits, and break free of the "education revolution" that brought us standardized testing, standardized thinking, and the narrowing of the curriculum to what could be measured and calculated in effect sizes—to what is known so far. The time has come to recognize that we must live in a culture of *and-also* rather than *either-or*. That the teaching of thinking skills must be integrated, not an add-on or something that we do if we have time. In the mythical and idyllic school of the Dr. Seuss (1998) book *Hooray for Diffendoofer Day!*, when the students and teachers become anxious about upcoming standardized testing and the threat of school closure if the students don't perform, a very wise teacher responds thus:

> ***Don't fret!***
>
> ***You've learned the things you need***<br>
> ***To pass that test and many more—***<br>
> ***I'm certain you'll succeed.***
>
> ***We've taught you that the earth is round,***<br>
> ***That red and white make pink,***<br>
> ***And something else that matters more—***<br>
> ***We've taught you how to think. (p. 26)***

## WHY THINKING PROTOCOLS?

Thinking, as previously stated, does not occur in isolation. It is a dynamic and social process, and protocols are needed to keep it on track and focused. Although this book focuses on developing or promoting specific types of thinking, it also recognizes the importance of developing students' ability to collaborate and communicate as they participate in meaning-making dialogue. Throughout life, membership in groups is inevitable and pervasive, and it is not enough to simply think critically or creatively in isolation (Johnson & Johnson, 2017). Thinking is not a one-way street. For example, one must be able to formulate and communicate one's thoughts in a logical sequence, consider other points of view, and reflect on possible errors in reasoning. In many instances, it may be necessary to defend one's position in a reasoned and controlled manner. For dialogue to be meaningful, it is important that boundaries and parameters are set so that classroom conversations don't stall, deteriorate into negative dialogue, or waste valuable instructional time by not producing a meaningful outcome. It is also important that all voices have an opportunity to be heard and all group members learn through the process of negotiation, positive contribution, decision making, conflict resolution, and product development.

Typically, a protocol is defined as a system of rules that outlines how something is to be done. This book focuses on protocols that support and structure dialogue for meaning making and thinking. Providing protocols for students as they engage in dialogue creates the conditions for the dialogue to flow, much like the banks of a river allow water to flow. Although there may be rapids, the occasional breaking of the bank, and moments of stagnation, this is only temporary. Protocols allow for the conditions to be righted, for the participants to consider multiple perspectives, turn taking, and ways to deal with stagnated dialogue or indeed moments when rapids appear and the conversations become robust and tumultuous. The protocols do not work in isolation but can be combined depending on need and context. For example, the protocols around creating norms can be combined with protocols for generating and testing ideas. The protocols for grouping students can be combined with protocols for inferring.

The protocols within this book are intended for deliberate practice and intentional application—not just to be time fillers or isolated activities. It is important that teachers consider the specific type of thinking they are wanting to foster and the context in which that skill is to be applied and then choose and match protocols accordingly. Without such deliberate practice, the protocols will not be effective and transfer of the skill beyond the immediate learning episode will be limited.

## STRUCTURE OF THE BOOK

Teachers have struggled to find a resource that brings together strategies for teaching thinking skills, ideas for grouping students, and ways to promote a more collaborative classroom environment. This book is in response to that need, drawing on ideas and strategies from many different areas and authors. Chapters within the book combine research and theory as background and rationale along with strategies and practical examples. The practical examples provided are drawn from real-world experiences across a variety of contexts. They have been tried and tested over many years, either from my own teaching and leadership experience or by the many teachers with whom I have worked in a career spanning decades.

The focus of chapter 1 is metacognition—what it is and how it can be developed. Metacognition is both a skill for learning and a skill for life. When well developed, it can be considered the gift that just keeps on giving. Chapter 1 also looks at the importance of self-efficacy in the learning process and how to deal with what Marzano (2017) refers to as unproductive habits of mind.

Chapter 2 delves deeper into the importance of dialogue for meaning making. It outlines practical strategies for managing and forming groups, identifying group roles, and establishing norms along with specific strategies for group dialogue.

Chapter 3 begins with research and theory on the importance of critical thinking and the specific skills that need to be fostered and explicitly taught. Skills addressed include interpreting, evaluating, reasoning, questioning, and inferring. Thinking protocols are provided for each skill along with practical examples for application.

Chapter 4 focuses on creative thinking. It includes a section on creative-thinking myths before teasing out the notion of creative thinking in more detail. The chapter provides protocols for students to generate and apply new ideas in specific curriculum contexts, see existing situations in a new way, identify alternative explanations, and see or make new links to generate new and positive outcomes.

Chapter 5 addresses protocols for problem solving and problem posing while chapter 6 deals with the emerging but vital consideration of ethical thinking. Just because I can do something, is it the correct thing to do? Is this problem a problem that needs to be addressed? Is this the best solution to the problem ethically? What other problems are overlooked by society?

The book concludes with a final call to action. A call for a true education revolution, as opposed to the rhetoric that brought us standardized testing and standardized thinking—a revolution that promised so much but delivered so little. It's time to stop tinkering around the edges of a broken system, to move from pure accountability with an input-output mentality to an era of thinking! And to embrace, rather than run away from, all of the challenges that might entail. The status quo can no longer prevail. After all, as Rollo May (2009) challenged, "The opposite of courage is not cowardice . . . [It] is automaton conformity" (p. 225).

# CHAPTER 1

# METACOGNITION: THE GIFT THAT KEEPS ON GIVING

***You're on your own. And you know what you know. And you are the one who'll decide where to go.***

***—Dr. Seuss***

## WHAT IS METACOGNITION?

Metacognition, when fully developed, is the gift that keeps on giving. Metacognitive skills and behaviors are skills for learning but also for life. Students with metacognitive skills have been shown to learn and achieve at higher levels than their peers, which increases the likelihood of academic success (Baker, 2010; Darling-Hammond et al., 2008; Holyoak & Morrison, 2005; National Research Council, 2000). Since metacognition has a strong goal-setting and monitoring function, it is also a skill that is important for success in life. It is through metacognition that people set goals, plan for how they will achieve these goals, monitor how close they are to achieving their goals, and decide whether to persist with their current strategies and approaches or to try something different. These are essential skills for success in life.

The notion of a higher level of cognition, or metacognition, was first introduced by the developmental psychologist John Flavell in the mid-1970s. The literal meaning of the term is cognition about cognition (Fleming & Frith, 2014)—in other words, thinking about thinking. Originally, John Flavell and Ann Brown defined metacognition as knowledge about cognition and regulation of cognition (Baker, 2010). Arthur L. Costa (2001b) describes metacognition as "our ability to know what we know and what we don't know" (p. 51). In more specific terms, "the metacognitive system has been described by researchers and theorists as responsible for monitoring, evaluating, and regulating the functioning of all other types of thought" (Marzano & Kendall, 2007, p. 53). Since metacognition is the skill that regulates all other types of thinking, it is the starting point for this book on thinking protocols.

Metacognition involves two main areas: (1) metacognitive knowledge and (2) metacognitive regulation. Metacognitive knowledge is our awareness of our own thinking. It involves:

- **Awareness of knowledge—**Understanding what we know, don't know, and want to know
- **Awareness of thinking—**Understanding the task at hand and being able to identify the steps needed to solve the problem
- **Awareness of thinking strategies—**Understanding the different approaches that could be used to solve the problem successfully

Metacognitive regulation is the ability to manage our own thinking processes. It necessitates (Gregory & Kaufeldt, 2015):

- Planning a task thoughtfully—identifying the problem, deciding on a strategy, organizing our thoughts, and predicting a possible outcome
- Monitoring and regulating the effectiveness of the strategies that we have decided to use
- Assessing and evaluating the results against a specific criterion

Metacognition involves self-regulation of our cognitive efforts. This self-regulation is the process by which goals are realized, regardless of whether the goal is to maintain the present circumstances or to make something happen (Carver, Scheier, & Fulford, 2008). In the classroom, self-regulation is described as the degree to which students are actively involved in their own learning process (Risemberg & Zimmerman, 1992). It is the extent to which they contribute to learning goals and exercise control over accomplishing those goals (Schunk, 2001). Self-regulation incorporates behaviors such as:

- ***Attending to and concentrating on instructions***
- ***Organising, coding and rehearsing information to be remembered***
- ***Establishing a productive work environment***
- ***Using resources effectively***
- ***Holding positive beliefs about one's capabilities, the value of learning, the factors influencing learning and the anticipated outcomes of actions***
- ***Experiencing pride and satisfaction with one's efforts (Wills, 2012, p. 21)***

When students have strong self-regulatory behaviors, they tend to be more proactive and guided by personally set goals (Zimmerman, 2002). Consequently, they are more likely to succeed academically and be optimistic about their future. They are also more likely to tolerate frustration and persist regardless of the challenges they may face, or the hard work involved (Bauer & Baumeister, 2011). By developing these behaviors, we can help students address what Marzano (2017) refers to as unproductive habits of mind: "Unproductive habits of mind are those that hinder us from completing complex tasks" (p. 42). They include giving up as soon as something becomes difficult or when an answer to a solution or problem isn't obvious or will take an extended amount of time to reach. Fortunately, these unproductive habits of thinking can be counteracted by developing stronger metacognitive behaviors, which include self-regulatory behaviors.

## DEVELOPMENT OF METACOGNITIVE BEHAVIORS

Metacognition is developmental, beginning in the early years and maturing over time (Walsh & Sattes, 2011). Typically, inner language, a prerequisite of metacognition, begins around age five while the more formal thought processes of metacognition develop around age eleven (Costa, 2001b). Maturation also plays a role in metacognitive growth. The prefrontal cortex of the brain is the portion of the brain involved in executive function, which includes the metacognitive processes of planning and monitoring (Baker, 2010). The term *executive functioning* has its origins in both cognitive psychology and neuroscience. From the field of neuroscience, we know that the prefrontal cortex area of the brain is the last to develop, with full maturation not complete until late adolescence or early adulthood (Gregory & Kaufeldt, 2015). Multiple firsthand experiences are needed for executive function development to provide opportunities to practice and improve the skills. Developmental delays and lack of practice opportunities may explain why limitations in metacognitive functioning are still apparent in secondary school and even university students (Baker, 2010). This highlights the need to give more attention to providing these opportunities to practice and use metacognitive skills throughout all levels of the school curriculum.

There is clear consensus among researchers that metacognitive skills are modifiable and that they can be enhanced through direct instruction (Baker, 2010; Sternberg, Jarvin, & Grigorenko, 2011). However, Costa (2001b) warns that we need to teach metacognitive skills in a way that does not create an additional burden on the student's ability to attend to the task at hand. The following five strategies for enhancing metacognition are recommended by Costa (2001b). They can be applied at any grade level and across any domain of learning.

### 1. STRATEGY PLANNING

*Before* a learning activity, teachers take the time to develop and discuss strategies and steps for dealing with problems, rules to remember, and steps to follow. At this stage, Costa (2001b) recommends that teachers discuss time constraints, purposes, and conditions under which students are to operate so that students can keep these in mind as they work. They can then evaluate their performance afterward.

*During* the activity, teachers invite students to share their progress, thought processes, and perceptions of their own behavior. They ask students where they are up to, what pathway their thinking has taken, and what changes they might make. Such an approach also serves as a diagnostic tool for teachers to uncover possible errors in reasoning or misconceptions students might have and provides opportunities for more targeted assistance and feedback.

*After* the activity, teachers ask students to reflect on how well they adhered to the initial ground rules, whether they followed the instructions, and how effective their strategies were, and to think about more efficient strategies that could be applied in the future.

## 2. QUESTION GENERATING

The self-generation of questions facilitates understanding by encouraging students to "self-check" (Costa, 2001b). They may check, for example, if the concept makes sense to them or whether they can relate what they are learning to what they already know. Importantly, they must then decide what strategies to apply to improve their understanding. Costa (2001b) suggests that in this way, students become more self-aware and actively involved in the learning process as they take greater control.

Jackie Acree Walsh and Beth Dankert Sattes (2011) used student question prompts in a cycle of student learning and thinking to develop metacognitive behaviors. The cycle in figure 1.1 is an adaptation of their original cycle. The practical questions within the cycle are useful in guiding students' thinking and helping them to develop the inner language of metacognition. In implementing this strategy, as with any strategy within this book, teachers should adapt the questions according to their own contexts and the age of their students.

## 3. CONSCIOUS CHOOSING

Helping students to explore the consequences of their choices and decisions before and during the process of deciding helps to develop metacognition (Costa, 2001b). Being conscious of their choices helps students to understand the causal relationships among their choices, their actions, and the results achieved. Such an approach also helps students to become aware of the impact their behavior may have on others or the world around them. Costa (2001b) suggests that a statement such as "The noise you are making with your pencil is disturbing me" is more effective for metacognitive development than a command such as "Stop tapping your pencil!"

The notion of conscious choosing aligns with William Glasser's (1998) choice theory. Glasser suggests that all we do is behave and that almost all behavior is

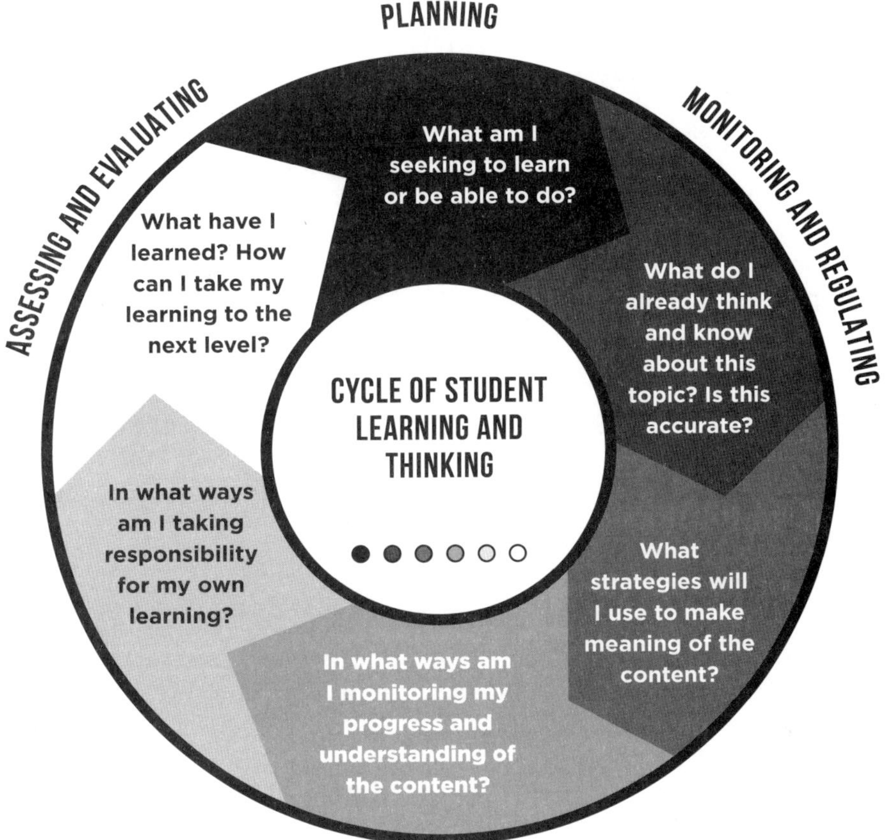


Source: Adapted from Walsh & Sattes, 2011, p. 8.

**Figure 1.1: Cycle of student learning and thinking.**

chosen. Our behaviors are a personal choice and are always within our control (Gregory & Kaufeldt, 2015). Helping students to realize that they have choices encourages them to accept personal responsibility for everything they do and understand that the only people whose behavior they can change are themselves (Glasser, 1998). Again, this is a very important mindset to develop as we prepare our students for their place in the world rather than just the world of work.

## 4. DIFFERENTIATED EVALUATING

This strategy also encourages students to be reflective by asking them to evaluate their actions based on two or more criteria. This might include what they liked or didn't like about an activity, what was positive about their behavior or what could be improved, or what the pluses or minuses of the group activity were. Students must also justify their responses.

## 5. MODELING

Costa (2001b) suggests modeling is one of the most effective strategies for developing metacognitive behaviors. He argues that students learn best by imitating significant adults around them and that teachers who openly demonstrate metacognition have a greater likelihood of developing students who are metacognitive. He suggests that teachers might:

- Share their planning by describing their goals and why they have chosen particular actions
- Make errors and then be seen to rectify the errors by getting back on track
- Admit that they may not know an answer and then discuss ways to find the answer
- Seek feedback on their actions from others
- Have a clearly stated value system and make decisions that are consistent with that value system
- Talk about their own strengths and weaknesses
- Demonstrate understanding and empathy by listening to and accurately describing the ideas and feelings of others

# METACOGNITION IN SPECIFIC ACADEMIC DOMAINS

Although some metacognitive skills are generic, others are more domain specific. A student may have high levels of metacognitive knowledge in reading, but that knowledge does not necessarily generalize to mathematics (Baker, 2010). This section focuses on reading, writing, and mathematics. Metacognitive skills in reading and writing will impact all literacy-based subject areas, including science, as students are required to read scientific texts.

## METACOGNITION IN READING AND WRITING

The goal or purpose of reading is always understanding. Proficient readers use their metacognitive skills to apply and adapt reading strategies to ensure the goal of understanding or meaning making is achieved. Stephanie Harvey and Anne Goudvis (2017) identify four phases of metacognitive knowledge in reading as readers move from less to more sophisticated ways of monitoring their strategy use and understanding.

1. **Tacit reading:** Readers do not have an awareness of how they think when they read.
2. **Aware reading:** Readers realize when meaning has been lost or they are confused, but they do not have enough reading strategies to address the problem.

3. **Strategic reading:** Readers use thinking and comprehension strategies, such as activating prior knowledge, questioning, inferring, visualizing, determining importance, summarizing, and synthesizing, to enhance understanding and acquire knowledge. They can monitor their understanding and apply reading strategies when meaning is lost.
4. **Reflective reading:** Readers are strategic about their thinking and can apply comprehension strategies flexibly depending on whether the purpose for reading is pleasure or learning. They can reflect on their thinking and revise their use of strategies.

As students move toward becoming the strategic, reflective readers described in the preceding list, they become increasingly more aware of their inner conversation and can quickly repair meaning if it is lost (Harvey & Goudvis, 2017). In this way, metacognitive knowledge becomes a process of comprehension monitoring. Rather than enhancing metacognition per se, the goal in reading instruction is to promote students' reading comprehension by increasing their metacognition. The research base for the effectiveness of such an approach is strong (Baker, 2010; Bruce & Robinson, 2002). One of the most successful strategies for increasing students' ability to monitor comprehension is reciprocal teaching, with effect sizes of 0.88 recorded (Marzano, 2017). An effect size can be used to indicate how much higher (or lower) the average score might be in a class where students use a particular strategy compared to a class where the strategy is not used (Marzano, 2007). An effect size of 0.88 is significant and translates to a percentile point gain of thirty-one (Marzano, 2009). This means that a class where the strategy of reciprocal teaching is being used may well outperform a class where it isn't being used by as many as thirty-one points on test scores.

Reciprocal teaching has been described as a dialogue between teachers and students for the purpose of jointly making meaning of text (Bruce & Robinson, 2002). The reciprocal-teaching strategies of predicting, clarifying, question generating, and summarizing are modeled by the teacher and then transferred to students as they gradually take on the role of teacher to lead discussions about a text (Palincsar & Brown, 1984). There are various approaches to the process of reciprocal teaching, but typically students are assigned one of the four strategies to apply when making meaning of a section of text. One student may take on the role of predicting, for example, predicting either what the purpose of the text might be or what might come next in the remaining sections of the text. Another student may take on the role of questioning as he or she makes connections to previous concepts learned or asks questions about what might be confusing or unclear. When all four strategy roles have been discussed, the roles are reassigned and a new section of text is read. In this way, students receive practice and feedback on each of the four strategies. Table 1.1 (page 16) shows the key words and thinking prompts that students might use as they engage with the process of reciprocal teaching.

Just as metacognition plays a role in the comprehension of text, it plays a role in the "production of text" (Baker, 2010, p. 207). Researchers have compared the

**Table 1.1: Reciprocal-Teaching Prompts**

| PREDICTING | QUESTIONING | CLARIFYING | SUMMARIZING |
| --- | --- | --- | --- |
| **Key words:** guess, infer, speculate | **Key words:** ask, examine, explore, inquire, evaluate, investigate | **Key words:** explain, define, monitor, refine, simplify | **Key words:** conclude, determine, review, synthesize |
| What have you already learned about this topic?<br>What is the purpose of this text? What is it trying to teach you or show you, and how can that help you work out what information might come next?<br>As you read the headings and titles and look at the pictures, can you predict what the text will discuss?<br>Explain the reasons for your predictions. Change your prediction if new information makes you think differently. | Ask questions using sentence stems that begin with who, what, where, why, when, and how.<br>What are the main ideas of the text?<br>What is confusing or unclear as you read the text?<br>How does what you are reading relate to what you are learning in class or to real life? | Are there any new terms or definitions? What do they mean?<br>Reread the text to gather more information.<br>Break down a complex idea into parts and examine each part individually.<br>Listen to your classmates' and teacher's ideas to refine your own understanding. Ask questions about what might seem unclear.<br>Draw a picture or diagram to map out a complex process or idea. | Determine the who, what, where, when, why, and how.<br>What is the most important information?<br>What do you think the author wants you to know?<br>How does what you have learned connect with what you already know?<br>Explain your conclusions about the topic. |

Source: From *Marzano Compendium of Instructional Strategies*. © 2016 by Marzano Resources, 555 North Morton Street, Bloomington, IN 47404, 800.733.6786, www.marzanoresources.com. All rights reserved. Used with permission.

differences in the metacognitive knowledge and control of "more-skilled and less-skilled writers" (Baker, 2010, p. 207). Typically, there are differences in "students' conceptions of writing and their knowledge of the writing process" (Baker, 2010, p. 207). For example, expert and novice writers will approach planning and revision processes differently. Experts are more likely to have overarching goals and will consider the best ways to communicate their message while revising at an overall level. In contrast, novice writers rarely have an overall plan and "revisions are typically made at a sentence-by-sentence level" (Baker, 2010, p. 207).

Writers who are metacognitively aware consider not only what they are trying to say but also the stages of the writing process. At each phase of writing—prewriting, writing (drafting or revising), and editing—the writer must consider four things.

1. What is the purpose (to inform, to entertain, to persuade)?
2. What do I know about what I am writing about? What do I need to research (to get my points across)?
3. What do I want to say about what I have learned?
4. Is my message coming across? Am I achieving my purpose? Is my writing clear and concise?

To increase students' metacognitive awareness and control in the writing process, various strategies are recommended by researchers (Baker, 2010; Bereiter & Scardamalia, 1987). Most of these strategies involve providing students with "prompts, cues and scaffolds," such as planning templates, to remind them of the actions required at each phase of writing (Baker, 2010, p. 207).

Another approach is to have students reflect on patterns in their writing behaviors rather than simply reflecting on one piece of writing. In this way, students identify the behaviors that work for them and those that impede the writing process. Reflective questions might include the following (ReadWriteThink, 2005).

- When you are writing, what is the easiest part for you? Why?
- When you are writing, what is most difficult for you? Why?
- Who reads your writing?
- What are the different purposes for your writing?
- What do you like to use when you are writing? Why do you use these things?
- What process do you use when you are writing?
- Do you get distracted when you are writing? Do you try to avoid it? What do you typically do instead of writing?
- What has influenced the way that you write? Why?
- If other people were watching you as a writer, what would they notice?
- How would you describe yourself as a writer?

## METACOGNITION IN MATHEMATICS

Just as students need to monitor their comprehension when they read, they must also monitor their cognitive processes when engaging in mathematical tasks. Specifically, they need not only mathematical strategy knowledge, such as the basics of algorithms, but also metacognitive awareness of strategies to help comprehend mathematical problems, organize information or data, plan solutions, carry out their plans, and check their results. The work of Alan Schoenfeld (1987; as cited in Baker, 2010) has been particularly influential in highlighting the importance of metacognition in mathematics. Schoenfeld has shown that many students do not reflect on the problem-solving strategies that they use and they rarely connect their solutions with the real world. Recognizing the importance of increasing students' metacognitive awareness, Kylie Meyer (2014) and Yvonne Reilly, Jodie Parsons, and Elizabeth Bortolot (2009) innovate on Annemarie Sullivan Palincsar and Ann L. Brown's (1984) reciprocal-teaching strategy described earlier. They show that the approach can be applied to mathematical problem solving to promote students' metacognitive awareness in mathematics. The researchers include "predicting, clarifying, solving and summarising as their key strategies or stages" (Meyer, 2014, p. 9). The four stages in a mathematics context are (Meyer, 2014):

1. **Predicting—**Predict the type of mathematical questions being asked, the mathematical operations needed, and what the answer might look like. Predictions are based on prior knowledge, the structure of the text (including headings, illustrations, or diagrams), and problem content.
2. **Clarifying—**List unfamiliar words, facts that are already known, and information that is needed to solve the problem.
3. **Solving—**Use a range of problem-solving strategies and show the working out using pictures, diagrams, numbers, or words.
4. **Summarizing—**Engage in self-reflection using questions such as, Can you justify your answer? How might you refine your approach if you had a similar problem to solve? How well did you contribute to the group when problem solving together?

## ASSESSMENT OF METACOGNITION

Monitoring students' metacognitive development can provide guidance for instruction and the types of strategies that are working most effectively (Ozturk, 2017). Linda Baker and Lorraine Cerro (2000) identify interviews and questionnaires as the most frequently used methods to assess metacognition. Usually, students are asked if they know or can do something or asked to think aloud about what they are doing and thinking as they solve a problem or read a text (Baker, 2010; Ozturk, 2017). Alternatively, students may be asked to complete checklists of strategies that they used to do a task.

Observations also play a key role in monitoring metacognitive development. According to Walsh and Sattes (2011), students are becoming more aware of their own thinking if they can describe their own inner language when they are thinking. They are able to identify the kind of thinking they are doing, list any steps or procedures they are using to do it, and tell the sequence of steps that they are taking and the roadblocks that they are encountering along the way (Swartz, Costa, Beyer, Reagan, & Kallick, 2007). As students develop systematic ways to solve problems—knowing where to begin and the steps to take and whether they are accurate or have errors in their thinking—they will persevere more often when faced with difficult tasks where the solution to a problem isn't immediately apparent (Costa, 2001b).

As we observe students' metacognitive behaviors, we must also consider the role of the self-system in learning because it is the self-system that influences students' level of engagement in a task and the amount of effort that they will put into it (Baker, 2010). If students don't think the task is important, or if they think their own skill set isn't enough to complete the task, they will give up or avoid the task completely. Consequently, they will not engage with the task metacognitively or at the necessary level of cognition. Central to the self-system is self-efficacy, which is positively associated with self-regulated learning, an important component of metacognition (Walsh & Sattes, 2011).

## THE ROLE OF SELF-EFFICACY IN LEARNING

Self-efficacy is an individual's belief about his or her capability to perform a task at a chosen level of achievement (Bandura, 1994). It is concerned not with the skills people have but rather with their personal judgments of what they can do with those skills (Bandura, 1994; Jinks & Morgan, 1999; Pajares & Schunk, 2002; Schunk, 2012). In other words, although students may indeed have the necessary skills to complete a task, they may not believe that these skills are enough to successfully complete the task. Self-efficacy answers the question, "Can I do this?"

Self-efficacy influences how people think, feel, motivate themselves, and act (Bandura, 1995). It has been shown to even influence how people establish goals. For example, if a person has a stronger perceived self-efficacy, he or she will set higher goal challenges and will have a stronger commitment to them. People with high self-efficacy tend to anticipate success, while those with lower self-efficacy will usually consider failure and what can go wrong—self-perceptions that may in turn lead to lower aspirations. Students with low self-efficacy will avoid tasks that they think are too difficult or become overly anxious and stressed (Linnenbrink & Pintrich, 2002, 2003).

Self-efficacy is linked to academic success because it influences behaviors that lead to success (Bandura, 1994; Jinks & Lorsbach, 2003; Schunk, 2012). Students with high self-efficacy will approach a challenge with confidence and are more likely to apply the most effective learning strategies (Walsh & Sattes, 2011). Importantly, if they encounter failure, they will not internalize this as lack of ability, inferiority, or bad luck but rather will view the failure as due to insufficient effort or skills they haven't acquired yet.

Further, students with high self-efficacy will try alternative strategies and persevere, while in contrast, students who doubt their ability will give up if their initial efforts are not successful. This begins a spiral whereby low self-efficacy causes less effort, resulting in lower success and a further decrease in self-efficacy (Jinks & Morgan, 1999). Fortunately, in a supportive classroom environment, self-efficacy can be improved.

# DEVELOPMENT OF SELF-EFFICACY

According to Albert Bandura (1994), the pioneer of the field, self-efficacy is developed through varying combinations of four sources of influence.

1. **Physiological indicators:** How do I feel?
2. **Vicarious or observational experiences:** How do I compare to others?
3. **Verbal persuasion:** What do others say about my skills?
4. **Mastery experiences (progress feedback):** Am I improving?

Each source is explored in more detail in the sections that follow.

## PHYSIOLOGICAL INDICATORS

When students experience symptoms that signal anxiety, such as nervousness, increased heart rate, or sweating, it can also convey to them that they lack the necessary skills to complete a task, thus negatively impacting their level of self-efficacy. When they experience decreased levels of anxiety during the completion of a task, self-efficacy can be raised (Schunk, 2003). To counter anxiety about task completion, the classroom culture should be one in which students feel comfortable making mistakes, support one another's learning, and demonstrate respect for each other (Walsh & Sattes, 2011). This is one of the reasons why it is important to establish class norms, which will be discussed in more detail in the next chapter (page 27).

## VICARIOUS OR OBSERVATIONAL EXPERIENCES

According to Pamela J. Gaskill and Anita Woolfolk Hoy (2002), children use observation as a source of comparison for their own performance, either to raise or to lower their self-efficacy. For example, if a child with low self-efficacy witnesses another child, who he or she considers to be of similar ability, successfully complete a reading task, the low-efficacy child will be more likely to believe that he or she will also experience success and be more motivated to participate. This strategy is most successful for those students who are unfamiliar with a task or those who have experienced difficulties and consequently hold doubts about their ability (Gaskill & Hoy, 2002; Margolis & McCabe, 2003, 2006; Schunk, 2001).

## VERBAL PERSUASION

Verbal persuasion is like a pep talk or specific performance feedback (Gaskill & Hoy, 2002). But there is feedback and there is *effective* feedback. If not well considered, feedback can have a negative impact and damage rather than enhance self-efficacy. For example, a teacher who responds to a student with the well-intentioned comment of "Well done" can have an unintended damaging effect. Students who are striving to improve can view a comment like this as "Well, I think you're dumb, and you can't do any better" (Wills, 2012). The feedback is broad rather than specific and does not provide any guidance as to how the student can improve—enforcing the belief students with low self-efficacy often articulate: "I can't, I'm dumb, and I can't improve." Perhaps the first step in developing a positive classroom culture is to rule out the words "I can't"!

Rarely do we seek students' viewpoints about effective feedback, but we should do so more often, as students have useful insights. For example, in an interview about feedback, one student responded that feedback from teachers is a problem when they just assign a grade but don't indicate how to improve the work. He went on to comment that in his opinion, teachers accept mediocre or average performance rather than encourage improvement. He explained, "Teachers just give a B—I can't see how to improve even though I know that there is something wrong. It's like teachers just accept performance rather than maximise performance" (Wills, 2012, p. 177). In some cases, students find it difficult to act on the feedback from teachers. One student explained in an interview, "When I hand in a draft they'll say, couldn't you have gone through it and edited it? Well no I can't, I can't see it [the mistakes]. I'll read through it and it makes perfect sense in my mind" (Wills, 2012, pp. 175–176). Research suggests that feedback can be more effective if it is *focused*, *timely*, *specific*, and *goal related*.

- Feedback should focus on effort that links to evidence of incremental gains in achievement (Jinks & Morgan, 1999). In such a way, students can identify that their improvements in achievement are related to effort rather than external factors, such as luck or an easier task.
- The greatest impact occurs when feedback is given immediately after a task or closely afterward. The longer the delay in providing feedback, the less impact the feedback will have on improving learning (Marzano, Gaddy, & Dean, 2000).
- Feedback should focus on the behavior to be reinforced by specifying it clearly (Gaskill & Hoy, 2002).
- Goal-related feedback has been shown to improve self-efficacy, particularly in reading (Guthrie, Wigfield, & VonSecker, 2000; Schunk, 2003; Schunk & Rice, 1991, 1992). For example, Dale H. Schunk and Jo Mary Rice (1991) investigate the role of feedback linked to the goal of using a comprehension strategy (finding the main idea). Their study shows that readers benefit from explicit feedback on their use of the comprehension strategy. It also finds that students who receive goal-related feedback are more likely to transfer the strategy into new contexts.

## MASTERY EXPERIENCES

The old saying, "Success leads to success," is true when it comes to developing higher levels of self-efficacy. However, this will only occur if students *value* the success they have experienced or the task they have mastered. If the task is perceived by the students as easy, they will place less value on it and attribute their success to external factors, such as the assistance they were provided, luck, or the suggestion that the task had been dumbed down. For their success to be valued, students need to experience success with tasks that are challenging yet attainable—difficult but not too difficult (Marzano, 2009). It is important that students have had to persevere and expend effort to succeed at the tasks (Walker, 2003). This condition for the effectiveness of mastery experiences or success links back to goal setting and feedback.

The effects of achieving goals or experiencing success are not automatic (Schunk, 2003; Schunk & Swartz, 1993). Goals need to be specific by clearly articulating the expected level of performance, they need to be temporarily close at hand in that they are achievable in the near future, and, as previously stated, they need to be viewed as challenging yet attainable (Schunk, 2003; Schunk & Swartz, 1993; Walker, 2003). As feedback is gained about progress toward these set goals, self-efficacy is increased (Schunk & Swartz, 1993).

Feedback that indicates evidence of incremental gains in achievement and links to effort is highly effective (Jinks & Morgan, 1999). In this way, students can identify that the improvements they have made and the success that they are experiencing are related to effort. Similarly, Carol Dweck (2000, 2007) suggests that praise given to the students as they work toward achieving these incremental gains should focus on the effort expended, the level of challenge, and the strategies used. A word of caution is offered by Spencer J. Salend (2011), who warns that praise should only be given when it has been legitimately earned. It should be spontaneous and specifically relate to the accomplishment. Feedback in the form of undeserved praise weakens teacher credibility and can reduce the effect of praise in the future (Pintrich, 2002). As Erik H. Erikson (1959) pointed out so long ago, children cannot be fooled by empty praise and condescending encouragement.

One highly effective strategy for developing self-efficacy is the use of proficiency scales, which were first described by Marzano in the books *Classroom Assessment and Grading That Work* (Marzano, 2006) and *Making Standards Useful in the Classroom* (Marzano & Haystead, 2008). The design of the scale allows students to set challenging yet attainable goals and to see their incremental gains as they work toward mastery of their goals. It also provides a platform for teachers to provide specific, performance-related feedback in a timely manner.

## PROFICIENCY SCALES

Proficiency scales are a continuum that articulates distinct levels of knowledge and skill relative to a specific topic. They can be thought of as a learning progression or a progression of learning goals from simple to more complex (Marzano, 2009). Scales articulate for teachers and students what proficiency looks like for a target goal or standard, the knowledge and skills students need to achieve the target, and how students might go beyond the target learning goal (Heflebower, Hoegh, Warrick, & Flygare, 2019). In this way, students can identify the goals they need to attain as they work toward a more complex goal. As they move toward proficiency, they can articulate the target learning goal they are working toward and the progression that they are making toward that goal. Most importantly, they can use the scale to reflect on the effectiveness of the strategies they are using, adaptations that they might need to make, whether the level of effort they are applying is enough, and what their next steps will be in the learning process. All of these are strong self-regulatory behaviors and indicators of metacognition.

A student in second grade was able to use a proficiency scale similar to the example shown in table 1.2 to express her learning at the current moment. When asked, "What are you learning?" she was able to respond with a full explanation of her target goal and where she was in her progression toward that goal. She responded, "I need to be able to count in twos, fives, and tens from zero and nonzero starting points. At the moment, I can count in twos from zero and nonzero starting points and fives from zero but not nonzero yet. So . . . I'm practicing . . ." This student displayed strong self-regulatory behaviors—she had a goal, she knew where she was in relation to that goal, and she had developed strategies to reach that goal.

**Table 1.2: Grade 2 Mathematics Proficiency Scale Example**

| | |
|---|---|
| **Score 4.0** | **More complex learning goal**<br>*Demonstrations of learning that go above and beyond what was explicitly taught*<br>I can:<br>■ Explain why an error has occurred and how it can be fixed<br>■ Identify when an error has been made when skip counting<br>■ Explain when skip counting might be useful |
| **Score 3.0** | **Target learning goal**<br>I can count in twos, fives, and tens from zero and nonzero starting points. |
| **Score 2.0** | **Simpler goals or prerequisite knowledge**<br>*Foundational knowledge, simpler procedures, isolated details, and vocabulary*<br>I can recognize or recall specific terminology, such as *skip count*, *number pattern*, *sequence* or *order*, *starting point*, and *nonzero*.<br>I can:<br>■ Count in tens from nonzero starting points<br>■ Count in tens from zero<br>■ Count in fives from nonzero starting points<br>■ Count in fives from zero<br>■ Count in twos from nonzero starting points<br>■ Count in twos from zero<br>■ Count in ones from any starting point |
| **Score 1.0** | **With help, the student can perform score 2.0 and 3.0 expectations.** |
| **Score 0.0** | **Even with help, the student cannot perform expectations.** |

Older students may use a scale like the one shown in table 1.3 to discuss their learning progression as they work toward the goal of selecting evidence from a text to show how events, situations, and people can be represented from different viewpoints. The wording in the scale has been adapted to account for the age of the students and the content area.

**Table 1.3: Secondary School Proficiency Scale Example Focusing on Viewpoints**

| | |
|---|---|
| **Score 4.0** | **In addition to score 3.0, the student makes in-depth inferences and applications that go beyond what was taught.**<br>I can discuss and suggest possible reasons for different viewpoints. |
| **Score 3.0** | I can select evidence from the text to show how events, situations, and people can be represented from different viewpoints. |
| **Score 2.0** | **There are no major errors or omissions regarding the simpler details and processes.**<br>I can recognize or recall specific terminology, such as *evidence*, *represent*, and *viewpoints*.<br>I can perform processes such as:<br>■ Discussing alternative views that have not been represented<br>■ Identifying possible alternative views that have not been represented<br>■ Choosing an event, situation, or person and representing different views<br>■ Identifying different views on an event, situation, or person<br>■ Identifying a viewpoint in text by highlighting parts of the text that show different views on an event, situation, or person<br>■ Identifying language used to represent events, situations, or people<br>But the student exhibits major errors or omissions regarding the more complex ideas and processes. |
| **Score 1.0** | **With help, the student has a partial understanding of some of the simpler details and processes and some of the more complex ideas and processes.** |
| **Score 0.0** | **Even with help, the student cannot perform expectations.** |

Please note that this is the generic form of the proficiency scale and score 0.0 would not be used on a scale developed for students. Typically, students performing at the 0.0 level would be working on an individual curriculum plan and using a proficiency scale created for a different level of proficiency.

For more information on the use and development of proficiency scales, see *A Teacher's Guide to Standards-Based Learning* (Heflebower et al., 2019), *The New Art and Science of Teaching* (Marzano, 2017), *A School Leader's Guide to Standards-Based Grading* (Heflebower, Hoegh, & Warrick, 2014), *Designing and Teaching Learning Goals and Objectives* (Marzano, 2009), *Classroom Assessment and Grading That Work* (Marzano, 2006), and *Making Standards Useful in the Classroom* (Marzano & Haystead, 2008).

## CONCLUSION

Metacognition is an essential skill as we prepare our students for their place in the world, not simply for their place in the world of work. We need to support students so that they are proactive and guided by personally set goals, optimistic about their future, and able to tolerate frustration and persist regardless of the challenges they may face or the hard work involved. These skills are foundational for any thinking skills program, and therefore foundational for developing the thinking skills and dispositions described in the chapters to follow.

# CHAPTER 2

# DIALOGUE FOR MEANING MAKING

***We internalize talk, and it becomes thought. We externalize talk, and it becomes our link to social reality. We elaborate talk, and it becomes our bridge to literacy.***

***—Donald Rubin***

## RESEARCH AND THEORY

Learning is fundamentally about making meaning. It involves struggle as we grapple with new information, connect it to what we already know, and integrate it into our existing knowledge base. It is about hearing other viewpoints, assessing evidence, questioning assumptions, considering implications, and analyzing concepts and objections. Learning is so much more than information stored in short-term memory or information bestowed by authorities and mostly found in books (Paul, 2001). Learning does not occur in isolation; it is a social process with dialogue at the center (Bandura, 1993; Bruner, 1986; Piaget, 1973).

Dialogue as a teaching tool can be traced back to the time of Socrates (Fisher, 2003, 2013). In the Socratic tradition, the teacher's role is facilitation, using dialogue to support a student's construction of knowledge, increasing student participation in education, and shifting the power base from the teacher to the student (Hajhosseiny, 2012). As students talk—grapple with their own ideas, seek to understand the viewpoints of others, and try to reconcile the two—they learn at deeper levels.

Instructional approaches that include cooperative learning and dialogue have been shown to positively impact students' active learning and higher-order thinking skills simultaneously (Derewianka, 2018; Hajhosseiny, 2012; Roy, 2013; Sedova, Salamounova, & Svaricek, 2014). In a series of meta-analyses conducted by David

W. Johnson and Frank P. Johnson (2017), the findings indicate that cooperative learning results in increased willingness of individuals to take on difficult tasks and persist despite difficulties; longer-term retention of learning; higher levels of reasoning, critical thinking, and metacognition; creative thinking evidenced by an increase in the frequency of new ideas generated, strategies designed, and solutions created; greater transfer of learning from one situation to another; more positive attitudes toward the tasks being completed; and increased time on task. In a summary of John T. Bruer's (1994) research, Courtney B. Cazden (2001) notes the following five hypotheses as to why dialogic approaches and cooperative learning are so effective.

1. Social interaction allows skilled thinkers to demonstrate thinking strategies to those who are less skilled.
2. Group interactions allow students to share the cognitive load of thinking because the group has more collective information and can trigger the recall of information from individual memories.
3. Dialogue requires both language comprehension and language production. Since language production is more cognitively demanding, there is a deeper level of information processing.
4. Interaction in a social setting sends the message that thinking is socially valued.
5. Thought, learning, and knowledge are social phenomena. Thinking is internalized dialogue.

Simply having students "turn and talk" is not in itself going to produce the desired effect of deeper levels of learning. Approaches with clear structures and well-designed tasks for promoting talk and interaction between learners are required to produce higher gains in achievement (Evidence for Learning, n.d.). "Effective group interaction is a product of interpersonal skill development—not luck" (Roy, 2013, p. 133). Johnson and Johnson (2017) claim that the basic components of effective groups are "positive interdependence, individual and group accountability, face-to-face promotive interaction, appropriate use of social skills, and group processing" (p. 108), which are detailed in table 2.1.

Even though research supports dialogic approaches to teaching, their presence in most classrooms is scarce (Sedova et al., 2014). Teaching by telling and learning by memorizing still predominate in education (Edwards-Groves & Davidson, 2017; Paul, 2001). The issue with such an approach is that it confuses information with knowledge and separates knowledge from understanding. In a world of game shows where the quick recall of regurgitated facts is prized as a sign of intellect, we need to slow down. Value the discussion, value cognitive dissonance, talk to understand rather than talk to position, and stop the "I know more than you" mentality. After all, if we work together, we know so much more. Life's problems cannot be solved with one-dimensional answers, and knowledge is not ready-made for passive absorption (Paul, 2001). According to Richard Paul (2001):

**Table 2.1: The Basic Components of Effective Groups**

| | |
|---|---|
| **Positive Interdependence** | Group members perceive that they are linked in such a way that they cannot succeed unless the others in the group succeed (and vice versa), and they must coordinate their efforts with the efforts of others to complete a task. |
| **Individual and Group Accountability** | This fosters a sense of responsibility to the group as a whole and to other group members and reduces the risk of individuals taking a free ride by not contributing fully to the group. Group accountability exists when the overall performance of the group is assessed against a standard of performance. Individual accountability exists when the individual performance of each group member is assessed against a standard. |
| **Face-to-Face Promotive Interaction** | Promotive interaction occurs when group members encourage and facilitate each other's efforts to achieve the group's goals. They might share resources or challenge each other's thinking and reasoning in respectful and supportive ways. |
| **Appropriate Use of Social Skills** | Interpersonal and small-group skills need to be taught. These skills include the ability to get to know and trust one another, communicate clearly and precisely, accept and support one another, and resolve conflicts constructively. |
| **Group Processing** | Groups need to periodically reflect on how well they are functioning and how they plan to improve the way that they work together. |

Source: Adapted from Johnson & Johnson, 2017.

> ***Only when students have a rich diet of dialogical and dialectical thought, do they become prepared for the messy, multidimensional real world, where opposition, conflict, critique, and contradiction are everywhere. Only through a rigorous exposure to dialogical and dialectical thinking, do students develop intellectually fit minds. (p. 428)***

# THE PLACE OF DIALOGUE IN THE COMMON CORE

The importance of providing opportunities for meaningful dialogue is recognized within the Common Core State Standards. Students in kindergarten are expected to be given opportunities to "participate in collaborative conversations with diverse partners about kindergarten topics and texts with peers and adults in small and larger groups" (SL.K.1; National Governors Association Center for Best Practices [NGA] & Council of Chief State School Officers [CCSSO], 2010a). Also, they are expected to "follow agreed-upon rules for discussions (e.g., listening to others and taking turns speaking about the topics and texts under discussion)" (SL.K.1a; NGA & CCSSO, 2010a) and "continue a conversation through multiple exchanges" (SL.K.1c; NGA & CCSSO, 2010a). These expectations continue as students age. In English language arts, third-grade students, for example, are expected to:

- "Engage effectively in a range of collaborative discussions (one-on-one, in groups, and teacher-led) with diverse partners on grade 3 topics and texts, building on others' ideas and expressing their own clearly" (SL.3.1; NGA & CCSSO, 2010a)
- "Come to discussions prepared, having read or studied required material; explicitly draw on that preparation and other information known about the topic to explore ideas under discussion" (SL.3.1a; NGA & CCSSO, 2010a)
- "Follow agreed-upon rules for discussions (e.g., gaining the floor in respectful ways, listening to others with care, speaking one at a time about the topics and texts under discussion)" (SL.3.1b; NGA & CCSSO, 2010a)
- "Ask questions to check understanding of information presented, stay on topic, and link their comments to the remarks of others" (SL.3.1c; NGA & CCSSO, 2010a)
- "Explain their own ideas and understanding in light of the discussion" (SL.3.1d; NGA & CCSSO, 2010a)

This requires that students can (Palmer, 2014):

- Listen to others one at a time
- Read and study before discussion and use content they studied in their comments
- Shift discussion away from opinion sharing
- Explain key ideas and how those ideas have affected their own thinking

By eighth grade, students are expected to:

- "Engage effectively in a range of collaborative discussions (one-on-one, in groups, and teacher-led) with diverse partners on grade 8 topics, texts, and issues, building on others' ideas and expressing their own clearly" (SL.8.1; NGA & CCSSO, 2010a)
- "Come to discussions prepared, having read or researched material under study; explicitly draw on that preparation by referring to evidence on the topic, text, or issue to probe and reflect on ideas under discussion" (SL.8.1a; NGA & CCSSO, 2010a)
- "Follow rules for collegial discussions and decision-making, track progress toward specific goals and deadlines, and define individual roles as needed" (SL.8.1b; NGA & CCSSO, 2010a)

- "Pose questions that connect the ideas of several speakers and respond to others' questions and comments with relevant evidence, observations, and ideas" (SL.8.1c; NGA & CCSSO, 2010a)
- "Acknowledge new information expressed by others, and, when warranted, qualify or justify their own views in light of the evidence presented" (SL.8.1d; NGA & CCSSO, 2010a)

This requires that students can (Palmer, 2014):

- Acknowledge information that others present
- Make connections among the ideas of multiple other people
- Demonstrate understanding of different perspectives
- Reply to others' questions

Given that research indicates the effectiveness of dialogue for learning and curriculum requirements, why is it that teacher talk still dominates in classroom practice? The answer is simple: the approach in practice, rather than in theory, is difficult. The reality is that teachers are faced with numerous challenges when implementing the approach. They want to ensure that valuable instructional time is not being wasted with discussions that are not effectively engaging all students in deeper levels of thinking, the exchange of ideas, and meaning making. A challenge for teachers, for example, can be students who dominate the conversation, monopolizing the discussion and limiting the opportunity for others to contribute and offer alternative perspectives. Some students may be reticent to contribute while others may be embarrassed or overly anxious about contributing. Teachers need strategies to ensure that these challenges are addressed while still allowing the continued flow of the conversation (Walsh & Sattes, 2015). Although no simple answers exist, establishing routines and norms for equitable participation and accountability and using protocols to structure and scaffold participation are strategies worth exploring (Walsh & Sattes, 2015). These strategies are explored throughout this chapter.

# THINKING PROTOCOLS

Effective groups working cooperatively or collaboratively require that all members of the group contribute. Therefore, the expectation that all students contribute to discussions needs to be clearly communicated. However, if students are unsure about the processes and expectations as they contribute to group discussions, they may experience anxiety (Gregory & Kaufeldt, 2015). To help reduce possible anxiety, a sense of routine is important. Routines create consistency and clarity about procedures for how the teacher and students work together in the classroom. Commonly understood routines can lower stress and distraction while also reducing potential conflict within the groups (Gregory & Kaufeldt, 2015). For routines to be effective, they need to be demonstrated, practiced, and monitored so that they become automatic over time (Gregory & Kaufeldt, 2015). Typically, routines are established for:

- How to work together or norms of participation
- Group roles
- Management of accountability, participation, and feedback
- How groups are to be formed
- What to do if there is uncertainty around the task or procedure
- What to do if a student needs assistance

Two important aspects of group interaction are differentiated roles and norms (Johnson & Johnson, 2017). Roles differentiate the responsibilities of members within the group while norms guide group members' behaviors and attitudes. The protocols and strategies described in this section will support the development of these routines.

## DEFINING GROUP ROLES

Group roles define the formal structure of the group and distinguish the tasks to be performed by each member of the group so that the goals of the group can be achieved. Group roles can also help to balance the level of participation of the group members so that participation is equalized—rather than monopolized by certain group members. Johnson and Johnson (2017) make the following recommendations for teachers to consider when assigning roles to maximize the interdependence of the group:

- ***Assign groups when students are comfortable working together.***
- ***Initially, assign simple roles to students, such as reader, recorder, and encourager of participation.***
- ***Rotate the roles so that each group member plays each role several times.***
- ***Add new roles to the rotation that are slightly more sophisticated, such as someone who will check for understanding (for example, asking group members to explain what they are learning).***
- ***Gradually add roles that do not occur naturally in the group, such as an elaborator of ideas (for example, relating what is being learned to previous learning). (p. 488)***

To manage group roles, teachers may consider strategies such as assigning group role cards or the development of a group résumé.

# GROUP ROLE CARDS

## SETUP

| | |
|---|---|
| **Number of participants** | Groups of four to five |
| **Time needed** | Five minutes |
| **Room arrangement** | Table groups or groups seated |
| **Materials** | Cards for each specific role |

## PROCESS

1. Use job cards for specific roles within the group that will enable the group tasks or goals to be completed or achieved. Example roles could be discussion facilitator, summarizer, questioner, and recorder. Each job card should describe the tasks or actions that need to be carried out by the group member assigned to each role. Example job cards are shown in figure 2.1.
2. Once students have carried out their role, rotate so that each group member experiences each role.
3. Ask students to reflect on how effectively they carried out their role and what they might need to do differently next time they have a similar role in a group.

| **NAME**<br>.................................... | **NAME**<br>.................................... | **NAME**<br>.................................... | **NAME**<br>.................................... |
|---|---|---|---|
| **Group facilitator** | **Group recorder** | **Group questioner** | **Group timekeeper** |
| My role is to make sure that everyone gets a chance to talk and that as a group we listen and respond respectfully. | My role is to take notes to make sure that all of our ideas are recorded. | My role is to come up with important questions for our group as we think about the topic or solve our problem. | My role is to help our group keep track of the time and stay on task. I also need to make sure that we have the materials we need and pack up in time. |

**Figure 2.1: Sample job cards.**

### APPLICATION

- Consider having students identify the roles that will be required.
- Encourage students to develop the role descriptions for each role identified.

## GROUP RÉSUMÉ

This strategy is adapted from Laura Lipton and Bruce Wellman (2016). Creating a group résumé is an engaging way of helping students to get to know one another more when they are about to begin working as a group.

### SETUP

| | |
|---|---|
| **Number of participants** | Groups of four to five |
| **Time needed** | Fifteen minutes |
| **Room arrangement** | Table groups or groups seated in a cluster |
| **Materials** | Chart paper for recording and markers |

### PROCESS

1. Explain that the group is to create a résumé for the group that details:
   - ❑ Group name
   - ❑ Background information
   - ❑ Interests or hobbies
   - ❑ Two things no one else would guess about the group members
   - ❑ One thing the group members have in common
   - ❑ Signatures
2. Have each group share the highlights of the group résumé.

### APPLICATION

- Use this strategy in conjunction with group role cards so that there are a recorder, group facilitator, spokesperson, and time manager.
- Use a countdown timer to indicate the time left for the completion of the task.
- Display the résumés.
- Instead of groups identifying what they have in common or what no one else knows about them, have groups list information about a topic—what they think they already know and what they are wondering about the topic.
- If the group is working on a longer-term project or problem-solving task, group members may list on the group résumé the specific talents, interests, or skills of each group member.

# ESTABLISHING NORMS

When groups are formed, a new social entity is formed, potentially with its own rules, attitudes, beliefs, and practices (Johnson & Johnson, 2017). For the group dynamic to contribute to a positive and productive learning experience, it is important that parameters are in place to guide how the group will interact and work together. Group norms provide a set of expectations for students' behavior within the group (Marzano, 2019). However, norms cannot be imposed on a group. Johnson and Johnson (2017) argue that norms should develop out of the interactions among the members of the group.

## NORM CREATION

### SETUP

| | |
|---|---|
| **Number of participants** | Groups of two to five |
| **Time needed** | Ten minutes |
| **Room arrangement** | Table groups or groups seated in a cluster |
| **Materials** | Recording materials |

### PROCESS

1. Ask students to write down the behaviors or norms that are most important to them.
2. Students then work together to compile and classify the norms into a list of the beliefs and attitudes that will help to guide their behavior in the group. Norms will vary depending on the structure and goal of the group. For example, the norms of groups that are formed ad hoc to brainstorm ideas will differ from the norms of groups established for a longer time period to work collaboratively on solving a problem.
3. Depending on the function or goal of the group, ask students to reflect on how to (Marzano, 2019):
   - ❏ Decide who speaks and when
   - ❏ React if they think of something to say while someone else is speaking
   - ❏ Make sure that they disagree respectfully
   - ❏ Make a decision as a group
   - ❏ Encourage everyone to participate

### APPLICATION

- Norms should be displayed and addressed whenever the group is meeting together.

- A class set of norms can be created to guide the way ad hoc groups interact. These should also be referenced regularly.
- Norms can be used as a basis for reflection and feedback for the group.
- As a teacher, lead the way and model the expected beliefs and behaviors as you engage in dialogue.
- Explicitly name and talk about the critical components of effective dialogue, such as respect for others and their ideas, the value of students' questions, a willingness to take risks and learn from mistakes, and tolerance for ambiguity (Walsh & Sattes, 2015).
- Although it is recommended that groups establish their own norms, table 2.2 provides some useful examples.

**Table 2.2: Examples of Group Norms**

| | |
|---|---|
| **General Norms** | Ask questions when you are curious or confused or need clarification.<br>Share what you are thinking—others can learn from you.<br>Monitor how often you are talking—do not take over the conversation.<br>Listen respectfully and ask questions to understand other group members' perspectives.<br>Encourage others to speak so that all voices are heard. |
| **Specific Elementary School Example Norms** | Listen carefully to other students.<br>Ask questions if you do not understand what someone else says.<br>Learn from one another.<br>Be sure everyone contributes.<br>Allow time to think—before and after someone speaks.<br>Ask questions when you are curious. |
| **Specific Secondary School Example Norms** | Be open and respect all points of view.<br>Listen with an open mind and expect to learn from one another.<br>Accept responsibility for active and equitable participation by each group member.<br>Check for understanding. Before you counter an idea, be sure you fully understand what has been said.<br>Allow think time—before and after a group member speaks.<br>Ask questions. |

Source: Adapted from Walsh & Sattes, 2015, p. 144.

## MANAGING ACCOUNTABILITY AND PARTICIPATION

True classroom discussion and group interaction require that teachers relinquish some control. This also requires a shift in perceptions about time. Often teachers believe that it is more efficient to just tell students what they need to know—that discussions and group work take time away from content coverage (Walsh & Sattes, 2015). Ironically, the endless pressure of pacing guides and high-stakes testing calls into question the use of group work and discussion—an approach that has been repeatedly shown to move students to deeper levels of understanding (Walsh & Sattes, 2015). The following strategies can address the issue of accountability, allowing groups to stay on task and actively participate in and self-reflect on their learning so that the time is productive rather than wasted.

## TALKING STICKS

The notion of *talking sticks* was first established by Spencer Kagan and Miguel Kagan (2009) as a way of regulating discussions and ensuring that all group members have an opportunity to contribute to group discussions.

### SETUP

| | |
|---|---|
| **Number of participants** | Groups of three to five |
| **Time needed** | Length of discussion |
| **Room arrangement** | Table groupings |
| **Materials** | Talking sticks—colored ice cream sticks (available from craft shops) or colored cardboard strips |

### PROCESS

1. Provide each group member with a different-colored talking stick.
2. Instruct group members to place their stick in the center of the table after they have contributed to the discussion. Once a group member's talking stick has been placed in the middle, he or she cannot say anything else until all group members have had an opportunity to contribute and place their stick in the center. Group members cannot interrupt and must practice respectful listening while another group member is speaking.
3. When all group members have contributed, the sticks are collected and redistributed so that the process can begin again.

### APPLICATION

- Colored pencils or any tangible articles can be used as talking sticks.
- Kagan and Kagan (2009) suggest the use of talking chips with different tasks assigned on each of the chips (share an idea, ask a question, make a suggestion). Group members contribute the appropriate chip during the discussion and must use up all of their chips.

## GROUP REFLECTION GUIDE

It is important that students are provided with ongoing coaching for interpersonal and group skills (Marzano, 2019). Reflective guides such as this one can foster those skills.

### SETUP

| | |
|---|---|
| **Number of participants** | Whole class working in groups |
| **Time needed** | Five minutes |
| **Room arrangement** | Table groups or groups seated in a cluster |
| **Materials** | Reflection guide |

### PROCESS

1. Provide the groups with a reflection guide. An example is provided in figure 2.2.
2. Discuss any issues or concerns that groups are experiencing and how these might be resolved.

| **Cooperative learning feedback guide**<br>**Group name:**<br>**Group members:** | |
|---|---|
| **Criteria** | **Comments** |
| All group members participated equally in group activities. | |
| As a group, we cooperated, managed our time, and solved problems that arose. | |
| We distributed the tasks and responsibilities evenly. | |
| We completed the tasks on time. | |
| All members of the group contributed to the final outcome. | |
| Other comments | |

Source: From *Marzano Compendium of Instructional Strategies*. © 2016 by Marzano Resources, 555 North Morton Street, Bloomington, IN 47404, 800.733.6786, www.marzanoresources.com. All rights reserved. Used with permission.

**Figure 2.2: Sample reflection guide.**

## GROUP PROCESSING

This process is recommended by Johnson and Johnson (2017) for groups to process how effectively they functioned in the completion of a task. Groups need to have time to reflect, identify strengths, recognize ineffective behaviors, and set goals for future participation in group work (Roy, 2013). When groups are provided with this type of processing time, they achieve more and retain information longer than groups not provided with time (Roy, 2013).

### SETUP

| | |
|---|---|
| **Number of participants** | Whole class working in groups |
| **Time needed** | Five minutes |
| **Room arrangement** | Table groups or groups seated in a cluster |
| **Materials** | None required |

### PROCESS

1. Upon completion of a task, explain that each group will reflect on the group member actions that were helpful or unhelpful for completing the task. Each group and each student within the group are given feedback on the task completed and the way the students participated in the group.
2. Provide reflective prompts, such as "How frequently did each group member explain how to solve a problem or clarify other members' explanations?" Students then analyze and reflect on the feedback.
3. Have students describe the action each member engaged in that contributed to the group's effectively completing the task.
4. Help individuals and the group set goals for improving the quality of their work.
5. Encourage the celebration of members' hard work and the group's success (Johnson & Johnson, 2017).

## SELF-REFLECTION CHECKLIST

The self-reflection checklist in figure 2.3 (page 40) is based on several sources (Frey, Fisher, & Everlove, 2009; Johnson & Johnson, 2017; Walsh & Sattes, 2015) and personal experience. It can be adjusted to suit the age of participants or to focus on specific skills. Students color the number of stars that reflects the level of their performance—one star for low effectiveness through to five stars for exemplary performance.

| Reflective question | Performance |
|---|---|
| I contribute to the discussion so that others can learn from me. | ☆ ☆ ☆ ☆ ☆ |
| I express my ideas clearly. | ☆ ☆ ☆ ☆ ☆ |
| I listen actively and wait before adding my own ideas or comments. | ☆ ☆ ☆ ☆ ☆ |
| I paraphrase what other students say. | ☆ ☆ ☆ ☆ ☆ |
| I piggyback on classmates' ideas or comments. | ☆ ☆ ☆ ☆ ☆ |
| I make connections between what I already know and what I am learning. | ☆ ☆ ☆ ☆ ☆ |
| I pose questions to clarify the thinking or reasoning behind other group members' comments. | ☆ ☆ ☆ ☆ ☆ |
| I wait to think about the meaning of others' comments. | ☆ ☆ ☆ ☆ ☆ |
| I identify similarities and differences between my own and others' ideas. | ☆ ☆ ☆ ☆ ☆ |
| I make comments that relate to the topic. | ☆ ☆ ☆ ☆ ☆ |
| I keep an open mind and think about ideas that are different from my own. | ☆ ☆ ☆ ☆ ☆ |
| I disagree in a respectful way. | ☆ ☆ ☆ ☆ ☆ |

**Figure 2.3: Sample self-reflection checklist.**

## ACTIVATE

Activate (www.lightspeed-tek.com/product/activate-system) is a commercial product that can assist teachers to manage groups and monitor students' on-task behavior during group discussions. The teacher wears a lightweight wireless microphone with an earbud and can speak to the whole class through a flat-screen speaker that distributes sound evenly across the room. Portable two-way audio pods placed in the center of group tables allow the teacher to speak and listen across up to six groups. Teachers can listen in on and record student group interactions in real time. The pod system also enables students to communicate directly with the teacher when they need clarification or have a specific question or problem to resolve. Teachers can also share group and individual insights and responses with the whole class via the pods through the whole-class speaker. In a trial of the system in Australia, teachers reported that the system (Wills, 2018):

- Increased their confidence in using student dialogue as an instructional tool
- Allowed for the effective management of collaborative learning opportunities while increasing student accountability and time on task

## ESTABLISHING THE CLIMATE

As students engage in collaborative or cooperative work, there is a tension between two types of learning: (1) process learning and (2) content learning (Frey et al., 2009). Diana Hulse-Killacky, Jim Killacky, and Jeremiah Donigian (2001) provide examples of process questions.

- Who am I?
- Who am I with you?
- Who are we together?

Alternatively, content questions may look like this.

- What do we have to do?
- What do we need to do to accomplish our goals?

As students answer the content questions, they consolidate academic knowledge, but in addressing the process questions, they gain a deeper understanding of themselves as learners and as members of a group (Frey et al., 2009). This self-knowledge of how and when they learn something new is an important aspect of metacognitive awareness, described in chapter 1 (page 9).

## QUICKWRITE

Delving straight into the process aspect of a discussion can be difficult or even daunting for students who are less confident. A strategy recommended by Frey and colleagues (2009) to help students gather their thoughts and formalize their ideas before engaging in a discussion is the quickwrite. A *quickwrite* is a very short writing opportunity of around one to five minutes in length in which students respond to a prompt that will be the focus of the discussion. The writing can then become a reference point or bridge over the pauses that less confident or reluctant students might experience as they work together to get the discussion flowing (Frey et al., 2009). The quickwrite prompt might focus specifically on content that will be discussed or be more general in nature. Quickwrites can occur before, during, or after a lesson. Example prompts are listed here (Frey et al., 2009).

- What is the best thing that you learned today?
- What was confusing for you?
- What do you already know about this topic?
- What did you do to help yourself learn today?
- What does a person who was absent today need to know about this lesson?
- I was proud of myself today when I . . .

## GROUP STRUCTURES

Although group interaction facilitates knowledge development, group size can impact the effectiveness of learning in groups (Marzano, 2007; table 2.3). In fact, Marzano suggests keeping groups small, recommending pairs and triads for most types of interactions.

**Table 2.3: Size of Groups and Effect Sizes**

| GROUP SIZE | NUMBER OF EFFECT SIZES | AVERAGE EFFECT SIZE | PERCENTILE GAIN |
|---|---|---|---|
| 2 | 13 | 0.15 | 6 |
| 2–4 | 38 | 0.22 | 9 |
| 5–7 | 17 | -0.02 | -1 |

Source: From *Marzano Compendium of Instructional Strategies*. © 2016 by Marzano Resources, 555 North Morton Street, Bloomington, IN 47404, 800.733.6786, www.marzanoresources.com. 

The larger the group, the more likely it will be that students are excluded from conversations or that group members are influenced by the most dominant speaker (Frey et al., 2009). Smaller groups also increase the accountability of the group members, making it more difficult for students to "hide" or not contribute. Johnson and Johnson (2017) also maintain that smaller groups are more effective but suggest that there is no ideal size for the group. They propose that a commonly made mistake is placing students in larger groups of four or five before the students have the skills to interact within the group competently. Group size, they claim, depends on TEAM (Johnson & Johnson, 2017).

### T = TIME

Time considerations depend on both the time available and the type of task to be undertaken. If only a short amount of time is available, groups of two or three are ideal because they take less time to create and operate faster with more "airtime" for each group member (Johnson & Johnson, 2017). If a quick exchange of ideas is required, pairs working in a think-pair-share (see page 53) are appropriate, while for the completion of a more complex project, a group of four may be required.

### E = EXPERIENCE WORKING IN GROUPS

The larger the group, the more skillful group members must be at managing interactions. As group size increases, the interpersonal and social skills required to manage the interactions among group members become more complex and sophisticated (Johnson & Johnson, 2017). Therefore, if students have not acquired the necessary skills, smaller groups would be best.

### A = AGE

Younger students benefit from participating in smaller groups until they develop the necessary interpersonal or social skills required for the more complex interactions that arise from participating in larger groups.

### M = MATERIALS AND EQUIPMENT AVAILABLE

The availability of materials needed or the specific nature of the task will determine the size of the group (Johnson & Johnson, 2017). For example, if there are only ten tablet computers available for a class of thirty students, groups of three are appropriate. Another consideration is how the materials will be distributed to maximize participation and achievement. Materials can be distributed to create interdependence by giving each group only one copy of the materials. Alternatively, materials can be distributed in such a way that each student has part of the materials needed to complete the task. The students must work together to synthesize the information to be successful (Johnson & Johnson, 2017).

## FORMING GROUPS

For the purpose of grouping students to engage in meaningful dialogue, heterogeneous groups are recommended over homogeneous or ability-based groups (Frey et al., 2009; Johnson & Johnson, 2017). Homogeneous groups are appropriate when specific support or accelerated instruction is required, but they do not lend themselves to more complex tasks such as problem solving, idea generation, and decision making. Heterogeneous groups typically allow for students to be exposed to a greater number of ideas, multiple perspectives, and differing problem-solving methods (Johnson & Johnson, 2017; Marzano Resources, 2016). However, the groups need to be structured thoughtfully to enhance the learning opportunity of all group members. Neville Bennett and Allyson Cass (1989) found that when groups have a higher number of high-achieving students compared with the number of lower-achieving students, the high achievers tend to take control of the task and complete it without regard for the needs of other group members who may need additional time or further clarification. They found that the ideal ratio is, in fact, one high-achieving student for every two lower-achieving students (Bennett & Cass, 1989).

Mixed groups are characteristically formed in one of three ways: (1) student choice, (2) random choice, or (3) teacher choice (Frey et al., 2009). Allowing students to form their own groups can increase student engagement. However, this strategy may be limiting if there are not a variety of student interests and skill levels within each group.

The random choice approach works well when the aim is to interact with a range of peers to explore attitudes and opinions. Once again, this strategy can be limiting if there is not a range of experience and interests to provide multiple perspectives and viewpoints.

Groups that are formed deliberately and thoughtfully by the teacher can create the optimum combination of students. It is recommended that teachers use assessment data to determine students' prior knowledge as a basis for their decision making when forming groups (Frey et al., 2009; Johnson & Johnson, 2017; Marzano, 2019). Based on these data, decisions can then be made in several ways.

Frey and colleagues (2009) recommend a version of Johnson and Johnson's (2017) stratified approach for assigning students to groups. Students are ranked according to their prior knowledge scores and their social skills, thereby producing a cumulative overall score. For example, a student might be given a rank of one for prior knowledge and a rank of twenty-two for social skills for an overall score of twenty-three. To create the groups, the students are ordered from highest to lowest based on the overall score. When forming groups of two in a class of twenty-six, the teacher would partner student 1 with the student at the middle of the rank order; in this instance, it would be student 13. Student 2 would be grouped with student 14, and so on. For groups of four, teachers would group students 1, 2, 13, and 14 to work together and students 3, 4, 15, and 16 to work together, and so on (Frey et al., 2009). This approach creates a heterogeneous group, yet group members are not so far apart in their prior knowledge to have trouble working together. Teachers still need to review the groups formed using this approach to consider other factors that might inhibit group compatibility (for example, students who have difficulty working together or who are disruptive).

Marzano Resources (2016) proposes another approach for assigning students to groups, once again based on assessment data. Students are placed into categories and then grouped according to instructional needs, time available, or purpose of the task. The approach can be used to create either homogeneous groups or heterogeneous groups. Table 2.4 depicts a sample grouping table recommended by Marzano (2019).

*Wheel grouping* is another method for categorizing students and then determining the composition of the group (see figure 2.4). It ensures a mix of higher- and lower-achieving students based on prior knowledge.

## USING AD HOC GROUPING STRATEGIES

The following grouping strategies can be used to form ad hoc groups depending on the nature of the task and the time available.

### LEARNING PARTNERS

Learning partners can be established in several ways. They are an effective way of ensuring that students become accustomed to discussing ideas with a range of students within the class rather than limiting their discussions to their group of friends. Establishing learning partners is also a great way of managing response rates to maximize the number of ideas shared and expressed.

**Table 2.4: Sample Grouping Table**

<table>
<tr><th></th><th>HIGH SCORES</th><th>MEDIUM-HIGH SCORES</th><th>UPPER MID-RANGE SCORES</th><th>LOWER MID-RANGE SCORES</th><th>MEDIUM-LOW SCORES</th><th>LOW SCORES</th></tr>
<tr><td>HIGH SCORES</td><td rowspan="3" colspan="3">High-performing homogeneous groups</td><td rowspan="2" colspan="3">Heterogeneous groups</td></tr>
<tr><td>MEDIUM-HIGH SCORES</td></tr>
<tr><td>UPPER MID-RANGE SCORES</td><td colspan="2">Low variance</td><td>High variance</td></tr>
<tr><td>LOWER MID-RANGE SCORES</td><td>High variance</td><td colspan="2">Low variance</td><td rowspan="3" colspan="3">Homogeneous groups</td></tr>
<tr><td>MEDIUM-LOW SCORES</td><td rowspan="2" colspan="3">Heterogeneous groups</td></tr>
<tr><td>LOW SCORES</td></tr>
</table>

Source: From *Marzano Compendium of Instructional Strategies*. © 2016 by Marzano Resources, 555 North Morton Street, Bloomington, IN 47404, 800.733.6786, www.marzanoresources.com. 

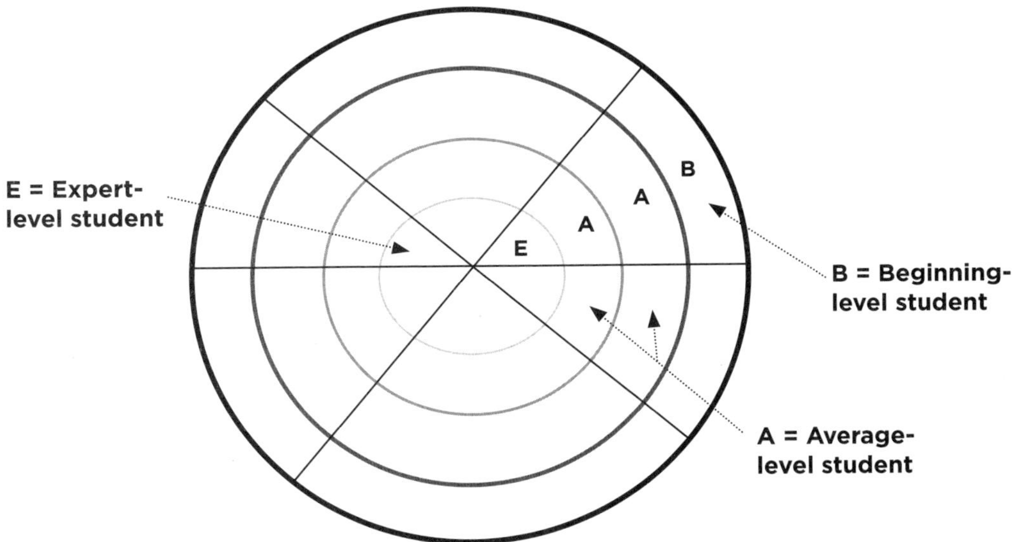


**Figure 2.4: Wheel-grouping approach.**

## MOVIE PARTNERS

### SETUP

| | |
|---|---|
| **Number of participants** | Groups of two to three |
| **Time needed** | Five minutes |
| **Room arrangement** | Standing groups |
| **Materials** | Notepaper to record different partners |

### PROCESS

1. Identify four popular, age-appropriate movie titles, and ask students to find a partner for each movie title provided.
2. At different times throughout the learning period, ask students to meet up with specific partners to discuss a topic. For example, students may be asked to meet up with their *Frozen* partner. At another time in the learning period, they may be asked to join with their *Guardians of the Galaxy* partner.
3. Each time students meet with their assigned learning partners, offer a new topic for discussion.

### APPLICATION

- Using music from the movie as the signal when it is time for students to meet up with their partner and then again when it is time for them to return to their table group adds to the engagement level of the strategy and is also an effective classroom management technique.
- With any variation, it is useful to have lively and relevant music playing and a countdown timer indicating the time remaining as students are establishing their learning partners. A variety of countdown timers are readily accessible online.
- Instead of movie partners, you could assign seasonal partners (winter, summer, autumn, spring), vacation destination partners (Paris, New York, London, home), or time-period partners (and play appropriate music for the period).

## BIRTHDAY MONTH GROUPS

### SETUP

| | |
|---|---|
| **Number of participants** | Small groups |
| **Time needed** | Five minutes |
| **Room arrangement** | Standing groups |
| **Materials** | None required |

### PROCESS

1. Direct students to group themselves according to their birthday months at designated points in the room. For example, students with birthdays in January, February, and March might move to one corner of the room; students born in April, May, and June might move to another corner of the room; and so on.
2. Give the students a prompt and have them discuss the idea with a partner or partners within that grouping.
3. Ask for each group to share responses with the whole class.

## INSIDE-OUTSIDE CIRCLE

The *inside-outside circle* strategy was originally developed by Kagan and Kagan (2009). When first introducing the strategy, model the process using a small group of students so that students are clear about what is expected. This strategy is an excellent way for students to share information and ideas or review content. It is definitely worth persisting even if it might take a little more time to establish the routine initially.

### SETUP

| | |
|---|---|
| **Number of participants** | Whole class |
| **Time needed** | Five to ten minutes |
| **Room arrangement** | Standing groups |
| **Materials** | None required |

### PROCESS

1. Ask students to form two concentric circles with an equal number of students in each circle.
2. Students forming the inner circle stand facing outward, and students forming the outer circle face inward (so that each person in the inner circle faces a person in the outer circle).
3. Ask a question or present a problem. Students discuss their thoughts, answers, and solutions with the person facing them.
4. At your cue, each person in the inner circle takes one step to the left so that everyone now faces a new partner. Partners again compare answers and solutions. Ask students to share what they discussed with their partners and how it changed (or did not change) their thinking.

### APPLICATION

- Put tape on the floor so students understand where to stand and where to move to on each cue.
- Ask students to identify similarities and differences among the perspectives of their different partners.

## GIVE ONE, GET ONE

*Give one, get one*, adapted from Lipton and Wellman (2016), sets up a process for the exchange of ideas and can be applied to a range of topics. As an interactive strategy, it allows for physical movement and facilitates the skill of paraphrasing as students share their partners' ideas rather than their own on each exchange. The ability to paraphrase is key to active listening and indicates the degree to which students are seeking to understand their peers' ideas and responses.

### SETUP

| | |
|---|---|
| **Number of participants** | Whole class |
| **Time needed** | Fifteen minutes |
| **Room arrangement** | Room for students to move and exchange ideas |
| **Materials** | Sticky notes or paper strips |

### PROCESS

1. Have students complete a response to a prompt on a paper strip or sticky note.
2. Upon completion, ask the students to circulate around the room, sharing the information on their own note or strip first and then exchanging paper strips or sticky notes with their peers. Upon each exchange, they leave with their partner's response and must then share that idea in the next exchange.
3. After two or three exchanges, ask students to return to their table group and share the information on the paper strips or sticky notes in hand.
4. Groups reflect and share themes and patterns to share with the full class.

### APPLICATION

- This strategy can be useful in teaching the writing process. Have students consider opening lines for a narrative, words to indicate emotion in different modalities, alternatives to *said*, oxymorons, and ideas for writing topics.
- Use music as a signal to change partners.

## DOUBLING UP

The *doubling up* protocol was adapted from Gayle Gregory and Lin Kuzmich (2007) and allows for multiple groupings and opportunities for students to hear multiple points of view and ideas.

### SETUP

| | |
|---|---|
| **Number of participants** | Minimum of four |
| **Time needed** | Thirty minutes |
| **Room arrangement** | Space for pairs to move and reform |
| **Materials** | Recording materials |

### PROCESS

1. Provide a prompt to think about, and ask each student to write down one or more ideas, solutions, or responses to the prompt.
2. The students then share their response with a partner.
3. Next, the two students meet with another pair to discuss their ideas or responses.
4. Students can then decide to add to or adjust their original response or idea.

### APPLICATION

Ask students to record why they changed or did not change their original response.

## FOUR CORNERS

The *four corners* protocol described by Lipton and Wellman (2016) is an easy yet effective way of grouping students according to interests or a common trait.

### SETUP

| | |
|---|---|
| **Number of participants** | Whole class |
| **Time needed** | Fifteen to twenty minutes |
| **Room arrangement** | Space for students to move to the four corners of the room |
| **Materials** | Labels for each corner |

### PROCESS

1. Prepare labels for each corner of the room. Labels might be food preferences (*Italian*, *Japanese*, *Mexican*, *Indian*), birth order (*youngest*, *eldest*, *middle*, *only child*), or favorite quotes.
2. Students consider the labels and decide which label is best suited to them. They may discuss why they chose that corner with those around them.
3. Once settled in their chosen corner, students can then create smaller clusters of two or three students.
4. Provide a discussion prompt once students have created groups of two or three.

### APPLICATION

- Once students are familiar with the process, the corners could be labeled for specific aspects of a topic for discussion. Students choose the corner that is of personal interest to them for further exploration.
- Provide a statement for students to consider. Label the corners *agree*, *strongly agree*, *disagree*, and *strongly disagree*. Students move to the corner that best describes their level of agreement with the statement. In some cases, it might be possible to have students who strongly agree discuss their viewpoints with the students who disagree, while those who strongly disagree have a discussion with those who agree. Students can then reflect on how their viewpoints differ and whether their thinking has changed during the discussion.

# FOCUSING AND SUPPORTING DIALOGUE

The following protocols can be used either to focus students' attention on the types of behaviors that are expected as they participate in group discussions or to structure discussions to ensure that groups stay focused and on task. Protocols such as these are guidelines for discussion, helping to provide structure and a safe environment for group members to contribute (City, 2014). Although many protocols exist, what follows is a selection of the protocols that I have used most often and found effective.

## FISHBOWL

The *fishbowl* protocol described by Marzano (2019) provides students with a model of what effective group work looks like through a focus group that demonstrates behaviors such as paraphrasing, pausing, clarifying, questioning, brainstorming, and using respectful language.

### SETUP

| | |
|---|---|
| **Number of participants** | Whole class |
| **Time needed** | Ten minutes |
| **Room arrangement** | Focus group |
| **Materials** | Recording sheet |

### PROCESS

1. Select a small group of students to demonstrate effective group work.
2. The rest of the class observes the model group's demonstration.
3. Discuss the effective group behaviors that the students observe the group using during the demonstration.
4. Focus students' attention on how the model group uses respectful language, demonstrates active listening, pauses to let another group member speak, asks a question, paraphrases other group members, clarifies another group member's statement, and offers a new idea.

### APPLICATION

- Rather than students observing the model group in real time, the group can be filmed and then viewed later to observe and discuss the expected behaviors.
- The same process can be used to have a model group demonstrate a particular protocol or thinking process that students will be asked to engage in.

## A–B EACH TEACH

The *A–B each teach* protocol is adapted from Lipton and Wellman (2016). It is a paired reading strategy that requires students to create short summaries and identify key points.

### SETUP

| | |
|---|---|
| **Number of participants** | Groups of two |
| **Time needed** | Ten to twenty minutes |
| **Room arrangement** | Table groupings |
| **Materials** | Texts at various levels focused on the topic that have two or more key sections of information |

### PROCESS

1. Students determine who is A and who is B.
2. Students each read their assigned section of text. For example, person A reads the first section, while B reads the second section.
3. On cue or when ready, each student teaches his or her assigned topic or section. Students should sit side by side with the text between them to ensure that the text is the focus of the conversation. Students must each provide a summary of the section that they have read along with key points.

### APPLICATION

Differentiate the content according to the reading level of the students.

## TRIAD CONVERSATIONS

The *triad conversations* protocol adapted from Gregory and Kuzmich (2007) allows for idea sharing or problem solving. It requires students to focus their attention on one person at a time and provides an audience for students' ideas or solutions.

### SETUP

| | |
|---|---|
| **Number of participants** | Groups of three |
| **Time needed** | Twenty minutes |
| **Room arrangement** | Table groups, groups seated in a cluster, or standing groups |
| **Materials** | Recording method for the recorder |

### PROCESS

1. Form groups of three.
2. Each student is assigned a letter: A, B, or C. Student A is the question asker, student B is the responder, and student C is the recorder.
3. In each round, the students take on new roles. In round two, student A will become the recorder, student B the question asker, and student C the responder. In round three, student A will become the responder, student B the recorder, and student C the question asker.
4. After each student has had an opportunity to respond, the group reflects on the ideas shared, information gathered, or solutions recorded to determine next steps or information to share with the whole class.

## APPLICATION

Table 2.5 shows some examples of questions that the question asker may put to the responder.

**Table 2.5: Questions for Triad Conversations**

| | |
|---|---|
| **Information Processing** | What did you find most interesting about what you have just heard or read?<br>Was there anything that confused you?<br>How did it connect with what you already know?<br>Is there anything you would like to know more about? |
| **Problem Solving** | What do you think the problem is?<br>How do you think we can solve this problem?<br>What might be our first step? |
| **Idea Sharing** | What is your idea?<br>How does your idea work?<br>What are the advantages of your idea?<br>What might be some possible problems that could be encountered? |

# THINK-PAIR-SHARE

The *think-pair-share* strategy was originally developed by Frank Lyman (1981) to support students who do not typically contribute responses. The process is highly effective because it provides students with time to think and prepare their answer before rehearsing their response with a classmate and finally sharing their thoughts with the larger group.

## SETUP

| | |
|---|---|
| **Number of participants** | Groups of two |
| **Time needed** | Ten to fifteen minutes |
| **Room arrangement** | Table groups with partners—side-by-side or across partners (as follows in figure 2.5, page 54) |
| **Materials** | Recording materials if required |

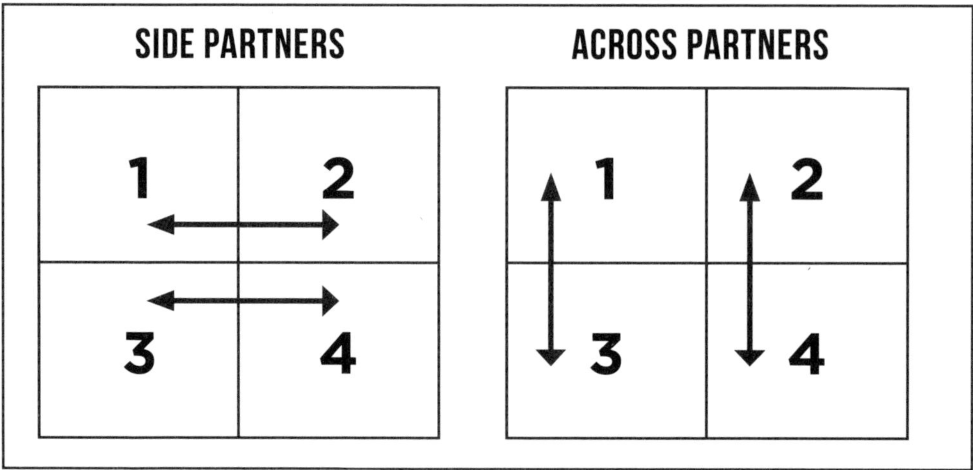


**Figure 2.5: Think-pair-share partner arrangements.**

### PROCESS

1. Group students in pairs and provide a prompt for students to discuss.
2. Students think about the prompt individually for a predetermined amount of time.
3. On cue, students each share their thoughts, ideas, and possible solutions with their partners.
4. Pairs come to a consensus about the solution or idea that they want to share.
5. Pairs are invited to share their solutions or ideas with the rest of the class.

### APPLICATION

The pairs can join with another pair to make a square and discuss the prompt among the four participants before sharing with the rest of the class.

## SAY AND SWITCH

This protocol is particularly useful for students to process and discuss information that they are learning or to generate new ideas.

### SETUP

| | |
|---|---|
| **Number of participants** | Groups of two |
| **Time needed** | Ten to fifteen minutes |
| **Room arrangement** | Table groups with partners—side-by-side or across partners or standing partners |
| **Materials** | Recording materials if required |

### PROCESS

1. Students decide who will be A and who will be B.
2. Students are given a topic for discussion or brainstorming.
3. Student A begins and has sixty seconds to tell student B what he or she knows about the topic or what ideas he or she might have.
4. Student B listens attentively. At the end of sixty seconds, student B then takes over the discussion and has sixty seconds to build on or add to what student A has said. Student B cannot repeat anything that student A has said.

### APPLICATION

- Depending on the topic or purpose, students may be given additional rounds for adding to, building on, or clarifying what has already been said in the first round.
- Reduce the time provided each round. For example:
    - Round one—Sixty seconds each
    - Round two—Forty-five seconds each
    - Round three—Thirty seconds each
- Students may wish to record their main points at the conclusion of the timed rounds.

## ROUND-THE-ROOM BRAINSTORMING

The *round-the-room brainstorming* protocol has been adapted from Gregory and Kuzmich (2007). It is an ideal strategy for sharing knowledge and ideas and is suitable for a wide range of age groups.

### SETUP

| | |
|---|---|
| **Number of participants** | Groups of three to four |
| **Time needed** | Twenty to thirty minutes |
| **Room arrangement** | Small groups with a chart for each group |
| **Materials** | Chart paper and a different colored marking pen for each group |

### PROCESS

1. Divide the class into groups—one group for each chart. Each group should stand in front of a chart. Each group selects a scribe. The scribe uses the assigned marking pen for all charts so that it is easier to attribute ideas to the appropriate group at the conclusion of the process. For example, one group may use a red marker for all charts,

which means that all red comments and ideas can be attributed back to this group.

2. The group brainstorms responses to the topic on the chart.
3. At your signal, the group moves to the next chart.
4. The group reads the responses from previous groups and adds additional ideas and responses. It may also respond to existing ideas with a specified code. For example, it places a tick to indicate that it agrees with the response or adds a question mark to indicate that it would like further clarification.
5. At the signal, the group moves and repeats the process.
6. When the group members reach the chart where they first started, they read the additional ideas and comments and clarify points as needed. They cluster ideas and decide on a way to synthesize and communicate the ideas.
7. Groups may then report out to the whole class or complete another walk around to view the completed charts.

### APPLICATION

The process could be used for generating ideas for different aspects of writing—for example, alternatives to using the word *said*, or words to describe feelings, settings, or characters.

## STAY AND STROLL

The *stay and stroll* protocol is a strategy that has evolved over a number of years in my work in both classroom and adult learning settings. It allows groups to share ideas with other groups, clarify their thinking, and receive feedback from other groups.

### SETUP

| | |
|---|---|
| **Number of participants** | Groups of three to four |
| **Time needed** | Twenty to thirty minutes |
| **Room arrangement** | Small groups |
| **Materials** | Recording materials |

### PROCESS

1. Provide groups with a prompt for discussion. Groups record their thinking—usually on large pieces of paper.
2. When groups are ready to share their ideas or responses, ask students to select one member of the group to stay. This person remains while all other members of the group stroll to view the work of other groups.

Group members who stay have the role of explaining or responding to questions posed by the members of other groups.

3. After students have had enough time to visit each group, they return to their original group to discuss patterns or trends that they noticed as they walked around. The student who remained behind reports on any questions or feedback provided by other groups.
4. Provide time for students to add to or refine their work based on their observations or feedback.

### APPLICATION

Use lively music and a two-minute timer as students move from group to group. This creates a sense of urgency with a time frame. A variety of timers can be accessed via YouTube for this purpose.

## CONCLUSION

The old adage that the person talking is the one doing the thinking is true. If we want our classrooms to be places of rich learning, we need them to be places rich with talk—rich with student dialogue. However, we are not talking about talk for talk's sake; we are talking about meaningful dialogue guided by the research-based principles and strategies described throughout this chapter. Protocols in subsequent chapters of this book can be used alongside these principles and strategies to facilitate different types of thinking as we stretch students to think critically and creatively and problem solve. It is time to shift the balance of talk in our classrooms!

# CHAPTER 3

# PROTOCOLS FOR CRITICAL THINKING

***Read not to contradict and confute; not to believe and take for granted; nor to find talk and discourse; but to weigh and consider.***

***—Francis Bacon***

## RESEARCH AND THEORY

In 2015, President Obama signed into law the Every Student Succeeds Act—a law that reauthorized and built on the Elementary and Secondary Education Act (1965) in its aim to ensure U.S. students all have equal educational opportunities. This act was a response to educators' and families' calls for "a better law that focused on the clear goal of fully preparing all students for success in college and careers" (U.S. Department of Education, n.d.). Critical thinking, the focus of this chapter, is certainly a desirable aptitude both for pursuing college and career and for participating actively as an informed citizen in a democratic society since critical thinking is the process of assessing available evidence to make decisions (Johnson & Siegel, 2010; Moon, 2008). To participate in a democracy, citizens need to be not only reasonably informed but also capable of "charting their own course in life" (Johnson & Siegel, 2010, p. xii). They need to be able to make informed decisions for the welfare of their society while not necessarily having specialist knowledge of the area or field for which the decision will be made. For example, they may need to consider the education policies of various political parties prior to an election without knowledge of the field of education. Rather than requiring expert knowledge, the decision-making process involves the ability to make a logical appraisal of the arguments that are put forward to weigh the pros and cons of each (Johnson & Siegel, 2010). This decision-making capability is the hallmark of a critical thinker since the focus of critical thinking is deciding what to believe or do through reasoning and reflective thinking (Ennis, 2001).

Within the classroom, critical thinking is also a meaning-making process (Naiditch, 2017). It is at the core of most intellectual activity that involves students learning to recognize or develop an argument, use evidence in support of that argument, draw reasoned conclusions, and use information to solve problems (Partnership for 21st Century Learning, 2015). Importantly, critical thinking is also viewed as self-directed, self-disciplined, self-monitored, and self-corrective thinking (Paul & Elder, 2008). Many years ago, futurist Alvin Toffler (1970) was quoted as claiming that the illiterate of the future would be not those who could not read or write but those who could not learn, unlearn, and relearn. Critical thinking as a process of self-corrective thinking is also a process of learning, unlearning, and relearning—skills required not only in the classroom but also in the world beyond (Naiditch, 2017).

Typically, critical thinking is conceptualized not only as skills but also as dispositions (Hajhosseiny, 2012). According to Robert H. Ennis (2001), effective critical thinkers are characterized by three broad dispositions. First, they care about making the right decision and having true beliefs. This involves:

- ***Seeking alternative hypotheses, explanations, conclusions, plans, and sources and being open to them***
- ***Endorsing a position to the extent that it is justified by the information available***
- ***Being well informed***
- ***Considering viewpoints other than their own (Ennis, 2001, p. 44)***

Second, critical thinkers tend to want to present a position honestly and clearly (Ennis, 2001). This involves:

- ***Being clear about the intended meaning of what is communicated***
- ***Determining and maintaining focus on the conclusion or question***
- ***Seeking and offering reasons***
- ***Considering the whole situation***
- ***Being aware of their own beliefs (Ennis, 2001, p. 44)***

Third, ideal critical thinkers need to be concerned about the dignity and worth of every person. Without this disposition, Ennis (2001) claims, critical thinking is less valuable and indeed potentially dangerous. Critical thinkers displaying this disposition will:

- ***Listen to others' views and reasons***
- ***Avoid intimidating or confusing others***
- ***Be concerned with the welfare of others (Ennis, 2001, p. 44)***

Clearly, the development of these dispositions cannot occur in isolation or in a situation where teacher talk predominates. Students need opportunities to listen to other points of view, and time to consider alternatives and explore possibilities.

## CRITICAL THINKING AND DIALOGUE

Fostering dialogue is viewed as part of the method for developing critical thinking, making it possible for students to take the perspective of others into account (Paul & Elder, 2008; Winsler, Fernyhough, & Montero, 2009). Accommodating multiple perspectives in this way also enables students to better understand a problem (Hajhosseiny, 2012; Sedova et al., 2014). However, as Jennifer Moon (2008) cautions, the way a person thinks is under the control of the individual—one person cannot make another think critically. What is possible, though, is that as teachers, we can foster critical thinking through the tasks we set, the habits we encourage students to form, the careful and deliberate feedback we provide, and the classroom atmosphere we create (Moon, 2008).

While there are several strategies for encouraging critical thinking, no one strategy is the "right" or only option (Moon, 2008; Naiditch, 2017). Nonetheless, the provision of cooperative learning opportunities and dialogue is considered essential for the development of critical-thinking skills (Hajhosseiny, 2012; Moon, 2008). It is through discussion and debate that students learn to listen, speak publicly, accept or reject, and develop an argument—all done in an organized and civilized manner (Naiditch, 2017). As students engage in discussions and develop arguments, they learn to present their thoughts logically, express themselves clearly, answer questions, and learn from others to revise their own arguments, reformulate them, and make them more convincing (Naiditch, 2017). These interactions help students to understand that there can be different views of the same idea. As multiple perspectives arise within the group, it can facilitate a shift from absolutist thinking or the tendency to limit our thinking to black-and-white terms (Moon, 2008).

## CRITICAL THINKING IN THE FRAMEWORK FOR 21ST CENTURY LEARNING

The process of critical thinking is intertwined with the content of thought or domain knowledge (Willingham, 2008). Consequently, critical thinking needs to be taught alongside content, rather than as an isolated skill (Naiditch, 2017). Beyer (2001b) cautions that stand-alone thinking-skills classes, unless linked directly and purposefully to systematic follow-up instruction in subject-matter courses, are not sufficient. For the improvement of thinking, the teaching of explicit skills must be complemented by a focus on the application of the skills across different subject-matter domains, or in the case of the Framework for 21st Century Learning, across nine key subjects: (1) English, reading, or language arts; (2) world languages; (3) arts; (4) mathematics; (5) economics; (6) science; (7) geography; (8) history; and (9) government and civics (Partnership for 21st Century Learning, 2015).

Working alongside the subject areas of the Framework for 21st Century Learning are the following vital 21st century skills (Partnership for 21st Century Learning, 2015).

- **Life and career skills:** Flexibility and adaptability, initiative and self-direction, social and cross-cultural skills, productivity and accountability, and leadership and responsibility
- **Information, media, and technology skills:** Information literacy; media literacy; and information, communications, and technology literacy
- **Learning and innovation skills:** Creativity and innovation, critical thinking and problem solving, communication, and collaboration

This book focuses on learning and innovation skills. Within the Framework for 21st Century Learning, the learning and innovation skills of critical thinking and creative thinking are not interchangeable (Partnership for 21st Century Learning, 2015). Indeed, critical thinking is believed to underpin creative thinking (Tactical Steps Education, n.d.b). For example, in subjects such as visual arts, typically viewed as the domain of creative thinking, a great deal of critical thinking is involved: as students analyze the works of famous artists, examine how different effects were produced, or make judgments about their effectiveness, they are thinking critically. Although critical thinking and creative thinking are linked, for practical purposes the two skills are addressed in separate chapters within this book.

## THINKING PROTOCOLS

According to Ken Kay (2010), founding president of the Partnership for 21st Century Learning, activities that foster critical thinking should require students to think, make small leaps of imagination, respond to changes and vagaries, and consider new possibilities. The following skills are included as examples of critical thinking: interpreting, analyzing, evaluating, reasoning, questioning, and inferring (Australian Curriculum, Assessment and Reporting Authority, 2018a; Partnership for 21st Century Learning, 2015). Thinking protocols that can support the process of critical thinking within various key subject areas of the Framework for 21st Century Learning are presented for these skills in the next sections of this chapter.

## INTERPRETING

The skill of interpretation goes beyond merely the summation of the words within texts (both written and spoken) as students engage in sophisticated levels of meaning making (Bellanca, Fogarty, & Pete, 2020). Interpretation is synonymous with integration since both deal with the distillation of knowledge down to its key characteristics (Marzano & Kendall, 2007). The process of integration involves the mixing of new knowledge that a student may experience and prior knowledge already residing in the student's permanent memory (Marzano & Kendall, 2007). When applied appropriately, it results in students being able to generate a statement of important or critical elements (Marzano & Kendall, 2007). Associated words are *clarify*, *communicate*, *comprehend*, *describe*, *explain*, *summarize*, and *understand*.

## SENTENCES, PHRASES, WORDS

The *sentences, phrases, words* protocol was adapted from Lipton and Wellman (2016) and requires students to dig deeper into a text to determine the critical aspects of what they have read, heard, or viewed. It helps students to collaboratively construct meaning and to clarify and extend their thinking. The sentences, phrases, words process is similar to the *three levels of text* protocol developed by Lois Brown Easton (2009) and often used by educators engaging in professional reading as a professional learning team.

### SETUP

| | |
|---|---|
| **Number of participants** | Groups of two to four |
| **Time needed** | Thirty minutes |
| **Room arrangement** | Table groupings |
| **Materials** | Text for interpretation<br>Sticky notes |

### PROCESS

1. Provide students with a text at an appropriate level of complexity to read individually.
2. Distribute sticky notes for students to use as they consider the text. On three separate notes, students record a sentence, a phrase, and a key word that they believe are important.
3. Upon completion, students share and discuss their responses in small groups. The following questions may be used to prompt discussion.
    - ❑ How are the responses similar?
    - ❑ How are the responses different?
    - ❑ Why could there be differences among what group members have considered as important or significant?
    - ❑ What is the relationship among the sentences, phrases, and words that have been selected?
    - ❑ What personal connections have you made between what you read or heard and your own experiences?
4. As a group, students then create a synthesizing statement to share with the class.

### APPLICATION

The sentences, phrases, words protocol can be applied across a range of subject areas and contexts where students are required to identify critical content and engage more deeply with texts. This can be seen when sixth- to eighth-grade students are required to "determine the central ideas or information of a primary or secondary source; provide an accurate summary of the source distinct from prior knowledge or opinions" (RH.6-8.2; NGA & CCSSO, 2010a) in history and social studies classes, or sixth-grade students are required to "integrate information presented in different media or formats (e.g., visually, quantitatively) as well as in words to develop a coherent understanding of a topic or issue" (RI.6.7; NGA & CCSSO, 2010a) in English language arts.

The sentences, phrases, words protocol can be easily differentiated to meet the needs of diverse groups of students by adjusting the complexity and length of the text that is provided to students.

## THREE-MINUTE PAUSE

The *three-minute pause* is a simple but effective protocol first established by Ralph Tyler and further developed by Jay McTighe (2019) and used extensively in his workshops on Understanding by Design. It allows students time to process and discuss information presented to them. Importantly, this protocol can be used by teachers to break up information that they present to students into smaller segments rather than overload students with too much information at one time. Marzano (2017) refers to this as breaking content into "digestible bites" (p. 30). The notion is that based on students' prior knowledge, teachers should carefully plan the delivery of content in smaller increments, stopping strategically to allow students time to process and interpret the information provided.

### SETUP

| | |
|---|---|
| **Number of participants** | Groups of two to four |
| **Time needed** | Three minutes |
| **Room arrangement** | Table groupings |
| **Materials** | Recording materials |

### PROCESS

1. Students individually record responses to the following prompts.
    - ❑ Identify three key points from what you have just read or heard.
    - ❑ Make two connections or record two pieces of additional information that you can add.
    - ❑ Create one clarifying question. Are there things that are still not clear? Are there confusing parts? Can you probe for deeper insights?

2. Upon completion, students share their responses in round-robin fashion.
3. After the task, you may choose to collect the responses as a formative assessment. Have students been able to identify the key points? Are there any misconceptions that need to be addressed?

# ANALYZING

The ability to analyze, according to James A. Bellanca, Robin J. Fogarty, and Brian M. Pete (2020), involves "the tedious task of taking ideas and objects apart, looking carefully at the various components, and then reorganizing the ideas by the similarities and differences found" (p. 19). It is embedded in exercises that require prioritizing, sequencing and delineating, comparing and contrasting, classifying and sorting, and discerning point of view and nuance (Bellanca et al., 2020). Throughout the Common Core State Standards, students are required to perform analyses. For example, in mathematics, they analyze data (NGA & CCSSO, 2010b); and in English language arts, they analyze literature to explore setting, theme, character, motivation, and relationships to plot (NGA & CCSSO, 2010a). The following strategies focus on prioritizing and delineating, with subsequent strategies focusing on comparing, classifying and sorting, and discerning points of view.

## ONE-WORD SUMMARY

The *one-word summary* is a form of limited word summary. As such, it forces students to distill information down to one key point and to prioritize critical content. This version of the strategy was developed by Rick Wormeli (Wormeli & Stafford, 2018).

The one-word summary is also an effective protocol for reviewing content at the end of a session. David Sousa (2001, 2011, 2017) reminds us of the importance of regular quick reviews such as this through his work on the primacy-recency effect. The premise of the primacy-recency effect is that during a learning episode, we remember best that which comes first (prime-time-1), second best that which comes at the end (prime-time-2), and least of all that which comes just past the middle (Sousa, 2001, 2011, 2017). Consequently, it is best to structure learning sequences with critical content at the beginning of the lesson (rather than administrative tasks, for example) and then a review of the critical content using a summarization strategy, such as the one-word summary, at the end (Sousa, 2011, 2017; Wormeli & Stafford, 2018).

### SETUP

| | |
|---|---|
| **Number of participants** | Whole class |
| **Time needed** | Ten to twenty minutes |
| **Room arrangement** | Table groupings |
| **Materials** | Recording materials |

### PROCESS

1. Ask students to write down one word that summarizes the key point of what they have just read or heard.
2. Students then explain their choice of word. This step is vital, as it is not the choice of a word but the rationale behind it that leads to learning (Wormeli & Stafford, 2018).
3. Collect the one-word summaries to analyze the words that students have chosen along with the rationales. This becomes an excellent formative assessment tool. Consider the words chosen. What patterns and trends are emerging? Have students identified critical content? Do the rationales indicate misconceptions?
4. Feed back to the class the most frequent word mentioned, most unusual word, or most convincing rationale.

### APPLICATION

An alternative approach is to have the class brainstorm a list of possible words and then narrow the selection down to three words from which students may choose. Students can argue for and against words as effective descriptions of the topic. In this process, students are analyzing the topic in a substantive manner. Once again, they provide a rationale for their word choice.

## SCRAMBLED SENTENCES

The *scrambled sentences* protocol referenced by Lipton and Wellman (2016) takes the one-word summary a step further. It is an effective way of bringing a learning experience to a close by capturing and sharing the most important information from the session—again a process of prioritization. The strategy creates high energy and interaction as group members create a collective synthesis of key words (Lipton & Wellman, 2016).

### SETUP

| | |
|---|---|
| **Number of participants** | Groups of four to five |
| **Time needed** | Ten to fifteen minutes |
| **Room arrangement** | Table groupings |
| **Materials** | Sticky notes |

### PROCESS

1. Distribute one sticky note per student. Ask each student to record a key word that captures an important idea from what has been read or discussed during the session.

2. Within their group, students share their key words. They eliminate any duplicate words and substitute them with other appropriate key words.
3. Ask the groups to create a sentence using their key words. They may add additional words if necessary but should try to limit the number of additional words used.
4. Have each group share its sentence.

## HEADLINES

The *headlines* protocol comes from the Visible Thinking research of Ron Ritchhart and Project Zero (n.d.d), a research center at the Harvard Graduate School of Education. It draws on newspaper-type headlines as a way of summing up and capturing the essence of an idea, concept, or topic. Typically, it works most effectively at the end of a class discussion or session after students have explored a topic in detail or have formed opinions about it.

### SETUP

| | |
|---|---|
| **Number of participants** | Individuals, then groups of two as part of a think-pair-share |
| **Time needed** | Ten minutes |
| **Room arrangement** | Table groupings |
| **Materials** | Recording materials |

### PROCESS

1. Ask students to create a headline that captures the most important aspect of the topic that should be remembered (think).
2. Upon completion, ask students to share their headline with a partner (pair).
3. Have students share a headline from someone else that they thought was particularly good at communicating the core of the topic (share).
4. Record headlines so that a class list of headlines is created. Alternatively, use a web-based application such as Padlet (https://padlet.com) for students to share their headlines. Simply have students double-click on the background of the Padlet wall to add their headline. This could be used to implement thinking protocols as homework where students are able to collaborate from anywhere.
5. Review and update headlines periodically as the class learns more about the topic.
6. Use a follow-up question such as, "How has your headline changed, or how does it differ from what you would have said?" to help students reflect on changes in their thinking.

### APPLICATION

Examples of headlines based on the topic of materialism might include "Materialism—the possession obsession," "Materialism possesses you," or "You don't need it; you want it!" (Rochester Community Schools, n.d.).

## COMPARING, CLASSIFYING, AND SORTING

The identification of similarities and differences among or between things or ideas is fundamental to most analysis processes (Marzano & Kendall, 2007). According to Robert J. Stahl (1985) and Barry K. Beyer (1988), as cited by Robert Marzano and John S. Kendall (2007), the critical characteristics of the process are:

- ***Specifying the attributes or characteristics on which items being matched are to be analyzed***
- ***Determining how they are alike and different***
- ***Stating similarities and differences as precisely as possible (p. 45)***

Research indicates that identifying similarities and differences is associated with gains in student achievement (Marzano, 2019). Indeed, effect sizes of 1.61 have been recorded (Dean, Hubbell, Pitler, & Stone, 2012; Marzano, Pickering, & Pollock, 2001). An sten to others' views and reaso effect size of this nature is significant and equates to a potential gain in student achievement of forty-five percentile points (Dean et al., 2012; Marzano et al., 2001). The following strategies can support student discussions utilizing this essential skill.

### SENTENCE-STEM COMPARISONS

This process is deceptively simple but should not be discounted in terms of effectiveness. In application, it can be used in any subject area or grade level and is a useful way of scaffolding students' thinking as they discuss comparisons. The basic sentence structure was introduced by Marzano in *The Art and Science of Teaching* (2007) and further developed in subsequent publications, such as *The New Art and Science of Teaching* (2017).

#### PROCESS

The basic sentence structure is as follows.

- ***A and B are similar because ____________________.***
- ***A and B are different because A ____________________ but B ____________________.***

### APPLICATION

An example of the application of this strategy could be the comparison of a comma and a period.

- ***A comma and a period are similar because ___________________________.***
- ***A comma and a period are different because a comma _____________________ but a period _____________________.***

Another example might be the comparison of fractions and decimals.

- ***Fractions and decimals are similar because ___________________________.***
- ***Fractions and decimals are different because fractions ___________________ while decimals ___________________.***
- ***Fractions and decimals are different because fractions _____________________ but decimals _____________________.***

Other terms suitable for comparison include:

- ***Metaphors and similes***
- ***Molecules and atoms***
- ***Primary sources and secondary sources***
- ***Excess post-exercise oxygen consumption (EPOC) and oxygen deficit***

The sentence-stem completion strategy is ideal for students to reflect on and discuss any key terms that they typically confuse. As students engage in the process, their understanding of the topic deepens (Marzano, 2007).

## COUNTERCLAIM

The process of classification is associated with examining similarities and differences (Marzano, 2019). *Counterclaim*, which uses the process of classification and categorization, was developed by Tactical Steps Education (n.d.b). Using this protocol, students categorize items and then revise their classifications after listening to differing points of view. Taking the process one step further, students must then reflect on their own understanding, make decisions, and justify their viewpoints or reasoning.

### SETUP

| | |
|---|---|
| **Number of participants** | Groups of three to four, then whole class |
| **Time needed** | Ten to twenty minutes |
| **Room arrangement** | Table groupings |
| **Materials** | Statement cards for classification<br>Opposing position cards for each end of the continuum (for example, healthy and unhealthy)<br>Display board |

### PROCESS

1. Select a relevant issue or topic based on the curriculum focus.
2. Write opposing positions for the topic on two cards and display them on opposite ends of a continuum on a whiteboard or wall.
3. Students work in groups of three or four to consider several statements about the issue or topic. Groups discuss each statement and decide where each statement should be positioned on the continuum.
4. A representative from each group places the statements along the continuum in the order that the group has decided on.
5. Other groups are encouraged to "counterclaim" the position of any of the statements placed on the continuum by presenting an argument to support their challenge. Members of the group that placed the original statement on the continuum have the right of reply. The group may or may not move the statement as a result of the challenge.

### APPLICATION

- **Villain and hero:** Write the names of historical figures on the statement cards (for example, Adolf Hitler, Pol Pot, Benedict Arnold, Harriet Tubman, Nelson Mandela, and Marie Curie). Students must decide if the figures are best described as villains or heroes.
- **Fact and opinion:** Write various statements on the statement cards. Students must decide if the statements are facts or merely opinions. Alternatively, students could determine if the statements show faulty logic or a credible argument.

## DOUBLE BUBBLE THINK-PAIR-SHARE

The *double bubble map* can be used to compare items, people, places, events, or concepts. This version of the map is from Marzano Resources (2016). This protocol combines the use of the double bubble map and think-pair-share (described in chapter 2, page 27).

## SETUP

| | |
|---|---|
| **Number of participants** | Individuals, then groups of two, then four |
| **Time needed** | Ten to twenty minutes |
| **Room arrangement** | Table groupings |
| **Materials** | Double bubble map template |

## PROCESS

1. Choose two topics to compare. Write the two things being compared in the large circles on the left and right sides of the double bubble map template.
2. Distribute the double bubble map template to each student.
3. Students use words or short phrases to describe what is similar about the two topics and record these in the circles in the middle that connect to both topic circles. They then record words and short phrases that describe what is different about the two topics in the applicable circles that only connect to one of the topic circles.
4. Students form pairs and compare their maps. As they compare their responses, they discuss their reasoning and add to or adjust their own maps.
5. Pairs then combine with another pair for further discussion and sharing.
6. Invite students to share their own ideas or the ideas that they have heard.

## APPLICATION

Figure 3.1 (page 72) features a filled-out version of the double bubble map template that compares mathematical expressions and mathematical equations.

Other examples for comparison include:

- **English language arts—**Novel studies or character traits
- **History—**Source and evidence
- **Geography—**Land formations, conservation, and preservation
- **Science—**Contact and noncontact forces
- **Visual arts—**Artworks from different social, cultural, and historical contexts
- **Music—**Rhythmic and harmonic patterns
- **Engineering and technology—**Materials, components, tools, equipment, and techniques

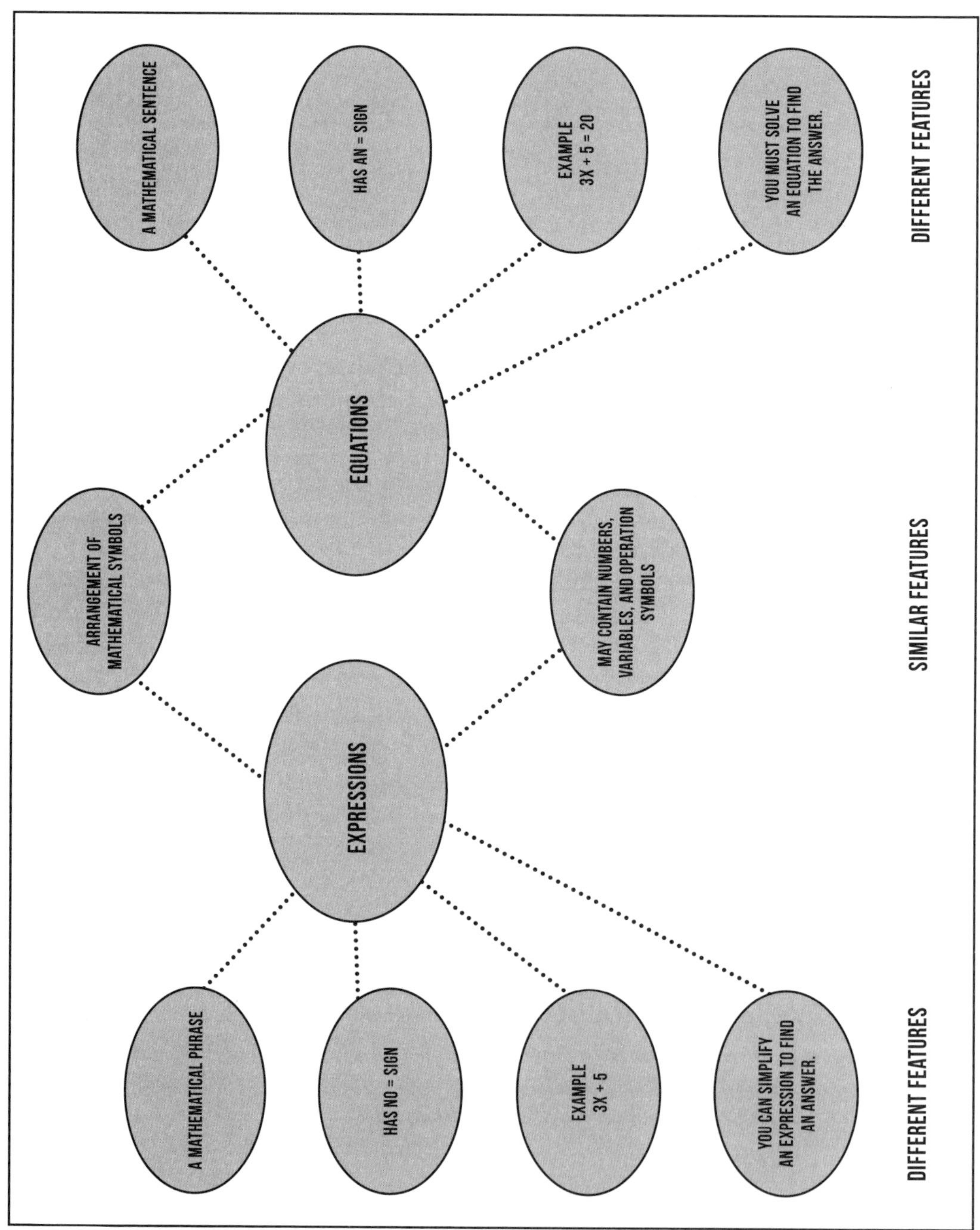


**Figure 3.1: Application of double bubble map think-pair-share.**

## INTER-VENN-TION

The *inter-VENN-tion* protocol developed by Lipton and Wellman (2016) is one that I have adapted and used extensively when working with teacher teams to compare current practice with new initiatives. In the classroom, it can be an effective way of scaffolding student discussions so that students can compare their thinking about a topic with the perspectives of other group members. It may also be used to ascertain prior knowledge about and prior experiences with a topic.

### SETUP

| | |
|---|---|
| **Number of participants** | Groups of two, then four |
| **Time needed** | Twenty to thirty minutes |
| **Room arrangement** | Table groupings |
| **Materials** | Blank paper<br>Template with a Venn diagram |

### PROCESS

1. Provide students with a topic prompt.
2. Individually, students record their responses on a blank piece of paper.
3. Upon completion, students form groups of two.
4. Students discuss their responses and complete the Venn diagram, placing information in the appropriate space on the diagram to indicate similarities and differences in experiences or perspectives.
5. If new information arises during the discussion, students can add the information accordingly.
6. After fifteen to twenty minutes, have pairs create quartets and share the discussion that has taken place and the similarities and differences that were identified.

### APPLICATION

- Model the process initially by having students record and compare information about themselves (for example, interests, family, or hobbies).
- Use this protocol at the beginning of a unit of study and then at a later stage for students to reflect on how their thinking has changed or deepened.

## EVALUATING

Evaluation is a form of decision making done at a very conscious and thoughtful level, unlike decision making that occurs quickly without much conscious thought (Marzano & Kendall, 2007). It involves making an assessment against a set of criteria and determining value and quality based on how well an object or action fulfills the criteria (Bellanca et al., 2020). Evaluation is a complicated process, as it requires the application of other thinking skills, such as analysis, synthesis, and comparison (Bellanca et al., 2020). The following strategies are useful for helping students to determine the criteria for making judgments, including considering different perspectives on how an evaluation might be formed and understanding the advantages and disadvantages of an action or object.

## CONSIDER ALL FACTORS (CAF)

Edward de Bono is one of the most influential people in the field of thinking skills and someone who has certainly had a huge impact on my own teaching and thinking. Through his work at Cambridge University, de Bono established the Cognitive Research Trust (CoRT) program for teaching thinking in schools. The *consider all factors* (*CAF*) protocol is a strategy within that program and an excellent tool for helping students to consider all aspects of a topic or action as they determine the criteria on which to base evaluations (CoRT Thinking, 2019b). Its use reduces the tendency to be satisfied with accepting the first considerations that come to mind immediately. Instead, when considering a new topic, students begin to think, "What am I missing?" Students might, for example, explore the topic of sleep and consider why it is so important. They would then complete the sentence, "After considering all factors, I think that . . ." I have also found that the CAF process is enhanced with the use of the decision-making matrix outlined in step 4.

### SETUP

| | |
|---|---|
| **Number of participants** | Groups of two, then four |
| **Time needed** | Twenty minutes |
| **Room arrangement** | Table groupings |
| **Materials** | Recording materials<br>Decision-making matrix template |

### PROCESS

1. Students work individually to list as many factors as possible that need to be considered on a specified topic or issue.
2. Working in pairs, students compare their lists and establish an agreed-on list of factors by adding to, combining, or refining their lists.
3. Pairs may then form quartets to repeat step 2, arriving at an agreed-on list for the quartet. Depending on the topic, you may wish to then have all groups share their lists to establish a list that is agreed on by the whole class.
4. Students use the decision-making matrix (figure 3.2) to record the factors to be considered and the alternatives for evaluation (Marzano Resources, 2016).

5. As a group of four, students consider the alternatives and the degree to which each one meets each of the criteria determined by the group.

   It is appropriate to assign a weighting system to criteria if the group decides that one or more criteria are more important than others. For example, one criterion may be assigned double points because it is viewed as more important while another criterion receives the single score of zero to three.

| **Factors for consideration** | **Alternatives** | | | |
|---|---|---|---|---|
| 0 = Does not meet criterion<br>1 = Slightly meets criterion<br>2 = Meets criterion<br>3 = Strongly meets criterion | | | | |
| | | | | |
| | | | | |
| | | | | |
| | | | | |
| | | | | |
| | | | | |
| | | | | |
| Totals | | | | |

Source: From *Marzano Compendium of Instructional Strategies*. © 2016 by Marzano Resources, 555 North Morton Street, Bloomington, IN 47404, 800.733.6786, www.marzanoresources.com. All rights reserved. Used with permission.

**Figure 3.2: Decision-making matrix template.**

## APPLICATION

- In health and physical education, students may determine the most important factors when developing a health plan and then evaluate alternatives.
- Elementary school students may use the process to consider all of the factors that judges from the Children's Book Council should contemplate when determining which picture book should be judged picture book of the year.
- In ninth- and tenth-grade history, students can consider all factors required to "cite specific textual evidence to support analysis of primary and secondary sources, attending to such features as the date and origin of the information" (RH.9-10.1; NGA & CCSSO, 2010a).

## CALL TO ACTION—CHALLENGES, SUCCESSES, ISSUES

As students engage with this protocol, originally developed by Tactical Steps Education (n.d.b), they examine an issue or problem presented as a call to action and outline the various ways it may be viewed. In this way, they can make reasoned judgments and explore options from a broader perspective.

### SETUP

| **Number of participants** | Groups of two or four |
|---|---|
| **Time needed** | Twenty minutes |
| **Room arrangement** | Table groupings |
| **Materials** | Recording materials |

### PROCESS

1. Provide students with a prompt in the form of a call to action. The prompt may be a current issue relevant to students, such as "All teenagers should learn about resources for anxiety and depression while they are in school." Younger students may consider a prompt such as "Plastic straws should be banned from all school cafeterias."
2. Ask students to create three columns labeled Challenges, Successes, and Issues. If more appropriate for the topic under discussion, the Issues column may be replaced with an Interesting Thoughts column.
3. Working in pairs or quartets, students discuss and record the challenges they foresee if the statement were to be enacted, the successes that may be possible if the action were to be taken up, and the possible issues that may arise out of the action.
4. Have groups of students compare their responses to gain other perspectives for consideration.

### APPLICATION

Table 3.1 shows an example of a completed call to action exercise. The table highlights how you might set up a template for students to use for this exercise.

## HOW I SEE IT

This protocol has been adapted from the Visible Thinking routine developed by Project Zero (n.d.a) called *circle of viewpoints*. It helps students reflect on diverse perspectives around a topic or issue. It helps to develop an understanding that people may think and feel differently depending on their background experiences or prior knowledge.

**Table 3.1: A Completed Call to Action**

| **Call to action:** All learner drivers in the United States should complete one hundred hours of driving experience prior to gaining their intermediate or provisional license. | | |
|---|---|---|
| **Challenges** | **Successes** | **Issues** |
| ■ It would place a heavy demand on parents or caregivers.<br>■ Other drivers who supervise may not be the best instructors in terms of road rules.<br>■ Learner drivers whose parents or caregivers do not drive are disadvantaged. | ■ Young drivers are more prepared and safer on the roads.<br>■ Research suggests that graduated driver licensing systems, which include longer practice periods, are associated with 26 to 41 percent reductions in fatal crashes and 16 to 22 percent reductions in overall crashes among sixteen-year-old drivers (Centers for Disease Control and Prevention, n.d.). | ■ People cheat the system.<br>■ Lessons with driving school instructors are expensive.<br>■ What about families with more than one teenager who needs to acquire the hours of driving experience?<br>■ Different states and provinces currently have different requirements. |

## SETUP

| | |
|---|---|
| **Number of participants** | Groups of four |
| **Time needed** | Twenty minutes |
| **Room arrangement** | Table groupings |
| **Materials** | Recording materials |

## PROCESS

1. Have students brainstorm a list of different viewpoints that may arise on a topic. The following questions may help students consider a range of possible perspectives.
   - ❑ How might this topic be viewed by someone from a different country, region, or time period?
   - ❑ Who (and what) might be affected?
   - ❑ Who is involved?
   - ❑ Who might care?
2. Ask students to choose one of the viewpoints from the list. Provide time for students to prepare to speak about the topic from that perspective. Encourage students to become actors, taking on the character of the viewpoint they have chosen.

3. Have students take turns within groups of four acting out their various perspectives. The following guiding prompts from Project Zero (n.d.a) may be useful for students as they share their chosen perspective.
    - ❏ I am thinking of . . . (identify the topic) . . . from the point of view of . . . (state the viewpoint you have chosen).
    - ❏ I think . . . (describe the topic from your chosen viewpoint).
    - ❏ A question I have from this viewpoint is . . .
4. As students share their viewpoints, their ideas can be recorded or written on a group chart so that a list of possible perspectives is created. Share the group charts through a process such as stay and stroll (as outlined in chapter 2, page 27).
5. The last guiding prompt asks students to think of a question they might have from their chosen viewpoint. Collect these questions for later class discussions, or ask students to write them down and answer them as they learn more about the topic.
6. Finish the protocol by having students reflect on new ideas that they have about the topic that they had not considered previously or new questions that have arisen through the discussions.

## THREE AS—AGREE, ARGUE, AHA

This protocol adapted from Lipton and Wellman (2016) is one that I typically use with adults in professional learning sessions but have adapted here for classroom purposes. It helps students to consider an issue in terms of positives and negatives and also to consider other people's perspectives or viewpoints.

### SETUP

| | |
|---|---|
| **Number of participants** | Groups of three to four |
| **Time needed** | Twenty minutes |
| **Room arrangement** | Table groupings |
| **Materials** | Recording materials |

### PROCESS

1. Introduce a topic for discussion or distribute a short reading.
2. Students record one thing about the topic or selection of text with which they agree and one thing about the topic or selection of text with which they might argue.
3. In round-robin fashion, students first share the things with which they are in agreement. They then discuss what values or beliefs they hold that may have influenced the choice of agreements.

4. Repeat step 3, but this time, students share the things with which they disagree. Once again, have students reflect on the values or beliefs they hold that may have influenced their responses.
5. Finally, students record their aha moments—new insights or perceptions that arose from their discussions.
6. Invite groups to share their insights with the whole class.

## AGREEMENT, DISAGREEMENT, IRRELEVANCE (ADI)

The *agreement, disagreement, irrelevance* (*ADI*) protocol by de Bono (CoRT Thinking, 2019a) helps students understand that in an argument, the two sides will not necessarily disagree about everything. Usually, there are some points on which they will disagree but others on which they will agree. There may also be some points that are completely irrelevant, and it does not matter whether they agree or not. ADI helps students to make a deliberate effort to find the points of agreement, disagreement, and irrelevance.

### SETUP

| | |
|---|---|
| **Number of participants** | Groups of two to three |
| **Time needed** | Twenty minutes |
| **Room arrangement** | Table groupings |
| **Materials** | Recording materials<br>Text for discussion and exploration |

### PROCESS

1. Select a relevant issue or topic and texts that represent both sides of the argument.
2. Have students interrogate the texts to determine points on which the two sides agree and disagree as well as points that are irrelevant.
3. Upon completion, have students consider their own thinking in terms of the points they agree or disagree with or points that may not have been raised by either side that they believe are important for consideration.

## TRUE FOR WHO?

The *True for Who?* protocol is another tool developed by Project Zero (n.d.e). It is an effective technique for supporting students to consider issues from different perspectives. As students engage in the process, they gain a deeper understanding of how an issue looks from different points of view and see how different viewpoints and experiences might influence the positions people may take in an argument.

## SETUP

| | |
|---|---|
| **Number of participants** | Groups of four to five |
| **Time needed** | Twenty to thirty minutes |
| **Room arrangement** | Table groupings |
| **Materials** | Recording materials |

## PROCESS

1. Choose a relevant topic or issue for consideration (such as climate change).
2. Highlight a claim that has been made about the topic or issue. (In the case of climate change, you might highlight a claim that climate change is a natural occurrence and not an outcome of human activity.)
3. In groups of four to five, students discuss the claim using the following prompts.
    - ❑ What kind of situation was the claim made in?
    - ❑ Who made it?
    - ❑ What were people's interests and goals?
    - ❑ What was at stake?
4. As a whole class, brainstorm a list of the different standpoints from which to look at this claim (such as scientist, politician, farmer, businessperson, industrialist, and conservationist).
5. In their original group of four or five, students choose a viewpoint and take on that persona or role. From this stance, students consider this question: Would this person think the claim is true or false, or would he or she be uncertain or even ambivalent? Why?
6. Have students speak in round-robin fashion from the viewpoint that they have chosen using the following prompts.
    - ❑ My viewpoint is . . .
    - ❑ I think this claim is true or false or I'm uncertain or unconcerned because . . .
    - ❑ The thing that would convince me to change my mind is . . .
7. Finally, students step back from the discussion and consider everything that they have heard. They then determine their own conclusion or stance and reflect on any new ideas or questions that may have emerged. A quickwrite (see chapter 2, page 27) could be used to capture their thinking.

# REASONING

The ability to reason is a crucial step in the expression of meaning and the communication of thinking (Bellanca et al., 2020). Consequently, it is a communicative skill that appears in all subject areas as an essential means for presenting information to others for consideration. According to the Common Core State Standards, by the end of fourth grade, students are expected to "identify the reasons and evidence a speaker provides to support particular points" (SL.4.3; NGA & CCSSO, 2010a). In providing their reason, students explain a situation or circumstance that made certain results seem possible or more appropriate. Typically, this is done in answer to simple yet extremely important questions such as, "What is your reason?" or "Why do you think that?" Bellanca and colleagues (2020) remind us that the act of reasoning has very clear rules: "A must follow B with a sufficient line of evidence. All the facts selected must contribute to the argument. No facts may be extraneous or unconnected" (p. 157). The protocols that follow in this section can assist students in this reasoning process.

## TRUE, FALSE, AND DARE

In a world where information is easily accessible and sometimes overabundant, we need to help our students separate the wheat from the chaff—in other words, work out what is worthwhile and true and what is rubbish to be discarded. The *true, false, and dare* protocol adapted from Stephen Bowkett (2007) helps students to assess the information with which they are presented to determine what is of value, what is irrelevant, and what is simply not true.

### SETUP

| | |
|---|---|
| **Number of participants** | Groups of two |
| **Time needed** | Fifteen to twenty minutes |
| **Room arrangement** | Table groupings |
| **Materials** | Text (spoken, written, visual, or multimodal) for consideration |

### PROCESS

1. Present students with a text to investigate.
2. Have students work together in pairs to consider the following questions adapted from Bowkett (2007).
   - ❑ How recent is the information? Has new information been presented since the text was created?
   - ❑ What is the source of the information? Are there other sources that would verify the information?
   - ❑ What is the author's purpose in presenting this information—is it to entertain, inform, or persuade?
   - ❑ How does the information build on what I already know or understand?

- ❑ Is the author putting forward a point of view? If so, what evidence is being used to support that point of view? Does the author offer other viewpoints, or does the author show a particular bias?
- ❑ Does the author present a logical flow of ideas?
- ❑ Does the information make sense, or do I have questions about what the author has presented?

3. Depending on time constraints, ask students to present their thoughts.

### APPLICATION

As you think about the questions in step 2, do not be fooled into thinking that these questions are only appropriate for older students. Even younger learners can respond to modified versions of these questions. It is important not to dumb things down for students; sometimes they will surprise you with their insights. You might consider a simplified version of the protocol for younger students, such as find the fib, described next.

## FIND THE FIB

*Find the fib* (developed by Kagan and Kagan [2009]) requires little to no preparation and can be used in all subject areas.

### SETUP

| **Number of participants** | Groups of two |
|---|---|
| **Time needed** | Fifteen to twenty minutes |
| **Room arrangement** | Table groupings |
| **Materials** | Recording materials |

### PROCESS

1. Ask students to write down three statements—two that are true and one that is a fib.
2. When students have finished writing, have them read their statements to a partner.
3. Partners must guess which statement out of the three is the fib.

### APPLICATION

You might employ this protocol after students have learned about a historical figure or time period, after students have finished a topic in science or geography (such as planets, the water cycle, or landforms), or after students have read a fiction text (for example, they may write about character traits or events).

## ERRORS IN REASONING

The analysis of errors in reasoning involves students consciously considering the validity of information and identifying any inaccuracies that have been presented (Marzano & Kendall, 2007). The world is filled with examples of errors in thinking—they can be seen in advertising, conversations, scams, or political speeches. The ability to identify errors in thinking is essential to reduce our students' vulnerability to manipulation and misinformation and to better inform their decision making and choices.

Rather than a protocol as such, Marzano (2016) provides a set of useful guidelines for students to consider the reasoning of others or their own reasoning. He categorizes typical errors into categories as outlined in table 3.2.

**Table 3.2: Strategies for Identifying Errors in Reasoning**

| STRATEGY | DESCRIPTION |
|---|---|
| **Identifying Errors of Faulty Logic** | The teacher asks students to find and analyze errors of faulty logic. Errors of faulty logic refer to situations in which a conclusion is not supported by sound reasons. Specific types of errors in this category include contradiction, accident, false cause, begging the question, evading the issue, arguing from ignorance, composition, and division. |
| **Identifying Errors of Attack** | The teacher asks students to find and analyze errors of attack. Errors of attack happen when a person focuses on the context of an argument, rather than the argument itself, in trying to refute the other side. |
| **Identifying Errors of Weak Reference** | The teacher asks students to find and analyze errors of weak reference. Specific types of these errors include using sources that reflect biases, lack credibility, appeal to authority, appeal to the people, and appeal to emotion. |
| **Identifying Errors of Misinformation** | The teacher asks students to find and analyze errors of misinformation. Two types of misinformation errors are confusing the facts and misapplying a concept or generalization. |
| **Practicing Identifying Errors in Logic** | The teacher uses practice exercises to help students identify errors in logic. Typically, these exercises will describe a scenario in a few sentences and ask students to identify the reasoning error present in the scenario. Students might select the answer in a multiple-choice or matching format or be asked to recall the answer from memory. |
| **Finding Errors in the Media** | The teacher provides students with footage of political debates, televised interviews, commercials, advertisements, newspaper articles, blogs, and other sources and asks them to find and analyze errors in reasoning that underlie the messages therein. |

continued →

| | |
|---|---|
| **Examining Support for Claims** | The teacher asks students to examine the support provided for a claim by analyzing the grounds, backing, and qualifiers that support it. *Grounds* are the reasons given to support a claim; *backing* is the evidence, facts, or data that support the grounds; and *qualifiers* address exceptions or objections to the claim. |
| **Judging Reasoning and Evidence in an Author's Work** | The teacher asks students to apply their knowledge of reasoning and argumentation to delineate and evaluate the arguments present in a text. Students read a text and identify the claim, grounds, backing, and qualifiers. Students must decide whether the reasoning is valid or logical (containing no errors) and whether the supporting evidence is sufficient and relevant. |
| **Identifying Statistical Limitations** | The teacher asks students to find and analyze errors that commonly occur when using statistical data to support a claim. The five major types of statistical limitations for students to be aware of are (1) regression toward the mean, (2) conjunction, (3) base rates, (4) the limits of extrapolation, and (5) the cumulative nature of probabilistic events. |
| **Using Student-Friendly Prompts** | The teacher uses prompts and questions phrased in nontechnical language to prompt students to look for certain types of errors (for example, asking students to look for "getting off topic" rather than "evading the issue"). |
| **Anticipating Student Errors** | The teacher identifies errors that students are likely to make during a lesson. During the presentation of content, the teacher alerts students to the potential problems. For example, when a teacher introduces the process for finding the area of a right triangle, he or she reminds students it is sometimes difficult to identify the base and height if the triangle has been rotated. |
| **Avoiding Unproductive Habits of Mind** | Unproductive habits of mind are those that hinder us from completing complex tasks. To counteract unproductive habits, the teacher reinforces the following productive habits of mind: staying focused when answers and solutions are not immediately apparent, pushing the limits of your knowledge and skills, generating and pursuing your own standards of excellence, seeking incremental steps, seeking accuracy, seeking clarity, resisting impulsivity, and seeking cohesion and coherence. |

Source: From *Marzano Compendium of Instructional Strategies*. © 2016 by Marzano Resources, 555 North Morton Street, Bloomington, IN 47404, 800.733.6786, www.marzanoresources.com. 

## WHAT MAKES YOU SAY THAT?

As students engage with this protocol from Project Zero (n.d.f), they must describe what they see or know and then provide an explanation. Not only is evidential reasoning (evidence-based reasoning) promoted as students share their interpretations, but as they listen to one another, they also begin to understand alternatives and multiple perspectives.

## SETUP

| | |
|---|---|
| **Number of participants** | Whole class, then groups of two to four |
| **Time needed** | Fifteen to twenty minutes |
| **Room arrangement** | Table groupings |
| **Materials** | Prompt for discussion—object or text (spoken, written, visual, or multimodal text)<br>Recording materials |

## PROCESS

1. Introduce the process by modeling the protocol as a whole-class discussion or by using the fishbowl strategy described previously in chapter 2 (page 27).
2. As students interpret the object or text provided, continually ask two follow-up questions so that students begin to automatically support their interpretations with evidence without even being asked.
    - ❑ What do you know? Or, depending on the context, what do you see?
    - ❑ What do you see or know that makes you say that?
3. Document the interpretations and evidence, taking note of the language that students use to justify their thinking. This document could be used later to create a rubric showing the elements of a good interpretation or what constitutes good reasoning. Students could use this rubric to self-reflect on their own interpretations at a later date.
4. Once students are comfortable with the process, move the discussions into smaller groups of two to four. Monitor students' use of the follow-up questions to ensure that they are providing reasoned evidence for their interpretations.
5. In these smaller groups, the documentation of the interpretations may take the form of sketches, drawings, mind maps, or writing depending on the context. These may then be displayed or reviewed and built on as the topic is further explored and students' understanding of the topic deepens.

## APPLICATION

The basic nature of the questions in this protocol means that it is very flexible and easily adapted for use with almost any subject area: looking at works of art or historical artifacts, interpreting a poem, making scientific observations and hypotheses, or investigating more conceptual ideas such as democracy or bullying (Project Zero, n.d.f).

When introducing a new topic, the protocol may also be useful for gathering information on students' general concepts and possible misconceptions. If used in this way, it is an effective formative assessment tool to highlight areas for clarification, gaps in understanding, or areas where students already have substantial prior knowledge and depth of understanding, thus informing the teacher's next steps for instruction.

# QUESTIONING

Questioning, as de Bono (2004) asserts, is an important aspect of listening and an important means of interaction between people in conversation or in any type of communication. Our questions "show attention and interest. They allow for the further exploration of certain points. They permit the clarification of any misunderstanding. They enable the speaker to elaborate on points which seem to be of interest to the listener" (de Bono, 2004, p. 72). Students typically have very little experience in school of asking questions, though it is an important skill; usually this is the domain of the teacher. Walsh and Sattes (2011) maintain that teachers ask, on average, fifty questions an hour in elementary and secondary classrooms. With so many teacher questions, is there any time remaining for students to be actively involved in questioning and, therefore, meaning making? Typically, the answer is no, indicating that a change is necessary. However, students struggle to formulate questions—probably because they have so little experience doing so in the school setting. The following strategies are effective approaches for supporting students to generate questions.

## QUESTION JUMBLE

This gamelike protocol provides a fun scaffold for students to develop questions. The potential combination of question stems encourages students to generate more complex questions, rather than restricting their questions to simple, literal questions, such as "Who is . . . ?"

### SETUP

| | |
|---|---|
| **Number of participants** | Groups of four |
| **Time needed** | Ten to fifteen minutes |
| **Room arrangement** | Table groupings |
| **Materials** | Two sets of cards per group (see figure 3.3) printed on different-colored cards to distinguish the two sets<br>Recording materials |

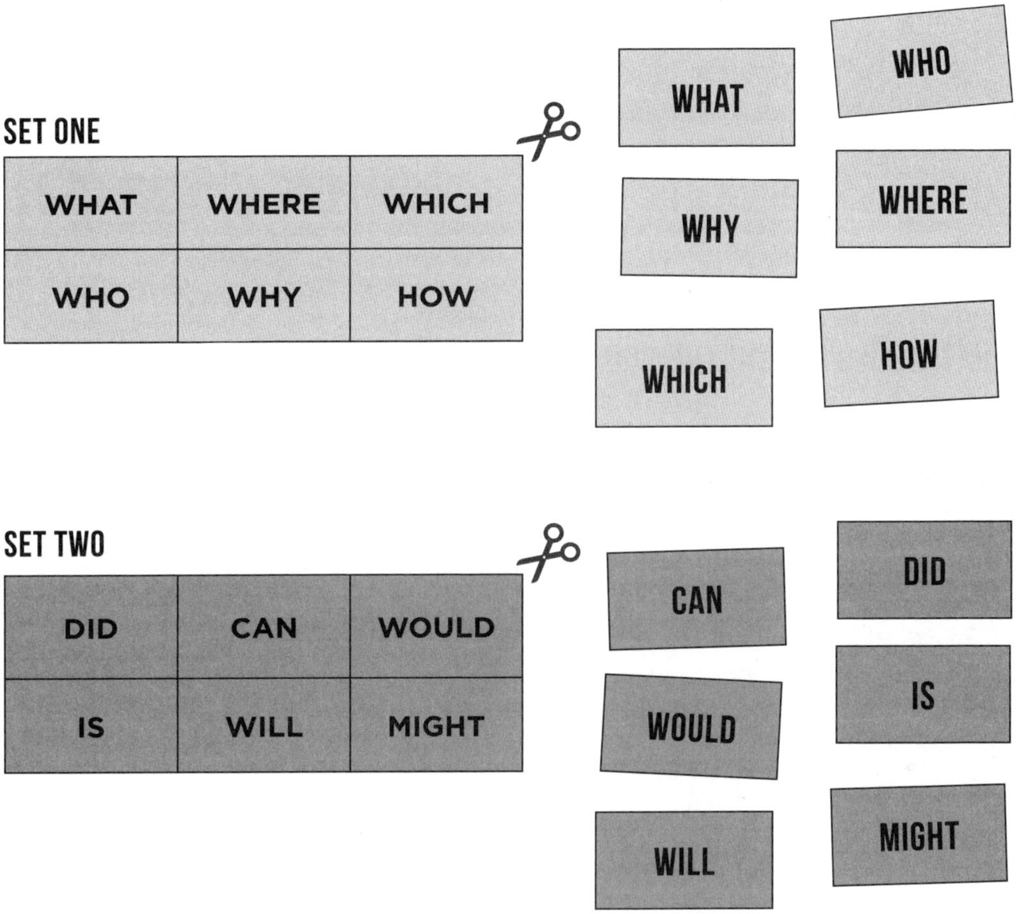

**SET ONE**

| WHAT | WHERE | WHICH |
|---|---|---|
| WHO | WHY | HOW |

WHAT
WHO
WHY
WHERE
WHICH
HOW

**SET TWO**

| DID | CAN | WOULD |
|---|---|---|
| IS | WILL | MIGHT |

CAN
DID
WOULD
IS
WILL
MIGHT

**Figure 3.3: Question jumble cards.**

## PROCESS

1. Provide students with a topic for discussion.
2. Working as a group, students take turns drawing a card from each set of cards.
3. Students then develop a question using the two words selected. For example, after reading a story, students might generate questions after selecting the How card from the first set and the Would card from the second: How would you help the main character of the story solve the issue of bullying? How would you change the ending of the story?
4. After each student has generated and recorded a question on paper, have students pass their questions to another group for that group to answer.

### APPLICATION

- Have students categorize questions as literal, inferential, or evaluative.
- Use the question starters to determine students' background knowledge and understanding of a topic.
- Use the process to formulate questions for a particular purpose, such as organizing an event, interviewing a guest speaker, or reviewing understanding after watching a program such as *CNN 10* (www.cnn.com/cnn10).

## WHAT WOULD WINNIE THE POOH ASK SPIDER-MAN?

This fun question-generation protocol from Bowkett (2007) can be pitched at any level of sophistication and age group.

### SETUP

| | |
|---|---|
| **Number of participants** | Groups of two, then four |
| **Time needed** | Ten to fifteen minutes |
| **Room arrangement** | Table groupings |
| **Materials** | Question grids for each group |

### PROCESS

1. Start this protocol with a simple level of sophistication by using a grid of four squares.
2. Above and beside the squares, write the names of cartoon characters, celebrities, or other well-known characters.
3. Where two characters intersect, students work in pairs to ask two questions from the perspective of each character. An example is provided in figure 3.4.
4. Upon completion of the questions, have pairs combine to answer the questions that they created in the grid. You may wish to have students provide feedback to each other on the quality of the questions that were created using a set criterion.

### APPLICATION

Once students are familiar with the process, increase the level of sophistication by replacing the cartoon characters with historical figures, prominent scientists, contemporary politicians, or characters from a novel study.

| | Winnie the Pooh | Snow White |
|---|---|---|
| **Spider-Man** | What would Winnie the Pooh ask Spider-Man?<br><br>What would Spider-Man ask Winnie the Pooh? | What would Snow White ask Spider-Man?<br><br>What would Spider-Man ask Snow White? |
| **Batman** | What would Winnie the Pooh ask Batman?<br><br>What would Batman ask Winnie the Pooh? | What would Snow White ask Batman?<br><br>What would Batman ask Snow White? |

**Figure 3.4: Sample question grid.**

# INFERRING

The most common way of thinking about the skill of inferring is the notion of reading between the lines. It is the search for meaning that is implied rather than stated explicitly—the meaning that resides just below the surface of what has been written or said. As humans, we are constantly making inferences; we make inferences about expressions, body language, and tone as well as texts that are read, viewed, or heard (Harvey & Goudvis, 2017). When we infer, we draw on our background knowledge and experiences, merging them with clues gleaned from what we have heard or read to draw a conclusion, predict an outcome, or surface a theme (Harvey & Goudvis, 2017). Although often linked to reading comprehension, the skill of inferring is cross-curricular, as can be seen in the following examples from the Common Core State Standards for mathematics (NGA & CCSSO, 2010b) and the Next Generation Science Standards (NGSS Lead States, 2013).

- In seventh-grade mathematics, students "use data from a random sample to draw *inferences* about a population with an unknown characteristic of interest" (7.SP.A.2; NGA & CCSSO, 2010b) and "use measures of center and measures of variability for numerical data from random samples to draw informal comparative *inferences* about two populations" (7.SP.B.4; NGA & CCSSO, 2010b).
- Middle school students learning about biological evolution "apply scientific ideas to construct an explanation for the anatomical similarities and differences among modern organisms and between modern and fossil organisms to *infer* evolutionary relationships" (MS-LS4-2; NGSS Lead States, 2013).
- When studying matter and its interactions, high school science students "plan and conduct an investigation to gather evidence to compare the structure of substances at the bulk scale to *infer* the strength of electrical forces between particles" (HS-PS1-3; NGSS Lead States, 2013).

The protocols that follow are practical strategies from a range of sources that can be used to develop the skill of inferring. First of all, students need to know what inferring actually is and what it means to infer. One very simple strategy for that is to teach students the formula for inferring from Harvey and Goudvis (2007): background knowledge plus text clues equals an inference, or "BK + TC = I" (p. 141).

## THE WHAT DO WE KNOW? WEB

The *What Do We Know? web*, based on the work of Bowkett (2007), helps students to move beyond being passive recipients of facts and to consider in more detail what they think they know in relation to a topic or concept.

### SETUP

| | |
|---|---|
| **Number of participants** | Groups of two, then four |
| **Time needed** | Fifteen to twenty minutes |
| **Room arrangement** | Table groupings |
| **Materials** | Web template |

### PROCESS

1. Create a template as per the web in figure 3.5.
2. Write a statement or fact in the center of the web. The limited space within the web means that the statement needs to be precise.
3. Moving out from the center of the web, students work in pairs to write a few things about what they know.
4. In the next section of the web, students record their first responses, including assumptions they might be making, associations they have made, and inferences they have arrived at as well as opinions, ideas, and beliefs.
5. Having considered what they think they know and how they may come to these understandings, students then generate a list of things that they want to know more about.
6. Ask students to move into groups of four to compare their responses. They may prioritize what they want to find out or adjust their web based on their discussions.

### APPLICATION

- This protocol can be adapted by simply choosing a specific example for your topic area.
- It may also be used as a formative assessment to determine students' prior knowledge or misconceptions.
- Throughout a unit of study, students may revisit their web to update their responses.

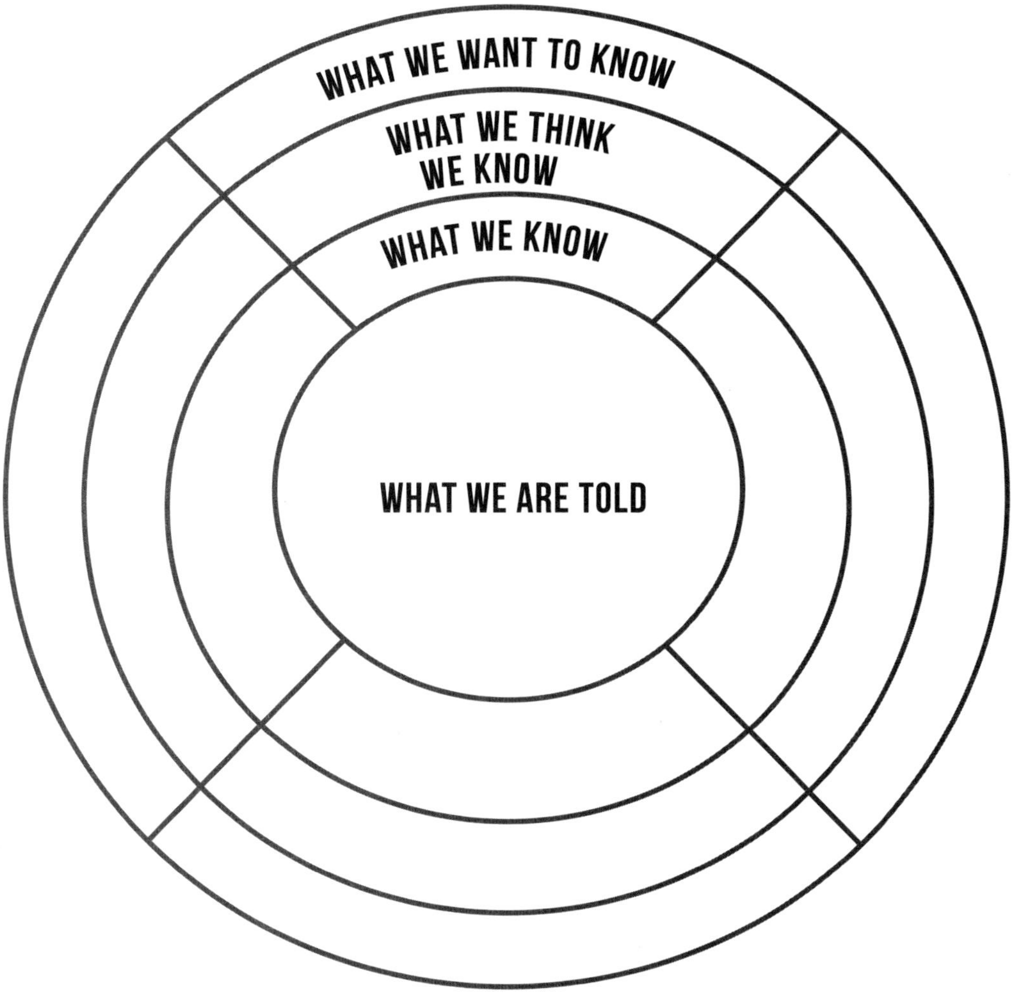

**Figure 3.5: Web template.**

## ICEBERG STRUCTURE

This protocol adapted from Bowkett (2007) uses the metaphor of an iceberg to encourage students to dig below the surface level of information that has been presented (the visible part of the iceberg) to consider the author's agenda, bias, omissions, and possible generalizations that may have been made (the submerged part of the iceberg). Students are also asked to consider their own interpretations of what the information means.

### SETUP

| | |
|---|---|
| **Number of participants** | Groups of two, then four |
| **Time needed** | Fifteen to twenty minutes |
| **Room arrangement** | Table groupings |
| **Materials** | Iceberg template |

### PROCESS

1. Present students with the iceberg template (figure 3.6) and an appropriate prompt. Explain the metaphor of the iceberg. For example, when we look at an iceberg, only a small part of the iceberg is visible. There is a large section of the iceberg that is submerged and not visible. Like sailors being cautious of icebergs and what they can't see, we must be cautious when information is presented to us. We must consider what assumptions, biases, or viewpoints underpin the statement or information—what lies hidden under the surface.
2. Have students work in pairs to dig deeper using questions such as the following.
    - ❏ What is the source of the information?
    - ❏ Are there other sources that can verify this information?
    - ❏ What is the author's purpose in presenting this information?
    - ❏ Is the author biased?
    - ❏ Whose viewpoints are represented? Whose viewpoint or perspective is missing?
    - ❏ Do the ideas flow logically?
    - ❏ Do I understand what has been presented?
    - ❏ What do I think it means? What is my opinion?
3. Ask students to move into groups of four to compare their responses. They may add to or adjust their responses based on their discussions.

### APPLICATION

Topics for consideration may include the following.

- "Truth is within ourselves" (a line from Robert Browning's [1835] poem "Paracelsus").
- "All we can know is that we know nothing. And that's the height of human wisdom" (text from Leo Tolstoy's novel *War and Peace*; Goodreads, n.d.b).
- "The three little pigs were good friends."
- "Global warming is a myth."

## CONCLUSION

Throughout any given day, thoughts cascade through our minds and the minds of our students. Often, these thoughts go unnoticed or are merely taken for granted (Bowkett, 2007). However, teaching thinking skills through the use of the protocols in this chapter and the chapters to follow increases students' ability to notice, understand, and work more effectively with their thoughts as they make sense of their world. In doing so, they ask, "What is important?" "What is logical?"

"How might others think about this issue?" and, most importantly, "What do I think about this issue or topic and why?" As Bowkett (2007) proposes, it is easy to feel a sense of security by teaching students facts and then testing them to make sure they know those facts. But what a slippery slope. . . . Although students might be able to mindlessly regurgitate facts or processes, do they truly understand?

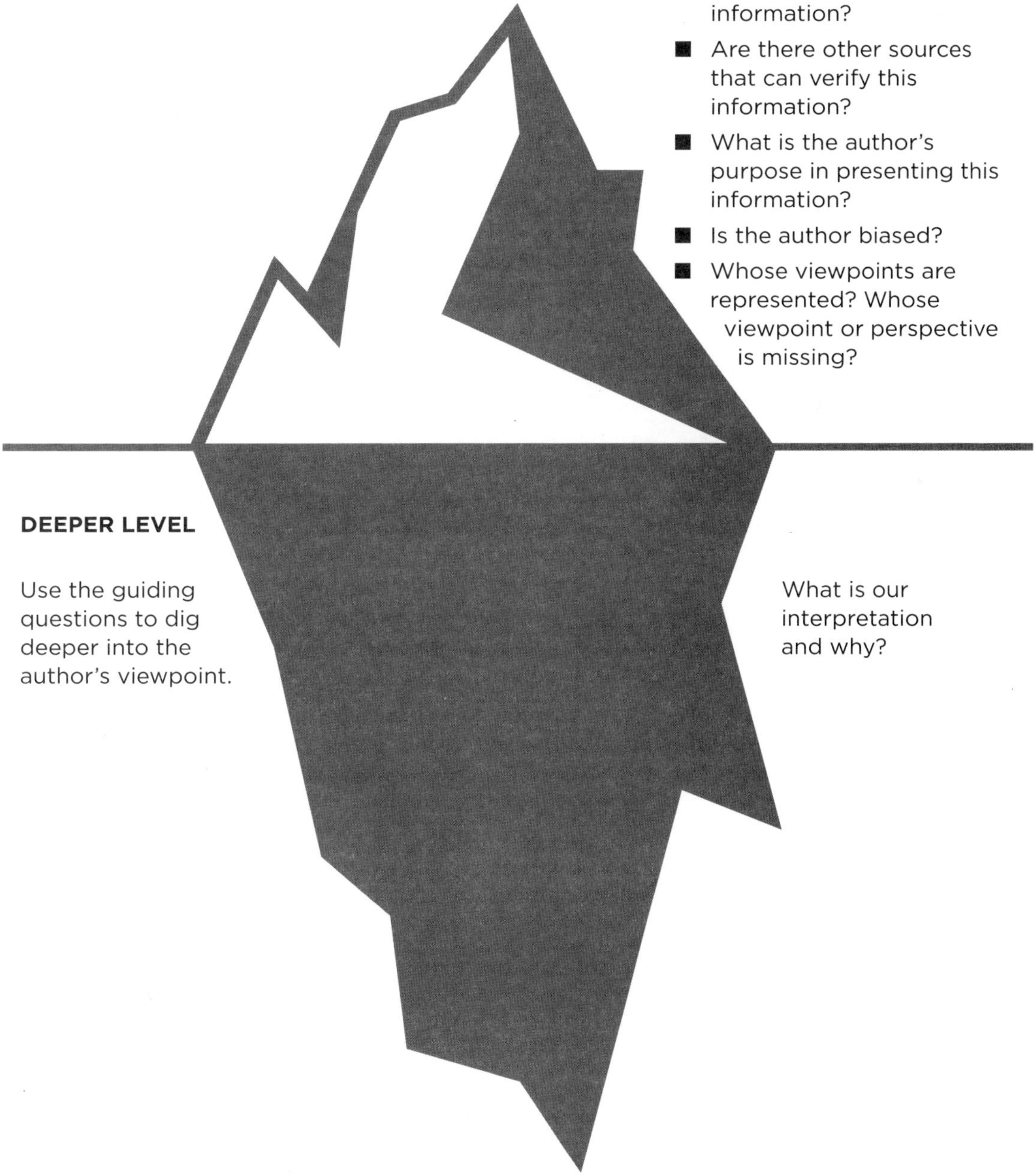

**Figure 3.6: Iceberg template.**

# CHAPTER 4

# PROTOCOLS FOR CREATIVE THINKING

***Think left and think right and think low and think high. Oh, the things you can think up if only you try!***

***—Dr. Seuss***

## RESEARCH AND THEORY

It might begin with a hunch or a new insight as you scribble on a napkin while pondering a problem. It might be a new way of doing something or the combination of existing ideas to create something original. It is a process, and it's the process of creative thinking. But creative thinking, although it may at times be spontaneous, isn't just free abandon and the generation of wild and crazy ideas. Creative thinking is "the process of having original ideas that have value" or, more specifically, have purpose (Azzam, 2009, p. 22). For example, coming up with one hundred ways to make a process more efficient isn't of value if one of them isn't selected and implemented or if the ideas are so far-fetched and impractical that they are ignored because there is no purpose for their use (Lucas & Spencer, 2017). Consequently, the process of creative thinking draws on the skills of critical thinking and, in particular, the skill of evaluation as ideas are considered, tested, and judged (Azzam, 2009; Lucas & Spencer, 2017; Sternberg & Grigorenko, 2016). As they consider what-if possibilities incorporating real-life problem solving, students engaged in creative thinking use both divergent and convergent thinking: divergent thinking as many different ideas or solutions are considered and then convergent thinking as a decision is made as to which idea or solution will provide the most efficacious results (Drapeau, 2014; Puccio & Murdock, 2001). Highly creative people are good at employing both types of thinking and at knowing when to swap between the two (Ostroff, 2016). Creative thinking isn't just the generation of elaborate products; it is also a way of thinking and an attitude toward life generally—a function of everything we do (Azzam, 2009; Drapeau, 2014; Sternberg & Grigorenko, 2016).

Creativity isn't a switch that's flicked on or off; it's a way of seeing, engaging with, and responding to the world around us (Judkins, 2015).

The terms *creativity* and *creative thinking* are often used interchangeably, but there are subtle differences. In simple terms, it is best to consider creativity "as an umbrella construct that subsumes creative thinking" (Puccio & Murdock, 2001, p. 67). Alternatively, you may see creative thinking as what you do when you are being creative and creativity as the outcome of that thinking (Lucas & Spencer, 2017). Although varying definitions of creativity and creative thinking exist, most draw on the foundational work of E. Paul Torrance (1974), where creative thinking is described as:

> ***a process of becoming sensitive to problems, deficiencies, gaps in knowledge, missing elements, and so on; identifying the difficulty; searching for solutions, making guesses, or formulating hypotheses about the deficiencies; testing and retesting these hypotheses and possibly modifying and retesting them; and finally communicating the results. (p. 6)***

Torrance proposes that another way of defining creative thinking is to draw on analogies (Shaughnessy, 1998). He refers to the following list as his "artistic definition" of creative thinking:

- ***Creativity is like wanting to know.***
- ***Creativity is like digging deeper.***
- ***Creativity is like looking twice.***
- ***Creativity is like listening to smells.***
- ***Creativity is like listening to a cat.***
- ***Creativity is like crossing out mistakes.***
- ***Creativity is like getting in deep water.***
- ***Creativity is like having a ball.***
- ***Creativity is like cutting holes to see through.***
- ***Creativity is like cutting corners.***
- ***Creativity is like plugging in the sun.***
- ***Creativity is like building sandcastles.***
- ***Creativity is like singing in your own key.***
- ***Creativity is like shaking hands with tomorrow. (as cited in Shaughnessy, 1998, pp. 442–443)***

Typically, creative thinking involves cognitive verbs such as *brainstorm, generate, connect, relate, design, create, produce, construct, elaborate, embellish, predict*, and *improve* (Drapeau, 2014). It is believed that creative-thinking skills enable us to cope with life's challenges and actualize our fullest potential (Puccio & Murdock, 2001). Mihaly Csikszentmihalyi (1996) advocates for creativity and creative thinking as ways of making day-to-day experiences more vivid, more enjoyable, and more rewarding, claiming that creativity and creative thinking banish boredom so that every moment is seen as holding the possibility of a fresh discovery. Perhaps it is for these reasons that creative-thinking skills are believed to promote well-being and good mental health as well as have the potential to even reduce the mental decline associated with aging (Puccio & Murdock, 2001). Similarly, acclaimed psychologist Abraham Maslow (as cited in Davis, 1989) stressed the value of what he termed *self-actualized creativity*, described as the mentally healthy tendency to approach all aspects of life in a creative fashion.

# CREATIVE-THINKING MYTHS

Possibly due to the multifaceted nature of creativity, there are many misconceptions about creativity, creative thinking, and what it means to be a creative person (Treffinger & Isaksen, 2001). Several of these misconceptions or myths are explored in the following sections.

## ONLY CERTAIN PEOPLE ARE CREATIVE

How many times do you hear people lament the fact that they are not creative? I can vividly recall a conversation I had with my son who is now a software engineer and at the time of our conversation was convinced that he was not creative but rather by nature a logical person who solved problems. Yet, he is creative—his work requires him to "successfully produce novel and useful responses to open-ended challenges and opportunities" daily, which is one of the definitions of creative thinking (Puccio & Murdock, 2001, p. 70). As a software engineer, my son produces novel and useful responses—it just happens to be with computer code.

Csikszentmihalyi (1996) describes two types of creative people: (1) *big-C* creative people and (2) *little-c* creative people. Big-C creative people are the people we typically think of as creative. They are the people who are distinguished in their fields and whose work often leads to change (Drapeau, 2014). Common examples include Einstein, Picasso, Mozart, Dickinson, and Gandhi (Lassig, 2012). Little-c creative people, on the other hand, are people who use creativity to affect their everyday lives (Drapeau, 2014). My son is a classic example of a little-c creative person. Indeed, everyone has the potential to engage in little-c creativity, albeit at different levels (Lassig, 2012). Little-c creativity may be as simple as a new floral arrangement or as complex as an original improvisation by a local jazz band (Gardner, 2006; Lassig, 2012).

Eminent developmental psychologist Howard Gardner (2006) also warns us against a one-size-of-creativity-fits-all view, proposing that although a person might be highly creative in one domain, he or she may not be viewed as creative in another realm. For example, a creative mathematician may be an atrocious debater, and vice versa.

## CREATIVITY IS AN INDIVIDUAL PURSUIT

Rather than the act of an individual, creative thinking almost always is a social activity and almost always takes place in response to an issue or problem facing an individual or group (Azzam, 2009; Drapeau, 2014; Lucas & Spencer, 2017). R. Keith Sawyer (2006) maintains that "creative insights typically emerge from collaborative teams and creative circles" (p. 42). Similarly, creativity expert Sir Ken Robinson (as cited in Azzam, 2009) makes the case that most original thinking comes through the stimulation of other people's ideas. Even people who work alone, he suggests, draw from the cultures they're part of and the influence of other people's thinking and achievements. Csikszentmihalyi (1996) argues that creativity is the interaction of three autonomous elements.

1. **The *individual*:** This person has mastered some discipline or domain of practice and is creating variations within that domain. The individual might be a musician creating a new piece of music or a software engineer writing a new program.
2. **The *cultural domain* in which the person is working:** This domain has its own models and rules. Even successful artists and innovators are often experts in the knowledge of their domains before diverging and breaking the rules of those disciplines. For example, Pablo Picasso was a student of classical painting before reimagining how to represent people and everyday objects in vivid colors and abstract shapes (Ostroff, 2016). After all, as Gardner (2010) suggests, "It's not possible to think outside the box unless you have a box" (p. 17).
3. **The *social field*:** This field provides the educational experiences and the opportunities to perform. Representatives from within the field determine whether an individual's creation has merit or value. It might be decided that the idea should simply be discarded because it is impractical or not new or novel but instead is something that already exists.

## CREATIVE IDEAS WILL SELL THEMSELVES

Robert Sternberg (2007) reminds us that not all new ideas are automatically accepted. Indeed, creative ideas are often viewed with suspicion and distrust, since people are typically comfortable with the ways that they already think and can be reticent to shift away from their current thinking (Sternberg, 2007). Not everyone, for example, can see the benefits of driverless cars. Although more and more people are beginning to see the advantages, the notion is still viewed as far-fetched and problematic by many people. Consequently, Sternberg (2007) maintains that we need to help students learn how to persuade other people of the value of their ideas. He suggests that if students complete a science project, they should be asked to present it and demonstrate why it makes an important contribution. Similarly, if they create a piece of art, they should be able to describe why they think it has value (Sternberg, 2007).

## CREATIVITY IS INNATE AND CANNOT BE TAUGHT

Researchers and practitioners generally agree that although creativity is complex and multifaceted, it can be taught and developed (Azzam, 2009; de Bono, 2007; Drapeau, 2014; Puccio & Murdock, 2001; Treffinger & Isaksen, 2001). In fact, research involving identical twins has shown that creativity is not an inherited skill but rather a skill that can be nurtured (Tactical Steps Education, n.d.b). Creativity, de Bono (2007, 2009) argues, is a skill that everyone can learn, practice, and use.

To teach creative thinking, you don't need to be creative yourself, but when teaching the generic skills of creative thinking, the classroom environment that is created is very important (Azzam, 2009). This is a safe and positive environment where unusual ideas are supported, choice is provided, multiple solutions are expected, and constructive feedback is given (Drapeau, 2014). Since "creativity demands emotional risk taking," students need to feel free to share their thoughts and ideas and understand that their ideas can be represented in different ways (Drapeau, 2014; Piirto, 2004, p. 417). An old anonymous quote describes this philosophy of risk taking perfectly:

> ***To laugh is to risk appearing the fool.***
> ***To place our ideas, our dreams, before a crowd is to risk their loss.***
> ***To live is to risk dying.***
> ***To hope is to risk despair. To try is to risk failure.***
> ***The person who risks nothing, does nothing, has nothing, and is nothing.***
> ***Only a person who risks is free. (as cited in VanGundy, 2005, p. 19)***

Modeling appropriate responses to creative ideas is essential in building students' understanding of what is and is not acceptable (Drapeau, 2014). Creative thinking will not become a habit in a classroom where "students are afraid of failure or making mistakes, overly focused on grades or worried about being different, or where they experience rejection, criticism, or bullying" (Drapeau, 2014, p. 13). For a range of strategies for developing classroom norms and expectations regarding respectful interactions, refer to chapter 2 (page 27).

## CREATIVITY IS TYPICALLY ASSOCIATED WITH THE ARTS OR SPECIFIC ACTIVITIES

Historically, certain subject areas, such as the arts, were considered to be the only areas where creative thinking was appropriate (Azzam, 2009; de Bono, 2007, 2009; Drapeau, 2014). However, it is important in all aspects of life and learning—without creative thinking in science, for example, new technology would not be developed (Tactical Steps Education, n.d.b). Creative thinking is essential for responding to the complex environmental, social, and economic pressures of the 21st century (Partnership for 21st Century Learning, 2019). Further, creative-thinking processes are fundamental to effective learning across all curriculum areas (Drapeau, 2014). Consequently, creative-thinking skills are included among the learning and innovation skills of the Framework for 21st Century Learning (Partnership for 21st Century Learning, 2019).

## CREATIVE THINKING IN THE FRAMEWORK FOR 21ST CENTURY LEARNING

In the Framework for 21st Century Learning, creative thinking involves students using various idea-generation techniques to create and refine worthwhile ideas, working creatively with others, and implementing innovations. This includes comprehending real-world limits to the implementation of new ideas, being responsive to diverse perspectives, incorporating group feedback, and viewing frequent mistakes as an inherent component of creativity and innovation (Partnership for 21st Century Learning, 2015).

Significantly, creative thinking in the Common Core State Standards (NGA & CCSSO, 2010a, 2010b) and the Next Generation Science Standards (NGSS Lead States, 2013) is not viewed as a side dish or an added extra if time permits. Rather, it is part and parcel of the main meal and full learning experience. Table 4.1 shows how creative thinking is experienced in specific subject areas within the Common Core State Standards and Next Generation Science Standards.

The Partnership for 21st Century Learning (2015) advises that activities that foster creative thinking and other 21st century skills should include both independent and collaborative tasks—such as the thinking protocols that follow. These protocols can be used both individually and collaboratively, albeit collaborative groups can use the individual strategies while individuals obviously are not able to fully engage with protocols originally designed for groups.

## THINKING PROTOCOLS

The thinking protocols in this section have been divided into two key areas of creative thinking: (1) generating ideas and (2) exploring possibilities. When exploring possibilities, the protocols typically involve a decision-making process as students determine the merits of their ideas.

**Table 4.1: Examples of Creative Thinking in the Common Core State Standards and Next Generation Science Standards**

| SUBJECT AREA | DESCRIPTION |
|---|---|
| **English Language Arts, History or Social Studies, and Technical Subjects** | Students think creatively about how they can best organize and structure their writing to support their writing's purpose, and about which words, phrases, and transitions will create cohesion and clarify relationships among their writing's claims, reasons, and evidence. They also think creatively to make visual displays or audio recordings when appropriate for presentations that they must give. |
| **Mathematics** | Students develop capacity in creative thinking as they learn to create equations describing numbers or relationships, generate patterns and equivalent expressions, make inferences, construct arguments, rewrite expressions in different forms, reason abstractly and quantitatively, and represent problems and data. |
| **Science** | Students learn that scientific knowledge results from imagination, creativity, and effort. They engage their creativity as they develop and use models, plan investigations, design solutions and improve designs, construct evidence-based explanations and claims, and communicate information. |

Source: Adapted from NGA & CCSSO, 2010a, 2010b; NGSS Lead States, 2013.

# GENERATING IDEAS

Brainstorming or generating ideas is the birthplace of all creative endeavors, big or small, where ideas are hatched and later incubated (Bellanca et al., 2020). The ability to generate many ideas is what the "father of creativity," E. Paul Torrance, refers to as *fluency* (Drapeau, 2014). The goal is to generate as many ideas as possible. Therefore, teachers should praise students for the number of ideas generated at this point rather than the quality of the ideas. The premise is that through quantity, it will be possible to find some quality responses (Craft, 2013; Drapeau, 2014). Arthur B. VanGundy (2005) also maintains that groups are more likely to arrive at a workable solution if they have more ideas from which to choose. Hence, he emphasizes the rule "No evaluation with generation!" (VanGundy, 2005, p. 9). Evaluation and prioritization are deferred until as many ideas as possible have been generated. Similarly, Gregory and Kuzmich (2007) suggest the use of the FLOW rules for idea generation.

- F = Free flow of ideas must occur.
- L = Let all ideas come out, even the crazy ones.
- O = Originality counts.
- W = Weigh up options later.

The following protocols are effective for improving students' ability to generate ideas.

## BRAINWRITING

Depending on the grade level and students you are teaching, the technique of *brainwriting*, as opposed to conventional brainstorming, can support students generating ideas. Brainstorming refers to the traditional verbal generation of ideas within a group setting. In contrast, brainwriting is silent as individuals within the group write down their initial ideas (VanGundy, 2005). Both approaches have merits, but an advantage of brainwriting is that students can express their ideas without worrying about what others think. Additionally, during brainwriting, four or five people can be generating ideas simultaneously as opposed to waiting while one person speaks, which is characteristic of traditional brainstorming sessions. Of course, the benefit of brainstorming is that we are typically social creatures and an idea generated by one person can spark other ideas among the group.

## BRAINSTORM AND CATEGORIZE

Bringing together the merits of both brainstorming and brainwriting, the *brainstorm and categorize* protocol is an approach that I have used extensively in my work. It was originally developed by Lipton and Wellman (2016) as part of their work supporting professional learning teams to become more effective. Not only is it useful for idea generation, it also can be used to activate prior knowledge and experiences (Lipton & Wellman, 2016). Hence, it is a useful tool for formative assessment.

### SETUP

| | |
|---|---|
| **Number of participants** | Groups of four to five |
| **Time needed** | Fifteen to twenty minutes |
| **Room arrangement** | Table groupings |
| **Materials** | Recording materials (Sticky notes work well.) |

### PROCESS

1. Direct the students to generate as many ideas as possible on a given topic by writing their ideas on slips of paper or sticky notes. Each idea should be written on a separate note.
2. After a designated amount of time, students share their responses with their group and organize their ideas into categories.
3. When the categories have been determined, the groups create a label for each category.
4. Have groups share their responses with other groups by using the stay and stroll (or gallery walk) protocol described in chapter 2 (page 27).

### APPLICATION

- In English language arts, students can generate ideas about what makes a good picture book and then create categories to combine the ideas, such as illustrations, plot, characters, and message. I have used this protocol as the basis for creating a rubric for writing a picture book, for providing peer feedback on student-created picture books, and for students to judge picture books produced by authors. This protocol can be linked to the decision-making matrix described in chapter 3 (page 75).
- For family and consumer sciences, students might brainstorm and categorize food preparation techniques.
- In the arts, students can generate a list of questions that they would like to ask a famous artist, playwright, or actor and then categorize the questions.
- During professional learning, educators can brainstorm and then categorize all the things that they do successfully at school to increase student learning and engagement along with the evidence that indicates that their assertion is correct. Educators might also brainstorm and categorize the characteristics of highly effective teachers.

## IDEA WEB

This protocol combines classic brainstorming with a mind map to extend the group's thinking and generate additional ideas. It is based on the *idea, category, web* strategy from Lipton and Wellman (2016) and the well-known lotus blossom diagram graphic organizer (see page 148). Unlike that of the lotus blossom diagram, the outcome is less structured, resembling a mind map rather than the typical grid format of the lotus blossom diagram.

### SETUP

| | |
|---|---|
| **Number of participants** | Groups of four to five |
| **Time needed** | Fifteen to twenty minutes |
| **Room arrangement** | Table groupings |
| **Materials** | Chart paper |

### PROCESS

1. Provide a prompt for discussion and direct students to work within their groups to generate as many ideas as possible for the topic. The ideas should be recorded on the chart paper in a nonlinear fashion.
2. After the initial brainstorming of ideas, have students consider each idea and tease it out further by building on or breaking down the original idea. These additions could be recorded in a different color and

should be linked to the parent idea with a line or arrow. This creates the web effect.

3. Upon completion, have students place a star on those ideas that warrant further exploration or that they wish to share with the larger group.

## APPLICATION

- It is best to model this process as a whole group first prior to having students work independently so that students become familiar with the process.
- When groups are working on idea generation such as this, I will often provide students with different-colored pens. This way, it is easier to see which students are contributing ideas as you move around the groups. An example of a final idea web on friendship is shown in figure 4.1.

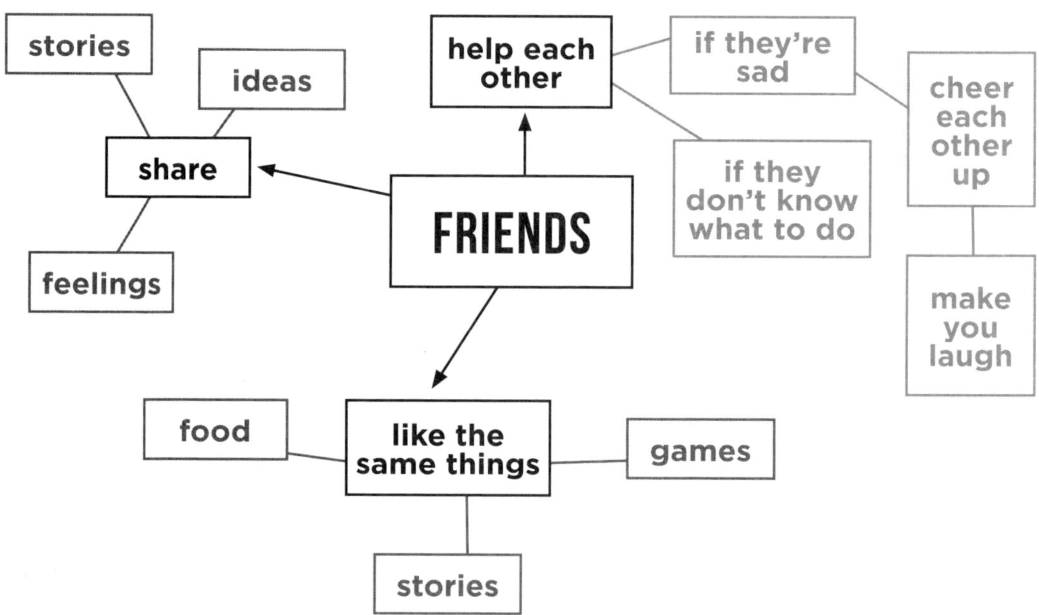


**Figure 4.1: Sample idea web.**

# PICTURE THIS

Our brains crave visualization (Taibbi & Iseminger, 2015). Although we know more now about the neurological functioning of the brain and its capacity to process visual stimuli to create mental images, the concept of *dual-coding theory* was first hypothesized by Allan Paivio in 1971. It is a theory tested over decades that shows that the formation of mental images enhances learning (Paivio, 2014). Similarly, Steven Pinker (2007) reminds us that to help students understand a topic, we need to show them how to picture it. The *picture this* protocol adapted from Chris Taibbi and Bob Iseminger (2015) is an excellent strategy for capitalizing on the brain's natural abilities. It is not only useful for generating new ideas but also a great way to reinforce content since the use of images results in a higher chance of the new concept's being embedded in long-term memory (Marzano, 2017).

## SETUP

| **Number of participants** | Groups of four to five |
|---|---|
| **Time needed** | Twenty to thirty minutes |
| **Room arrangement** | Table groupings |
| **Materials** | Pictures that depict or in some way reflect the topic for discussion (preferably images students have not seen previously) |

## PROCESS

1. Provide each group of students with a picture for discussion. Depending on the topic or context, you may wish to use the same picture for each group or a different picture for each group.
2. As a group, students generate and record as many words as possible that come to mind when they see the picture.
3. After some time has passed, bring the groups together as a whole class to share and explain their word choices and reactions.
4. At this stage, you might have students predict what the focus of the lesson or discussion is based on the picture or pictures provided. Alternatively, you may share the reason for choosing the pictures.

## APPLICATION

- When choosing pictures to share, you will find that there are many royalty-free picture websites, such as Pixabay (https://pixabay.com).
- In language classes, direct students to generate only certain parts of speech that are associated with the picture (for example, verbs, nouns, or adjectives).
- In English language arts classes, upon completion of this exercise, have students consider which words are synonyms for each other or classify the words according to modality (for example, powerful versus weak words). The words could also form the basis for students to compose a descriptive paragraph.
- In art classes, have students imagine what is outside the frame of the picture and create an extension of the image.
- In history classes, display a picture of a historical event and ask students to imagine the conversation between two or more people within the image.

## QUICK DRAW

*Quick draw*, adapted from Tactical Steps Education (n.d.b), also uses the brain's natural ability to create images. As students visually represent their thinking, they are encouraged to experiment and think outside the box, thus breaking out of the limitations of their thinking.

### SETUP

| | |
|---|---|
| **Number of participants** | Groups of four to five |
| **Time needed** | Fifteen to twenty minutes |
| **Room arrangement** | Table groupings |
| **Materials** | Recording materials |

### PROCESS

1. Organize students into small groups and present them with a problem to solve (for example, drivers do not always stop for pedestrians on crosswalks).
2. Give students four to five minutes to sketch as many ideas as possible. They may annotate their sketches if they feel more detail is needed.
3. Have students explain their sketches to the rest of their group members. At this point, emphasize that it is the idea that is important rather than the quality of the sketching.
4. Students may add suggestions to improve the idea or develop it further. Allow time for group members to each share his or her sketch and receive feedback.
5. If appropriate, have the group create a solution to share with the rest of the class.

### APPLICATION

This protocol can be adapted for many different contexts since most, if not all, subject areas have a problem-solving component. Teachers of mathematics, for example, might have students sketch out a mathematical problem, while engineering and technology teachers might have students create a sketch to solve the problem of having limited lighting in a room. Elementary teachers might have students create a sketch to solve a problem within their classroom or school, such as how to encourage more students to use the designated waste containers, reduce water wastage, or create less garbage.

# EXPLORING POSSIBILITIES

Exploring possibilities involves flexible thinking and the ability to go beyond what is expected by extending existing ideas and building on them. It entails associating ideas by connecting, uniting, and combining different ideas and relating and linking them to each other (Bellanca et al., 2020). Rather than generating many ideas, which was the goal for idea generation, the aim is to generate different kinds of responses (Drapeau, 2014). Brainstorming, therefore, becomes more specific and focused with starter phrases that might include the following.

- In what way might . . . ?
- List different ways to modify . . .
- Describe many possible changes to . . .
- What are different ways to improve on . . . ?
- How might you add to, expand on, or build on . . . ?

Anna Craft (2013) maintains that the process of exploring possibilities is also about helping students imagine what might be through asking "what if" and behaving "as if," in the manner outlined in the following *what if?* protocol. There is also a decision-making element as students determine the value and appropriateness of the responses they have created.

## WHAT IF?

What-if thinking or possibility thinking is believed to generate novelty and, therefore, sits at the core of creative thinking (Lucas & Spencer, 2017). Anna Craft, Teresa Cremin, Pamela Burnard, Tatjana Dragovic, and Kerry Chappell (2012) describe *what-if thinking* as driving creativity in the classroom. Although sometimes fantastical, it encourages predicting, speculating, philosophizing, and asking open and divergent questions. But it is this type of questioning, where assumptions are challenged, that creates the impetus for cultural, technological, and other forms of advancement (Sternberg & Grigorenko, 2016). Initially, the ideas may not be accepted; for example, when Copernicus asked the question, "What if the Earth revolves around the sun?" the idea was viewed as preposterous because everyone assumed that the sun revolved around Earth. It wasn't until many years later that people finally saw, thanks to Copernicus, the error in their original assumptions. What-if thinking resulted in scientists Robin Warren and Barry Marshall finding a new way of treating stomach and intestinal ulcers as they hypothesized, "What if ulcers are caused by bacteria, not by stress and lifestyle as is commonly assumed?" As a result of their discovery in 2005, ulcers can now be cured with a short-term course of medicine and antibiotics. As Marcel Proust stated so eloquently, "The real voyage of discovery consists not in seeking new lands, but in seeking with new eyes" (as cited in VanGundy, 2005, p. 13). The process of this protocol is very simple. It is basically stopping to ask, "What if . . . ?" thereby shifting the focus away from what exists already to what might be possible.

## SETUP

| | |
|---|---|
| **Number of participants** | Individuals or groups of two to four |
| **Time needed** | Fifteen to twenty minutes |
| **Room arrangement** | Table groupings |
| **Materials** | Recording materials |

## PROCESS

1. Establish a supportive learning environment. This is essential when teaching what-if thinking. It requires an environment in which:
   - ***Children's experiences and ideas are highly valued***
   - ***Dialogue between children and between teachers and children is encouraged***
   - ***An ethos of respect is nurtured and children as well as teachers experience meaningful control, ownership, relevance and innovation in learning (Craft & Chappell, 2014, p. 408)***
2. Students may work individually or in small groups of two to four, depending on the task, group dynamic, or topic, to consider a predetermined what-if prompt or to create their own what-if questions.

## APPLICATION

An example of the application of this strategy could incorporate the following prompts.

- What if gravity didn't exist for ten minutes every day (Bowkett, 2007)?
- What if there were no time zones in the world and we adopted the concept of universal time?
- What if adolescents were able to inform education policy?
- What if the Allies did not have victory over the Nazis in World War II?
- What if no one could get access to money for one month?
- What if anyone could go to college?
- What if wishes came true for one day only?
- What if animals could speak? What would they say?

# ABC GRAFFITI

New concepts or ideas are also generated when students associate ideas by connecting, relating, and linking ideas to each other (Bellanca et al., 2020). The *ABC graffiti* protocol developed by Bellanca and colleagues (2020) is an effective tool for helping students associate ideas by using the alphabet as an advance organizer.

## SETUP

| Number of participants | Groups of four to five |
|---|---|
| **Time needed** | Ten minutes |
| **Room arrangement** | Table groupings |
| **Materials** | Chart paper for recording and marking pens |

## PROCESS

1. Provide students with a topic for consideration.
2. Distribute chart paper and different-colored marking pens to each group.
3. Direct students to work within their groups to fill in one idea or association for each letter of the alphabet.
4. After approximately three minutes, have students move around to view the other groups' responses. Using their designated marking pen, they can add to the other groups' responses. Since each group has a different-colored pen, it is easy to see which groups added responses and how many associations or links they were able to make beyond their initial responses.

## APPLICATION

Figure 4.2 shows a partially completed response to the topic of marine life.

| A<br>Atlantic Ocean | H | O<br>otters | V |
|---|---|---|---|
| B<br>beaches | I | P<br>Pacific Ocean | W<br>whales |
| C<br>coral | J<br>jellyfish | Q | X |
| D<br>dolphins | K<br>kelp | R | Y |
| E<br>ecosystems | L | S<br>sharks | Z |
| F<br>fish | M | T<br>turtles | |
| G | N | U<br>unique animals | |

**Figure 4.2: Partially completed ABC graffiti activity.**

## A PICTURE PAINTS A THOUSAND WORDS

This protocol was inspired by the work of Tony Ryan (2019), who is well known for his thinkers keys developed in the 1980s and still used extensively today. The keys are a set of prompts to generate different types of thinking (Ryan, 2019). In this protocol, the picture key has been applied to encourage creative thinking by exploring possibilities.

### SETUP

| **Number of participants** | Individuals, then groups of two to three |
|---|---|
| **Time needed** | Ten to fifteen minutes |
| **Room arrangement** | Table groupings |
| **Materials** | Picture prompts<br>Recording materials |

### PROCESS

1. Provide students with a set of pictures of diagrams, such as the ones displayed in the Application section.
2. Ask students to generate as many ideas as possible for what the diagrams could be in relation to a particular topic. Ask, "If the topic is ______________________________, what could these diagrams represent?"
3. Upon completion, have students share their responses within their small group and then with the whole class.

### APPLICATION

There are many ways in which you might use this protocol. Figure 4.3 shows an example for the question, If the topic is thinking skills, what could these diagrams represent?

## SCAMPER

According to mythology, the Roman god Janus had two sets of eyes—one set looking ahead, one set looking back (Sorman-Nilsson, 2009). The *SCAMPER* protocol helps students behave in the same way by looking at what already exists (looking back) to create something new (looking ahead).

Brainstorming pioneer Alex Osborn first initiated the notion of using perspective changes on what already exists to develop new ideas (VanGundy, 2005). He developed a list of seventy-three questions designed to create new perspectives. In 1972 Bob Eberle organized some of these questions into the SCAMPER mnemonic (substitute, combine, adapt, modify, put to another use, eliminate, and reverse) that is widely used in classrooms and businesses today.

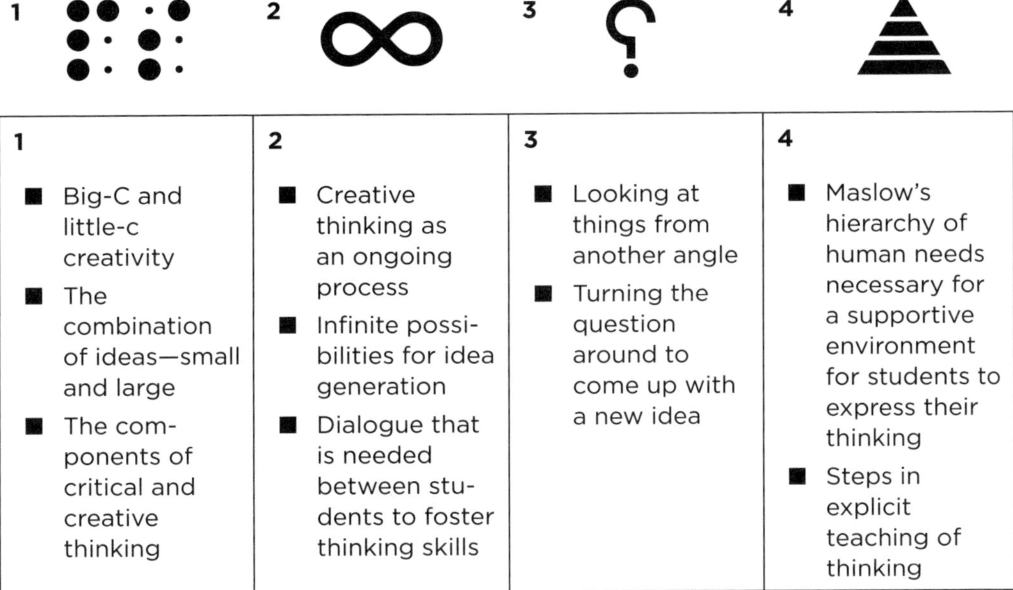


| 1 | 2 | 3 | 4 |
|---|---|---|---|
| ■ Big-C and little-c creativity<br>■ The combination of ideas—small and large<br>■ The components of critical and creative thinking | ■ Creative thinking as an ongoing process<br>■ Infinite possibilities for idea generation<br>■ Dialogue that is needed between students to foster thinking skills | ■ Looking at things from another angle<br>■ Turning the question around to come up with a new idea | ■ Maslow's hierarchy of human needs necessary for a supportive environment for students to express their thinking<br>■ Steps in explicit teaching of thinking |

**Figure 4.3: Sample picture prompts and corresponding completed picture key.**

## SETUP

| | |
|---|---|
| **Number of participants** | Groups of two to four |
| **Time needed** | Fifteen to twenty minutes |
| **Room arrangement** | Table groupings |
| **Materials** | Recording materials |

## PROCESS

1. Consider a product that could be improved, an issue that needs to be resolved, or a process that needs to be adjusted.
2. Have students work in small groups to answer the questions in table 4.2 (page 112). If teaching younger students, only provide the questions that are most appropriate for the product or issue in focus. Questions may also be altered or added if needed depending on the topic and age of the students. The sentence stems after each question set can be used to help students formulate their ideas.

**Table 4.2: The SCAMPER Mnemonic and Associated Questions**

| | |
|---|---|
| **Substitute** | What can we substitute? What can be used instead? Who else could be involved instead? What other ingredients could be added? What other approach could be used?<br>*Instead of . . . we can . . .* |
| **Combine** | What can we combine or bring together?<br>*We can bring together . . . and . . . to . . .* |
| **Adapt** | What can we adapt to use as a solution? What can we copy from?<br>*We can adapt . . . in this way . . . to . . .* |
| **Modify** | Can we change the item in some way? Can we change the color, sound, or shape? What other changes could we make?<br>■ **Magnify:** What can we add, make bigger, or exaggerate?<br>■ **Minify:** What can we remove, make smaller, or shorten?<br>*We can change . . . in this way . . . to . . .* |
| **Put to Other Uses** | How can we put the item to different or other uses? Can we use it in a new way?<br>*We can reuse . . . in this way . . . by . . .* |
| **Eliminate** | What can we eliminate or remove?<br>*We can eliminate . . . by . . .* |
| **Reverse** | What can be reversed or rearranged in some way?<br>*We can reverse . . . like this . . . so that . . .* |

## APPLICATION

SCAMPER can be used in many ways across the curriculum, including to:

- Adapt an existing story, rhyme, or fairy tale (English language arts or drama)
- Create new products or recipes (engineering and technology or family and consumer sciences)
- Adapt a music score or artwork (art or music)
- Create a backpack for surviving a natural disaster or find a solution for helping an endangered species (science)
- Adapt an existing game to maximize participation (health and physical education)

Teachers of younger students might prefer to use a simplified version of SCAMPER created by Tony Ryan (2019) known as the BAR thinkers key. Here, students focus on just three prompts: What can I (1) make bigger, (2) add to, or (3) replace?

## COMBINATION CAPERS

*Combination capers* is a protocol whereby two unconnected items are combined to create something new. It draws on a strategy first put forward by de Bono (2007). A classic example of the application of this approach is that of Art Fry, the inventor of Post-it Notes. Needing to find a way to locate his church hymns easily in his book, he used a scrap of paper and the "failed" glue produced by his colleague Spencer Silver at 3M to fashion a bookmark that would stay in place without ruining the pages. The combination resulted in the now widely used sticky notes.

### SETUP

| | |
|---|---|
| **Number of participants** | Individuals or groups of two to four |
| **Time needed** | Fifteen to twenty minutes |
| **Room arrangement** | Table groupings |
| **Materials** | Cards with pictures of objects<br>Paper strips (two different colors)<br>Recording materials |

### PROCESS

1. Create a collection of cards with different objects on each card. You will need two cards for each student or for each group of students if students are working in groups.
2. Distribute the cards to each student or group of students.
3. Students must combine the two objects on their cards to come up with a new idea. They must explain how their idea has value. For example, shoes and wheels would combine to create gym shoes that act as roller skates; a table and bag might result in a bag that can be turned into a portable table.

### ALTERNATIVE PROCESS

This process adapted from de Bono (2007) is similar but combines objects and adjectives. The emphasis is on the creativity of "what can be" rather than "what is" (de Bono, 2007).

1. Give students two different-colored pieces of paper.
2. On one piece of paper, students write the name of an object; on the second piece, they write an adjective. The adjective must start with the same letter that started the object, such as *terrifying* (adjective) and *table* (object).
3. When complete, have students place the papers in two separate boxes—one for the objects and one for the adjectives.

4. Shake both boxes to mix up the words.
5. Students take a new piece of paper from each box. This means that they now have a new object and a new adjective. They must then combine their two words to create a new idea. For example, if they get the word *happy* and the word *soap*, they might come up with the idea of soap that when used emits a vapor that makes people feel happy.
6. Students share their ideas within their small group. The group can then choose one idea to share with the rest of the class.

### APPLICATION

For combination capers, you may specify that the idea must have value as a business idea or must benefit the environment or people in some way. Younger students might draw their new idea.

For the alternative process, you could allow younger students to choose from preprinted adjectives and pictures of objects. Once again, students could draw their ideas and explain their ideas within their small group.

## CONNECT AND SOLVE

The *connect and solve* protocol created by Patti Drapeau (2014) is similar to combination capers described earlier in this chapter (page 113), but this time the characteristics of random words are used to solve or address a problem.

### SETUP

| **Number of participants** | Groups of four to five |
|---|---|
| **Time needed** | Fifteen to twenty minutes |
| **Room arrangement** | Table groupings |
| **Materials** | Recording materials<br>Sticky notes |

### PROCESS

1. Determine a topic or issue that will be the focus.
2. Have the class generate a list of nouns. Record each noun on a separate sticky note.
3. Each group chooses three nouns by selecting the sticky notes off the board or randomly choosing the nouns from a container.
4. Students choose one noun out of the three to work with.
5. Working within their small group, students generate a list of characteristics associated with their noun. Next, they make as many connections as possible between the characteristics of their noun and the topic or problem that is to be addressed.

6. Using the connections generated, students come up with a solution to the problem or issue.
7. Students may choose one connection to explore further or present to the class.

## APPLICATION

The process might be used to:

- Solve a problem faced by a character in a story (such as in the example of a completed exercise shown in table 4.3)
- Resolve an environmental issue
- Address a community issue, such as homelessness

**Table 4.3: Connect and Solve Example**

| | |
|---|---|
| **Topic** | In the book *Sunday Chutney*, written by Aaron Blabey (2009), the main character, Sunday Chutney, has lived in many different locations and each time must attend a new school, meaning that she is always the new student. The issue for discussion might be to determine ways for Sunday Chutney to cope with always being the new student or how she might be able to make friends quickly. |
| **Nouns** | *Dog, shoes, bottle* |
| **Chosen Noun** | *Dog* |
| **Characteristics of Chosen Noun** | Friendly, loyal, curious, independent, active |
| **Connections** | **Friendly:** Sunday Chutney could be very friendly each time she moves to a new school, increasing her chances of making new friends.<br>**Loyal:** Sunday Chutney might stay in touch via social media with all the friends that she makes at the different schools that she attends.<br>**Curious:** Sunday Chutney could talk to her parents about the impact that moving from place to place has on her and find out if they might be able to settle in one place for longer periods of time.<br>**Independent:** Sunday Chutney could be homeschooled and enroll in a distance education program so that she doesn't have to attend different schools.<br>**Active:** Sunday Chutney could choose a sport and join a team each time she moves. |

# IDEAS IN A BOX

The original name for *ideas in a box* was *morphological analysis*. It was developed by Fritz Zwicky, an astrophysicist and aerospace scientist who used the method for structuring and investigating scientific problems (Ritchey, 1998). This simpler version of the process is taken from VanGundy (2005). In this protocol, new ideas are generated in a systematic way by identifying and investigating a set of possible relationships or configurations contained in a given problem. Although not overly creative, the process does ensure that multiple possibilities are generated and considered.

## SETUP

| | |
|---|---|
| **Number of participants** | Groups of four to five |
| **Time needed** | Fifteen to twenty minutes |
| **Room arrangement** | Table groupings |
| **Materials** | Recording materials |

## PROCESS

1. Define a problem or issue for investigation.
2. Have groups determine possible attributes of the problem or issue and record these in the top row of a grid.
3. Under each heading, students record possible solutions.
4. Working in groups, students use the completed grid to generate a list of possible combinations and determine which one will be practical, most appropriate, or worth investigating further.

## APPLICATION

In a STEM activity, students may consider how to create a new container and may consider material, shape, and how the container will be closed (table 4.4). Students identify that the combination of an open, metal, cube-shaped container may be more appropriate than a cardboard, hexagonal prism-shaped container closed with clips. They also consider the impact of combining a variety of materials to create a cylindrical container closed with shoestring ties.

**Table 4.4: Sample Ideas in a Box Grid for Creating a New Container**

| SHAPE | CLOSURE | MATERIAL |
|---|---|---|
| Cylinder | Clips | Cardboard |
| Cube | Clamps | Plastic |
| Rectangular prism | Adhesive | Metal |
| Hexagonal prism | Open | Combination |
| | Ties | |

Ideas in a box is also a great way to create story plots, and rumor has it that it is an approach often employed by the writers of serial dramas. A very simple version for young students is included in table 4.5, where the main character is a frog. The headings chosen are Time, Mood, Setting, and Appearance. Based on the following matrix, one story might be about a lonely, wart-covered frog who finds himself in the city as the sun is setting. An alternative could be to use possible heroes, villains, problems faced by the characters, and locations as the headings.

**Table 4.5: Sample Ideas in a Box Grid for Creating a Story Plot**

| TIME | MOOD | SETTING | APPEARANCE |
|---|---|---|---|
| In the morning | Happy | Backyard | Green |
| Late in the afternoon | Sad | Forest | Slimy |
| In the middle of the day | Annoyed | River | Wart-covered |
| As the sun is setting | Lonely | City | Spotted |

## SYNECTICS

Developed by William Gordon (as cited in Taibbi & Iseminger, 2015), synectics attempts to produce creative solutions to problems using metaphorical modes of thinking. The term *synectics* is of Greek origin and refers to the combination of different and apparently irrelevant elements. It requires the consideration of familiar content, concepts, or objects in a new way by using three different types of analogies: (1) direct analogy, (2) personal analogy, and (3) compressed conflict. Since the easiest to apply in a classroom situation is direct analogy, it is the focus of this protocol.

### SETUP

| | |
|---|---|
| **Number of participants** | Groups of two to four |
| **Time needed** | Fifteen to twenty minutes |
| **Room arrangement** | Table groupings |
| **Materials** | Prompts<br>Provocative questions<br>Recording materials |

### PROCESS

1. Ask students to make comparisons between two concepts or objects based on descriptors not normally associated in that context. Taibbi and Iseminger (2015) offer the following examples:
   - ***Which is more restful—a circle or a line segment? Why?***
   - ***Which is more fragile—a democracy or a monarchy? Why?***

- ***Which is more circular—happiness or sadness? Why?***
- ***How is the electromagnetic spectrum like a piano? Why? (p. 37)***

2. Have students work within their small groups to create and record several responses.
3. Alternatively, provide students with a stimulus, such as an image, and ask them to generate and record comparisons between the image and the topic presented (for example, "Friendship is like water because . . ." or "Writing is like a river because . . .").

### APPLICATION

For protocols such as synectics and CSI (see the next section), students need to be able to deal with a level of ambiguity. Students who are more literal in their thinking may struggle with the protocol, but rather than avoiding the use of the strategy, provide additional modeled responses and encouragement for these students (Taibbi & Iseminger, 2015). As Robert J. Sternberg and Elena L. Grigorenko (2016) remind us, the period in which ideas are developing tends to be uncomfortable. Without the ability to tolerate ambiguity, individuals are more likely to accept less than optimal solutions (Sternberg & Grigorenko, 2016). You should also remind students that in synectics, there are no right or wrong answers, just possibilities, but they need to be able to justify their answers.

## CSI—COLOR, SYMBOL, IMAGE

This protocol adapted from Project Zero (n.d.b) requires flexible thinking as students create abstract symbols and images to represent important or insightful ideas from what they have read, watched, experienced, or heard. It can be used to enhance students' comprehension or to reflect on previous events or learning.

### SETUP

| | |
|---|---|
| **Number of participants** | Individuals, then groups of two to four |
| **Time needed** | Fifteen to twenty minutes |
| **Room arrangement** | Table groupings |
| **Materials** | Recording materials<br>Stimulus |

### PROCESS

1. Provide students with a stimulus for discussion. It might be an informational text, a video, or even a previous lesson or experience.

2. Direct students to make a note of things that they find interesting, important, or insightful. When finished, they must choose three items that are most significant for them.
3. For one of the three items, students choose a color that they feel best represents or captures the essence of that idea.
4. For another item, students choose a symbol that represents the idea. If the idea is about staying on track, two parallel lines could be used. A circle could be used to represent the idea of wholeness or something that never ends.
5. Finally, students choose an image that represents the third idea (for example, an image of a sunrise to represent a new beginning).
6. Upon completion, have students share with their group the colors, symbols, and images that they chose. Group members must also each explain their choices.

### APPLICATION

For younger students, consider using one of the aspects rather than all three. When discussing the concept of bullying, a teacher of first-grade students asked which color would represent bullying. Students responded with colors such as blue, black, and red and then explained why they chose their colors—red because people who bully make you feel mad and you go red in the face.

Another alternative is to use the process to represent one concept. For example, if the concept being explored is the growth mindset hypothesized by Dweck (2000), students would choose a color, symbol, and image that best capture the essence of the idea. They might choose the color yellow because people with a growth mindset are optimistic and yellow is a bright color. People with a growth mindset are risk takers who have a go, so the Nike symbol might be used. And finally, an image of a seedling captures the idea of growth.

## CONCLUSION

Teaching for creativity is about encouraging students to experiment, innovate, and explore new avenues (Azzam, 2009). It's about giving students not the answers but the tools to find the answers and what possibilities exist. Although creative thinking can't easily be reduced to a number on a test in this era of accountability, that doesn't make it any less valuable. But then, not everything of value can be easily measured. As an essential skill for problem solving, astute decision making, and innovation development in the future world of our students, creative thinking is vital (Bellanca et al., 2020).

Acclaimed creative-thinking theorist and researcher Torrance (in Henderson, Presbury, & Torrance, 1983) provides the following inspirational "Manifesto for

Children" for developing creativity (figure 4.4). Although directed at children, the manifesto provides sound advice for all.

## MANIFESTO FOR CHILDREN

- Don't be afraid to fall in love with something and pursue it with intensity.
- Know, understand, take pride in, practice, develop, exploit, and enjoy your greatest strengths.
- Learn to free yourself from expectations of others and to walk away from the games they impose on you.
- Free yourself to play your own game.
- Find a great teacher or mentor who will help you.
- Don't waste energy trying to be well rounded.
- Do what you love and can do well.
- Learn the skills of interdependence.

Source: Adapted from Henderson, Presbury, & Torrance, 1983.

**Figure 4.4: Manifesto for children.**

The skills and attitudes developed through explicitly teaching creative thinking are a strong foundation for problem solving and ethical thinking—the focus of the next two chapters.

# CHAPTER 5

# PROBLEM SOLVING AND PROBLEM POSING

***Sometimes the questions are complicated and the answers are simple.***

***—Dr. Seuss***

Each and every day, we face a range of problems to solve—some are simple and clear cut, such as remembering a password, while others are more complex, such as working out how to get to work on time when you realize that your tire is flat. Rarely, though, do we consider the process behind our thinking as we work toward a solution. Fundamentally, as we problem solve, we draw on our creative- and critical-thinking abilities as we analyze and interpret the situation (critical thinking), generate ideas and alternatives (creative thinking), and then evaluate the most worthwhile solution (critical thinking). But what is the starting point of problem solving? Does problem solving start with a problem to solve? Or does it start with a question whereby a problem is posed? The answer is both.

More often than not, problem solving begins with a problem. But there are differing definitions of exactly what constitutes a problem. Some believe that a problem can be viewed as a way of overcoming a difficult obstacle to achieve a goal (Marzano & Heflebower, 2011; Marzano & Kendall, 2007; VanGundy, 2005). Others take the process a step further, suggesting that a problem is a gap between a current state and a desired state of affairs—a gap between where you are and where you want to be (MacCrimmon & Taylor, 1976, as cited in VanGundy, 2005).

When the problem is clear—the current and desired states are known and how to close the gap is understood—the problem is described as *well structured* (Fields, 2006; Simon et al., 1986; VanGundy, 2005). Forgetting a password would be a well-structured problem: the current state is not being able to gain access, the desired state is access, and generally the solution is resetting the password. Generating ideas about possible solutions for such problems is usually a waste of time because there is only one plausible solution that can be agreed on. Typically, puzzle-type problems or problems presented to students in mathematics would be categorized as well-structured problems.

On the other hand, problems can be described as *ill-structured* or *ill-defined* when there are many options and no clear-cut way to proceed. These problems, such as stopping cyberbullying, are messy and usually require learners to express personal opinions or beliefs and make judgments (Beghetto, 2017; Bellanca et al., 2020; Fields, 2006). Life, with all of its twists and turns, is full of ill-structured, messy problems. Unfortunately, well-structured, clearly defined problems, the usual fare of classroom problem solving, do little to prepare students for solving the ill-structured problems of the real world (Antonenko, Jahanzad, & Greenwood, 2014; Beghetto, 2017). This can lead to students experiencing discomfort and frustration when asked to discuss and address problems where goals are unclear and multiple options are available (Antonenko et al., 2014; Drapeau, 2014; Sternberg & Grigorenko, 2016).

Whether well-structured or ill-structured, problems introduce a level of uncertainty and challenge. After all, it's the uncertainty that makes a problem a problem (Beghetto, 2017). Providing students with opportunities to deal with uncertainty in a supportive environment is important if students are to become comfortable with problem solving rather than anxious and frustrated. Ronald Beghetto (2017) suggests one simple way of doing this is to be less structured and planned when presenting problems to students and to create more open-ended tasks. For example, consider traditional mathematics instruction, where students are taught an approach for solving a problem and then given a set of similar problems to solve using the same procedure. Beghetto (2017) suggests making a small tweak to the procedure by asking students to come up with as many different ways of solving the problem as they can. Consequently, "students learn that even problems with fixed solutions can be approached in many different ways" (Beghetto, 2017, p. 22). The technique encourages students to become more actively involved and true problem solvers rather than passive "answer-getters" (Flynn, 2017, p. 27). Furthermore, students begin to realize that if they get stuck trying to solve a problem, there are probably other ways to solve it. Consequently, they are more likely to persist rather than give up when they experience difficulty (Beghetto, 2017).

Yet another way of thinking about problems is to view them as possibilities (Costa & O'Leary, 2013; Greene, Heyck-Williams, & Gray, 2017; Spencer, 2017). Indeed, industrialist Henry J Kaiser (as cited in Greene et al., 2017) said that "problems are only opportunities in work clothes" (p. 48). Such an approach draws on creative-thinking skills since problems are viewed as barriers that force you to try a different approach (Spencer, 2017). The barriers or constraints force you to think divergently by finding ways to work around the problem, using things in new ways, or connecting ideas. John Spencer (2017) provides the following questions for students to help them to reframe a problem as a potential opportunity:

- ***What is a different angle to this problem? What are we failing to see right now?***
- ***What hidden opportunities does this challenge offer? Could there be a positive side to this that we're failing to see?***
- ***What parts of these limitations should I actively resist or try to remove? What parts should I accept and work around?***
- ***What part of this can I tweak or change slightly?***
- ***Is there some kind of material or resource within this system that I can use differently?***
- ***What parameters can I work within? (p. 41)***

These questions help students to define the problem so that they can then move on to considering possibilities.

As previously stated, problem solving can also start with a question. Art Costa and Pat Wilson O'Leary (2013) maintain that "one of the distinguishing characteristics of humans is our inclination and ability to find problems to solve" (p. 194). Indeed, good problem solvers are often good problem finders, seeing the world in terms of problems to be fixed and finding opportunities for solutions (Tishman & Clapp, 2017). Nobel Prize–winning physicist Isidor Rabi (as cited in Costa & O'Leary, 2013) claims that he became a physicist and won the Nobel Prize because he was valued more for the questions he was asking than for the answers he was giving. But as Shari Tishman and Edward P. Clapp (2017) argue, students are not likely to ask questions or seek problems to solve if they don't have a sense of agency—a belief that things can be changed. They need to develop a can-do spirit so that they have the confidence to believe that they can overcome or solve problems that they see within their worlds (Tishman & Clapp, 2017). Hence, it is important for teachers to create the conditions that contribute to a positive affective climate for problem solving, such as promoting confidence, taking risks, facing uncertainties, accepting failure, and being persistent in overcoming obstacles (Lassig, 2012).

## CONSIDERATIONS

While problem solving is complex, the implementation of the following considerations can assist students to become more effective and confident problem solvers.

## CHUNKING

The process of chunking simply involves breaking something complex into smaller, more manageable pieces or chunks to avoid overload (Marzano, 2007; VanGundy, 2005). Students commonly feel overloaded or overwhelmed during the problem-solving process because they tend to find it difficult to establish a starting point, particularly when the problem is ill structured or open ended. By teaching students the basic principles of problem solving, we can ensure that they can apply these principles to almost any ill-defined problem to create a structure to follow with smaller steps or chunks on which to focus. Nobel Prize winner Herbert Simon (as cited in VanGundy, 2005) asserts that the goal of all problem solving is to make problems well structured so that a routine response can be used. By breaking problems down into smaller parts or subgoals, students make problems more manageable, clearer, and less daunting. For example, consider the problem of providing fresh food for homeless people in the local area. Smaller subgoals to be addressed might include learning more about the nutritional benefits of various types of foods, determining how these foods might be sourced and then stored, and establishing the most effective ways for distributing the food. From the subgoals, students can then determine an agenda of what must be done by when before moving on to the next subgoal (Beghetto, 2017).

## PROVIDING CHOICE

Students need opportunities to make choices to develop the skills to approach problems and stretch their minds to think in new ways (Beghetto, 2017; Ostroff, 2016). Choice has also been shown to increase interest and motivation (Ostroff, 2016; Tomlinson, 2017). Although choices cannot always be offered, Sternberg (2007) points out that students will only learn to choose and choose wisely if they are given choices. If a mistake is made in choosing a problem to solve or in taking an approach to solve the problem, this should be viewed as an important learning opportunity and part of the process. In this way, students learn to recognize the mistake and then redefine their choices. Choices do not have to be totally open-ended to be effective; although the choices can be completely student initiated, the approach can be as simple as providing two or three options from which to choose (Drapeau, 2014). Although teacher structured, it is still centered on students' thinking (Seeley, 2017).

## EXPLORING BACKSTORIES

Students can benefit from learning from accomplished problem solvers and the ways they went about successfully solving problems (Beghetto, 2017; Sternberg & Grigorenko, 2016). In doing so, they go beyond the *what* of the solved problem and learn about the *why*, *how*, *when*, and *where* of getting to the solution (Beghetto, 2017). By going behind the scenes of the problem-solving process, they can see the messiness of the original problem, the obstacles that were overcome, the various options tested, possible mistakes that were made, and even failures that were experienced. A classic example comes from the 1995 movie

*Apollo 13*, which dramatizes the aborted 1970 lunar mission. An onboard explosion affects the spacecraft's oxygen supply and electrical power, creating the extremely complex problem of getting the three astronauts back home safely. When carbon dioxide nears dangerous levels, ground control must quickly devise a way to extend their oxygen supply. The problem is that ground control can only use the materials that the astronauts can access. Ground control staff, under pressure of time and the potentially fatal consequences of failure, try out various options before finally succeeding. Scenes such as this help students to see the value of persistence and that it may take many attempts before a solution is reached.

## ALLOWING FOR MISTAKES AND REVISION

Typically, we try to protect our students from failure. Consequently, we have generations of students who give up when a problem becomes difficult (Flynn, 2017). Yet problem solving often requires divergent thinking and working through multiple iterations—where mistakes are made and revisions are required (Spencer, 2017). As it turns out, the growth mindset research from Dweck (2007) indicates that students benefit from struggling in a productive way with something challenging, such as a difficult mathematical problem (Boaler, 2015). When students struggle with a problem, their effort should be praised even if they are not entirely successful (Sternberg & Grigorenko, 2016). Teachers should point out the aspects of the students' approach that were successful, discuss why they were successful, and then indicate other ways to confront similar problems or challenges (Sternberg & Grigorenko, 2016). In this way, students become more confident problem solvers with higher gains in achievement (Flynn, 2017).

## CREATING LEGACY CHALLENGES

Beghetto (2017) proposes the concept of legacy challenges as a way of addressing complex problems that are not time bound or confined to the walls of the classroom. "A legacy challenge represents an issue, problem, or situation that requires us to develop an ongoing solution and pass that solution on from one group of young people to the next" (Beghetto, 2017, p. 24). This concept is similar to an approach taken at a school in central Queensland in Australia, where each year the departing twelfth-grade students work on a landscaping project throughout the year to enhance the grounds as their legacy. Legacy challenges may be more socially oriented, such as at another Australian school, where each year senior secondary students work alongside a charity organization to run a soup kitchen. Four questions are worked through to design legacy challenges:

1. ***What is the problem?***
2. ***Why does it matter?***
3. ***What are we going to do about it?***
4. ***What lasting legacy will our work addressing this problem leave? (Beghetto, 2017, p. 24)***

## TEACHING PROBLEM-SOLVING SKILLS STARTING IN THE EARLY YEARS

Learning how to problem solve is a key developmental milestone in early childhood (Fettig, Schultz, & Ostrosky, 2016). Problem solving has been shown to help children to remain calm during tough situations, quickly repair social relations, and get their needs met in safe and fair ways (Fettig et al., 2016). Without these skills, children tend to use aggression to solve interpersonal problems, with their aggression becoming more predictable and difficult to alter after the foundation years (Joseph & Strain, 2010). Continued aggression ultimately leads to peer rejection and poor mental health in adulthood (Joseph & Strain, 2010). Although formal problem-solving instruction may not occur, teachers can "sabotage" or create activities throughout the day to encourage younger students to generate solutions (Fettig et al., 2016). Adults also need to help younger children clearly reframe problems because they will often define the problem as the other person's problem (Joseph & Strain, 2010). For example, you can redefine "They won't let me play" as the problem "I want to play with them." Although subtle, Gail E. Joseph and Phillip S. Strain (2010) insist this reframing will help children generate more appropriate solutions.

## THE PROBLEM-SOLVING PROCESS

While the shape of the process in terms of time and structure may vary, there are particular steps that are typically taken in the problem-solving process. In a study conducted by Rebecca A. Roesler (2016) that established a model of problem solving in music, five component skills were identified. Later, through a literature review of relevant studies, it was concluded that these component skills can be applied to problem solving in other domains (Roesler, 2016). The five component skills are:

1. Establish goals
2. Evaluate performance
3. Conceive and consider options
4. Generalize and apply principles
5. Decide and act

A simplified version (Joseph & Strain, 2010) more appropriate for younger learners is:

1. What is my problem?
2. What are some solutions?
3. What would happen next?
4. Give the solution a try!

Each of the components outlined by Roesler (2016) requires significant metacognitive skills, such as problem identification, strategy selection, self-monitoring, evaluation, and self-correction (Westwood, 2016). Metacognitive questions and thoughts might include:

- What needs to be worked out in this problem? *Problem identification—establishing the goal*
- How will I try to do this? *Strategy selection—conceiving and considering options*
- Is this working out OK? *Self-monitoring—evaluating performance*
- How will I check if my solution is correct? *Evaluation*
- I need to correct this error and then try again. *Self-correction—evaluating performance*

Based on Roesler's (2016) original model and a synthesis of research on problem-solving processes, I have adapted the process so that it is easier to communicate to students (Antonenko et al., 2014; Beghetto, 2017; Bellanca et al., 2020; Beyer, 2001b; Goodwin, 2017; Marzano & Heflebower, 2011). To make it easier for students to remember, I have used the mnemonic CREATE because problem solving requires the creation of a solution.

- C = Clarify the problem.
- R = Reflect.
- E = Explore possibilities.
- A = Apply and decide.
- T = Take action.
- E = Evaluate.

A detailed description of each component and suggested protocols for each are included in the next section.

# THINKING PROTOCOLS

As problem solving is a ubiquitous human activity, and the skills in problem solving are critical for success in many fields, it is essential that problem solving is explicitly taught (Bellanca et al., 2020; Beyer, 2001b; Drapeau, 2014; Flynn, 2017; Marzano & Heflebower, 2011; Roesler, 2016; Sternberg, 2001). Understandably, Roesler (2016) observed that when learners exhibit a deficiency in any one or several of the components of problem solving, they will have trouble solving problems. The protocols in this section provide suggested strategies for addressing each component of the problem-solving process.

## CLARIFY THE PROBLEM

This component involves defining and clarifying the task or problem so that the problem becomes more manageable (Beghetto, 2017; Beyer, 2001b; Roesler, 2016). Sternberg (2007) describes this component as taking a problem and turning it on its head. "Many times in life individuals have a problem and they just do not see how to solve it" (Sternberg, 2007, p. 8). There are many ways teachers can encourage students to define and redefine problems for themselves rather than—as is so often the case—do it for them (Sternberg, 2007). In the process, students need to establish a goal and desired outcome, deconstruct the task, and clarify what the problem means or entails. Typically, students will need to ask questions.

- What are we being asked to do?
- What is meant by . . . ?
- How can we break this problem down into more manageable parts?
- What are the limitations or constraints that we must work within?
- Who is affected by this problem?
- Why is this a problem?
- Who can help us?

The following protocols can be used to help students work through these questions.

## SAY IT AGAIN, SAM!

This protocol, adapted from Tactical Steps Education (n.d.a), is simply designed to help students clarify the problem by restating it in simpler language. It helps students to deconstruct the problem by focusing on key words.

### SETUP

| | |
|---|---|
| **Number of participants** | Individuals, then groups of two to three |
| **Time needed** | Fifteen to twenty minutes |
| **Room arrangement** | Table groupings |
| **Materials** | Recording materials |

### PROCESS

1. Provide students with a problem to be tackled. Depending on the situation or focus, students may generate their own problem or question to address.
2. Have students identify the key words or phrases by underlining, circling, or highlighting them.
3. Ask students to focus on the key words and discuss what they mean.

4. Have students record their responses on either a teacher- or student-created framework.
5. Upon completion, have students compare or share their responses with other groups before sharing with the whole class.

## APPLICATION

The application in figure 5.1 shows an example framework that students can use to tackle a question, such as the question featured.

**Question:** What is the *best way* to *donate* to the *volunteer firefighters* after *devastating wildfires* in local communities?

| OPTIONS | PROS | CONS | DEFINE | IDENTIFY |
|---|---|---|---|---|
| | | | | |

**Figure 5.1: Example Say It Again, Sam! framework.**

# WHAT'S THE PROBLEM? WHAT'S NOT THE PROBLEM?

Originally created by Mel Silberman (1999) and later adapted by Lipton and Wellman (2016), this protocol is especially useful for ill-structured, messy problems that continually recur. It helps identify the underlying causes of a problem or issue.

## SETUP

| | |
|---|---|
| **Number of participants** | Groups of four to five |
| **Time needed** | Fifteen to twenty minutes |
| **Room arrangement** | Table groupings |
| **Materials** | Sticky notes<br>Recording sheet |

## PROCESS

1. With students, identify a persistent or recurring problem.
2. Pose two prompts and have students individually write brief responses on separate sticky notes.
    - ❑ What's the problem? What specifically is wrong?
    - ❑ What is not the problem?
3. In their groups, students share their responses to "What is not the problem?" and create a synthesizing statement. They record the statement on the group recording sheet (figure 5.2, page 130).

4. Students then consider their "What's the problem?" responses to identify what specifically is wrong. Then, using the discussion prompts on the recording sheet, students have a deeper discussion about the problem and record their responses on the recording sheet to share with the larger group.
5. Have students share and compare responses and possible solutions to determine a course of action.

<table>
<tr><td colspan="2">Recurring issue or problem:</td></tr>
<tr><td>What's the problem?</td><td>What is not the problem?</td></tr>
<tr><td colspan="2">Why does this problem occur and recur?<br>Which is caused by . . .<br>Which is caused by . . .</td></tr>
<tr><td>Who is affected by this problem?<br>Which then affects . . .<br>Which then affects . . .</td><td>Who is not affected by this problem?<br>Which then affects . . .<br>Which then affects . . .</td></tr>
<tr><td>Where does this problem occur?<br>It occurs there because . . .</td><td>Where does this problem not occur?<br>It does not occur there because . . .</td></tr>
<tr><td>When does this problem occur?</td><td>When does this problem not occur?</td></tr>
<tr><td colspan="2">The issue seems to be . . .</td></tr>
<tr><td colspan="2">A solution might be . . .</td></tr>
</table>

**Figure 5.2: Recording sheet template.**

## APPLICATION

Figure 5.3 is an example of a completed recording sheet.

<table>
<tr><td colspan="2">Recurring issue or problem: Fighting and bullying on afternoon buses</td></tr>
<tr><td>What's the problem?<br>Pushing and shoving once the bus arrives and fighting while on the bus</td><td>What is not the problem?<br>Students waiting for the bus</td></tr>
<tr><td colspan="2">Why does this problem occur and recur?<br>Older or bigger students push younger or smaller students out of the way to get on the bus first.<br>Which is caused by a need to get on the bus first to get a seat.<br>Which is caused by an overcrowded bus.</td></tr>
<tr><td>Who is affected by this problem?<br>Younger, smaller, or quieter students<br>Which then affects their parents when students arrive home upset.<br>Which then affects the staff at the school when parents complain.</td><td>Who is not affected by this problem?<br>Students who get on the bus and get a seat<br>Which then affects the students who are pushing in.<br>Which then affects the bus driver if fights break out.</td></tr>
<tr><td>Where does this problem occur?<br>On the buses traveling north from the school<br>It occurs there because the buses are typically overcrowded, and students are pushing to get a seat because the trip home is almost sixty minutes.</td><td>Where does this problem not occur?<br>On the buses traveling south from the school<br>It does not occur there because fewer students travel in that direction and there is more room on the bus, so everyone has their own seat.</td></tr>
<tr><td>When does this problem occur?<br>In the afternoons</td><td>When does this problem not occur?<br>In the morning on the way to school</td></tr>
<tr><td colspan="2">The issue seems to be overcrowded buses in the afternoon traveling north.</td></tr>
<tr><td colspan="2">A solution might be to lobby the bus company to provide additional buses on the overcrowded routes.</td></tr>
</table>

**Figure 5.3: Sample completed recording sheet.**

# FIVE WHYS

This protocol is based on a technique that was originally used within the Toyota Motor Corporation as a critical component of internal problem-solving training (Ohno, 1988). Taiichi Ohno (1988) maintained that by asking *why* five times, the nature of a problem as well as its solution becomes clearer. It is also a way of challenging the status quo to determine if the approaches used are the most effective or if they are the way things have always been done and the efficacy of the approaches has not been challenged. Since its original conception, the technique has become widely used in many different fields, including business management and education.

## SETUP

| | |
|---|---|
| **Number of participants** | Individuals or groups of two to three |
| **Time needed** | Ten to fifteen minutes |
| **Room arrangement** | Table groupings |
| **Materials** | Recording materials |

## PROCESS

1. Provide a five whys recording sheet for each student, or simply model the setup for the students.
2. Have students write the *why* question at the top of the sheet.
3. Direct students to answer by writing their first response underneath. Next, students ask, "Why?" of their first response and write the second response. This process is repeated at least five times or until a root understanding of the initial question is reached.
4. Individual sheets can be shared or discussed within the small groups of two or three and then with the full class.

## APPLICATION

- This protocol can be used in many different scenarios. It might be used to explore a problem faced by a character in a story or uncover the root cause of a historical event (such as World War II).
- The technique is also an effective way of uncovering students' misconceptions. You can see an example of this with a group of seventh-grade students struggling in mathematics. In this example, only three questions were needed to uncover an underlying issue. I don't think for a moment that the students were taught that when you divide by ten, you take away the zero. What probably occurred is that they were typically provided with questions where this approach or thinking worked. Consequently, they overgeneralized the incorrect approach. Although they had answered correctly previously, their correct answers were

derived from faulty reasoning. Whatever the case, the five whys process uncovered an underlying misconception of the concept of place value.

**Question 1:** What is 706 ÷ 10?

*Answer: 76*

**Question 2:** Why is the answer 76?

*Answer: Because when you divide by 10, you take away the 0.*

**Question 3:** Why do you take away the 0 when you divide by 10?

*Answer: Because that's what we were taught last year.*

- The following example was used by Taiichi Ohno (1988).

**Question 1:** Why did the welding robot stop?

*Answer: The circuit has overloaded, causing a fuse to blow.*

**Question 2:** Why is the circuit overloaded?

*Answer: There was insufficient lubrication on the bearings, so they locked up.*

**Question 3:** Why was there insufficient lubrication on the bearings?

*Answer: The oil pump on the robot is not circulating enough oil.*

**Question 4:** Why is the oil pump not circulating enough oil?

*Answer: The pump intake is clogged with metal shavings.*

**Question 5:** Why is the intake clogged with metal shavings?

Answer: *Because there is no filter on the pump.*

## REFLECT

This component requires students to explore the features of the task or situation (Beghetto, 2017). In doing so, they reflect on and determine the current state of reality and how it differs from the desired state or outcome they are wanting to achieve—turning "what it is" into "what it should be" (VanGundy, 2005). It also requires students to articulate what is known and what needs to be learned about the problem and the sources of information that they have available (Goodwin, 2017; Roesler, 2016). As students reflect, they ask questions.

- What is the current reality or situation?
- What do we already know about this problem?
- What extra information do we need?
- Where can we find out more information?
- Is this information reliable?

## RIGHT ANGLE

This protocol adapted from Gregory and Kuzmich (2007) is a useful reflective tool for looking at an issue or problem. It helps students reflect on what is currently known about the issue and possible opinions and reactions. In this way, students are able to separate facts from opinions and recognize potential gaps in their understanding of the issue.

## SETUP

| **Number of participants** | Groups of four to five |
|---|---|
| **Time needed** | Fifteen to twenty minutes |
| **Room arrangement** | Table groupings |
| **Materials** | Right angle recording template |

## PROCESS

1. After identifying a focus issue or problem, distribute the right angle recording template (figure 5.4) to each group.
2. At the right-hand side of the right angle, have students record the facts related to the topic or issue.
3. At the bottom, have students list opinions.
4. Remind students that in steps 2 and 3, they need to be mindful of the difference between facts and opinions and place the statements in the correct place on the template.
5. Upon completion, have students create a list of questions for further investigation.
6. Share the responses and questions for further investigation.

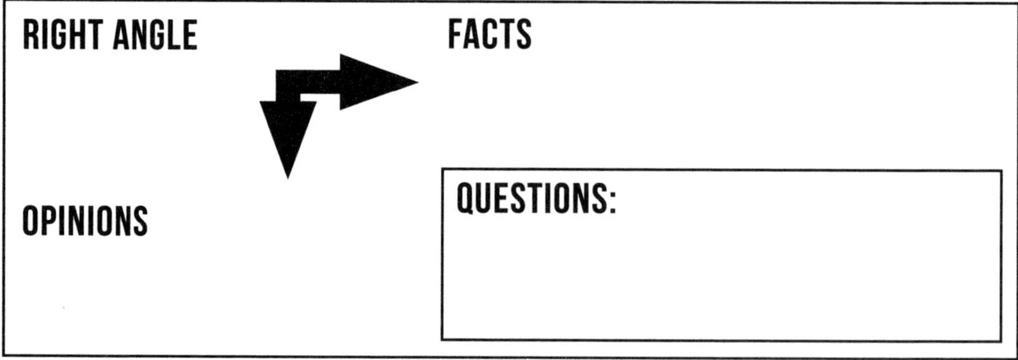


Source: Adapted from Gregory & Kuzmich, 2007.

**Figure 5.4: Right angle recording template.**

## APPLICATION

- This protocol can be used for any issues where there is the potential for facts to be clouded by opinions. Topics might include content-specific issues or relevant current events, such as the debates around controlled burning to reduce the threat of wildfires, and immunization.

- In the example shown in figure 5.5, students propose that they should be able to listen to music while they are studying or working.

### RIGHT ANGLE

**Issue:** Listening to music while working or studying

### FACTS

- The human brain cannot effectively multitask (Marzano & Heflebower, 2011).
- Performance deteriorates during multitasking (Marzano & Heflebower, 2011).

### OPINIONS

- Listening to music helps you learn.
- It is possible to multitask.
- I can block background noise.
- Younger people are good at multitasking.
- Multitasking can be distracting.

### QUESTIONS:

1. Do different types of music make a difference?
2. Are there tasks that could be completed successfully while listening to music?

**Figure 5.5: Sample completed right angle recording template.**

## HERE'S WHAT! SO WHAT? NOW WHAT?

Adapted from Lipton and Wellman (2016), this protocol helps students consider an issue by determining what they already know about the issue and what their next steps will be to address it.

### SETUP

| **Number of participants** | Groups of four to five |
|---|---|
| **Time needed** | Ten to fifteen minutes |
| **Room arrangement** | Table groupings |
| **Materials** | Recording template |

### PROCESS

1. Determine a topic to explore. Each group might work on the same issue, or alternatively, each group might have a different topic or issue to explore.
2. Provide each group with a template and explain the purpose of each column.
    - ❑ **Here's What!** State the issue or specific facts.

- ❑ **So What?** State what is already known or inferences that can be made.
- ❑ **Now What?** Record implications, predictions, or next steps.

3. Ask students to work in groups to complete each column on the recording sheet.
4. Upon completion, share the findings or conclusions with the full class.

### APPLICATION

Although this protocol can be used in many different ways across the curriculum, the example in table 5.1 shows the use of the protocol to plan out what can be cooked or created from a school's kitchen garden. The Here's What! column has been used to identify the specific produce that will be harvested from the garden; the So What? column identifies the dishes that can be prepared; and the Now What? column records implications in terms of the kitchen skills students will need to learn. The resource used for this example is Stephanie Alexander's (2008) *Kitchen Garden Cooking for Kids*.

**Table 5.1: Example Here's What! So What? Now What? Recording Template**

| HERE'S WHAT! | SO WHAT? | NOW WHAT? |
|---|---|---|
| Produce to be harvested:<br>■ Lettuce<br>■ Rhubarb<br>■ Beets<br>■ Herbs | Menu:<br>■ Three-cheese ravioli with herb butter<br>■ Green salad with beets and croutons<br>■ Rhubarb custard tart | Kitchen skills:<br>■ Making pasta<br>■ Making salad dressings<br>■ Shallow frying<br>■ Practicing oven safety |

## POSING QUESTIONS

This protocol inspired by Costa and O'Leary (2013) is far less structured than previous protocols and simply asks students to generate questions about a problem—not solve the problem or generate solutions, just pose questions.

### SETUP

| | |
|---|---|
| **Number of participants** | Groups of four to five |
| **Time needed** | Ten to fifteen minutes |
| **Room arrangement** | Table groupings |
| **Materials** | Recording materials |

## PROCESS

1. Determine a specific problem for discussion.
2. Direct students to work in groups to generate as many questions as possible about the problem.
3. Students may record the questions on a group recording sheet to share with the full class.

## APPLICATION

Costa and O'Leary (2013) suggest that one way to build ownership of asking questions is to have students work within their groups to create questions they want to answer in preparation for an upcoming test or assessment. Upon completion, the groups share their questions. When students have similar questions, it is reassuring, or if questions are posed that are unclear, it is an opportunity for further discussion and clarification. As a follow-up, the questions could be used for further group investigation as a review activity.

As students become more confident asking questions and posing problems for discussion, Costa and O'Leary (2013) suggest that the following types of questions should be heard.

- From whose point of view are you seeing this?
- What evidence do you have for . . . ?
- How do you know that is true?
- What do you think would happen if . . . ?
- If that is true, what might happen when . . . ?

They suggest that younger students might become more alert to phenomena in their environment and begin to recognize discrepancies and inquire about their causes by posing questions such as the following (Costa & O'Leary, 2013):

- ***Why do cats purr?***
- ***How high can birds fly?***
- ***Why does the hair on my head grow so fast but the hair on my arms and legs grow so slowly?***
- ***What would happen if we put a saltwater fish in a freshwater aquarium? (p. 195)***

# FISHBONE

This protocol uses the common fishbone diagram to explore cause and effect in a visual format. The approach was originally devised by professor Kaoru Ishikawa in the 1960s and published in his book *Introduction to Quality Control* in 1990. Sometimes known as the *Ishikawa diagram*, the tool is particularly useful when groups need to identify and analyze the underlying causes of a problem or challenging situation.

## SETUP

| | |
|---|---|
| **Number of participants** | Groups of two to three |
| **Time needed** | Ten to fifteen minutes |
| **Room arrangement** | Table groupings |
| **Materials** | Fishbone diagram template |

## PROCESS

1. Identify a problem where underlying causes need to be examined.
2. Have students brainstorm possible causes of the identified problem. Alternatively, groups can use the original categories identified by Ishikawa (1990) to guide discussions: environment, materials, people, methods, measurements, and machines.
3. Have each group complete its own diagram. Place the problem in the box at the right side of the diagram (the head), and then fill in the specific causes for each category along the spine of the fish diagram.
4. Upon completion, circle the specific causes that the group considers to be the major contributors to the problem (Lipton & Wellman, 2016).
5. If needed, assign different groups to address the selected areas of concern.

## APPLICATION

The example in figure 5.6 is based on a school group whose first kitchen garden was not as successful as expected.

Younger students may use a simpler version of the template, simply linking cause and effect. To support thinking, teachers may provide some of the information, requiring students to fill in the missing information as shown in figure 5.7. The example in figure 5.7 centers on the plains bison (World Wildlife Fund, n.d.).

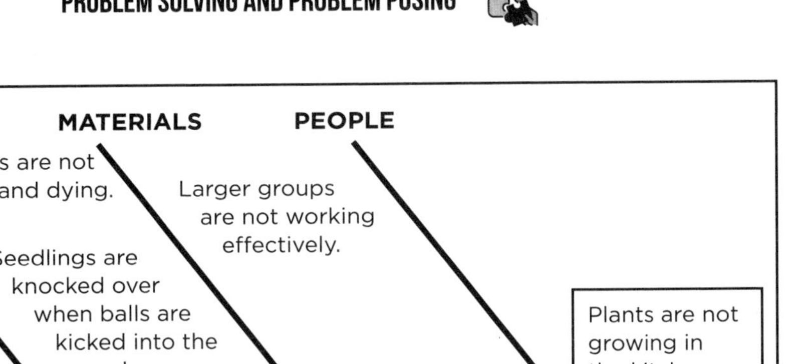


**Figure 5.6: Sample completed fishbone diagram.**

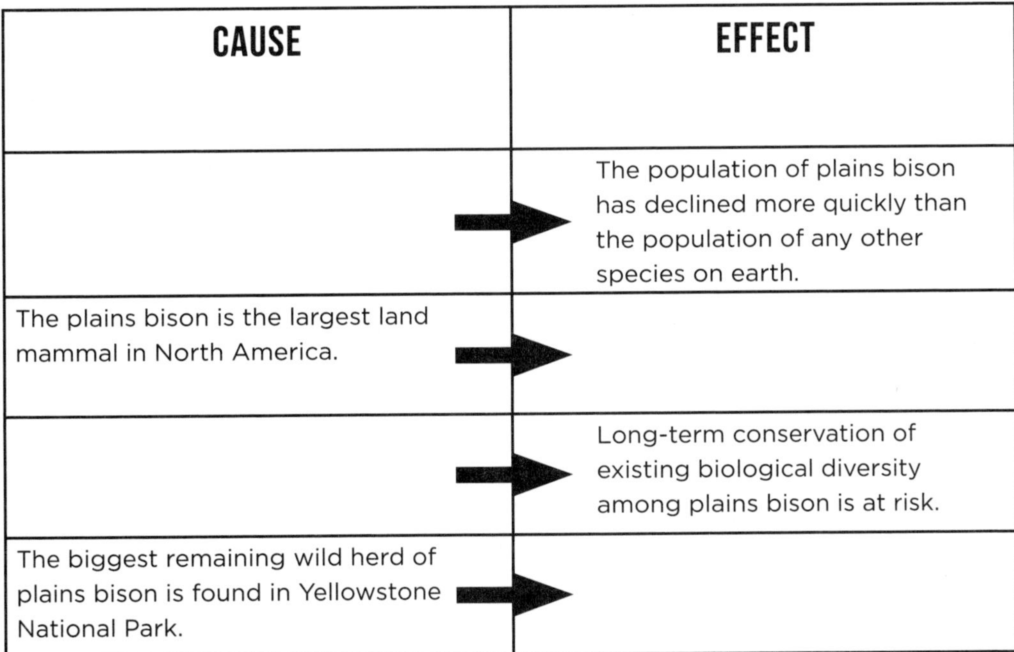

| CAUSE | EFFECT |
|---|---|
| | The population of plains bison has declined more quickly than the population of any other species on earth. |
| The plains bison is the largest land mammal in North America. | |
| | Long-term conservation of existing biological diversity among plains bison is at risk. |
| The biggest remaining wild herd of plains bison is found in Yellowstone National Park. | |

**Figure 5.7: Simplified fishbone template.**

## EXPLORE POSSIBILITIES

This component requires students to create or consider multiple possibilities that might lead to the accomplishment of their goal (Beghetto, 2017; Roesler, 2016; VanGundy, 2005). As students explore possibilities, they ask questions, including the following.

- What are all the possible options?
- What would change if we looked at the problem from a different perspective?
- What is an alternative explanation for . . . ?
- How is this similar to or different from other problems we have solved?
- How can we build on another idea?

As this component requires divergent thinking, some of the creative-thinking protocols described in chapter 4, such as SCAMPER (page 110), connect and solve (page 114), or ideas in a box (page 116), could be used to support students' thinking.

## CIRCLE OF OPPORTUNITY

This thinking protocol is an adaptation of VanGundy's (2005) use of the strategy for exploring possibilities within the business environment. It is based on the random combination of problem attributes to develop a creative solution to a problem.

### SETUP

| | |
|---|---|
| **Number of participants** | Groups of two to three |
| **Time needed** | Fifteen to twenty minutes |
| **Room arrangement** | Table groupings |
| **Materials** | Circle of opportunity template<br>Dice |

### PROCESS

1. Determine an issue to be addressed (for example, student seats are uncomfortable).
2. Distribute the circle of opportunity template to each group.
3. Have students generate a list of twelve attributes that are related or unrelated to the problem. Related attributes reflect the major problem attributes. (In the case of uncomfortable seats, these might be hard plastic, inflexible backing, height, noise as they are moved, lack of storage, or a need for seats to be stacked for storage.) Unrelated

attributes are those that are common to many problems—color, texture, materials, cost, single use versus multiple use, and size.

4. Have students place the twelve attributes on the circle of opportunity template. Figure 5.8 shows a circle of opportunity for the seating example.
5. Direct students to roll the dice to create the random combinations. First, they roll one die to get the first attribute and brainstorm associated ideas. For example, if a one is rolled, they might think of various colors or combinations of colors.
6. Next, students roll the two dice to determine the second attribute. Again, they should brainstorm associated ideas. For example, if the combination results in a ten, they would consider various textures (soft, fluffy, or slippery).
7. Students then combine the two attributes for consideration. In the chair example, if a five and then a combination making ten are rolled, they would consider a chair that would be made from textured material but with a flexible back.

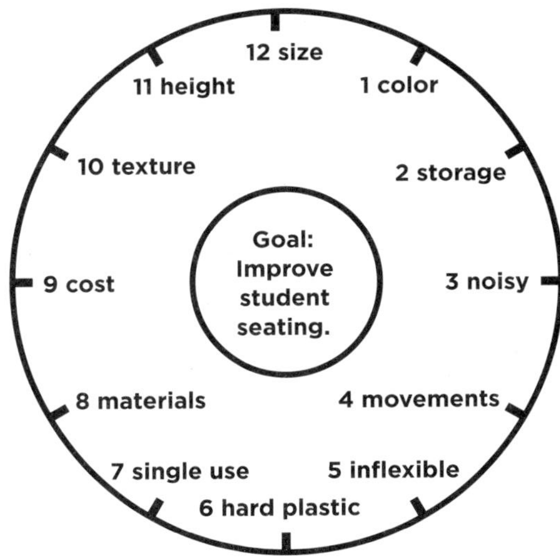


**Figure 5.8: Sample completed circle of opportunity—designing a chair.**

## APPLICATION

Another application might be students designing a new schoolbag (figure 5.9). They would follow the same process. Combinations and considerations might include:

- A padded handle with contrasting colors
- A handle that includes a charging port for a cell phone
- Expandable pockets for different purposes—carrying a laptop or books

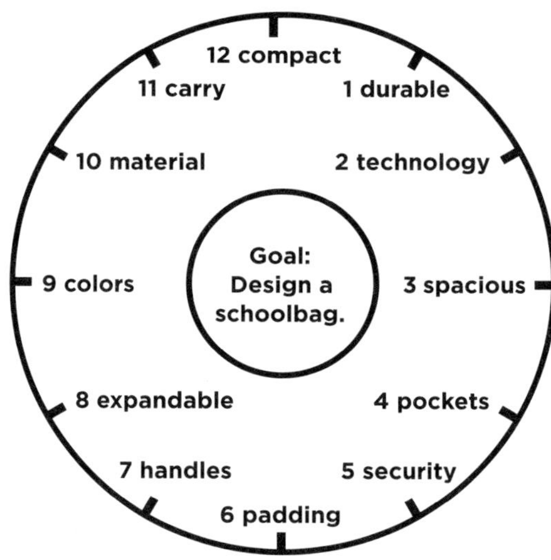


**Figure 5.9: Sample completed circle of opportunity—designing a schoolbag.**

# APPLY AND DECIDE

Having considered multiple options, students now need to apply criteria to determine the best course of action to follow (Beghetto, 2017). This component also requires them to use evidence and reasoning to justify their solution or decision and consider the consequences of their decision. In the process, students will need to ask the following questions.

- What are the criteria that need to be met?
- What is the best solution?
- What will happen if . . . ?
- Why is the solution better than . . . ?
- What are the advantages and disadvantages of . . . ?
- How can we justify . . . ?

This component requires more convergent thinking, so it is possible to use some of the critical-thinking protocols described in chapter 4 (page 95). Consider implementing the brainstorm and categorize protocol (page 102) or the decision-making matrix protocol (page 75).

## COMPASS POINTS

The *compass points* protocol described here is adapted from Project Zero (n.d.c). It is an excellent protocol for helping students to look at the pros and cons of an idea before finally deciding on its utility.

## SETUP

| | |
|---|---|
| **Number of participants** | Groups of four to five |
| **Time needed** | Fifteen to twenty minutes |
| **Room arrangement** | Table groupings |
| **Materials** | Sticky notes |

## PROCESS

1. Model the process first with the whole class and explain what is required for each direction of the compass point, as shown in table 5.2.
2. Once students are familiar with the process, present them with a topic, issue, or idea for discussion.
3. Have students write their responses for each compass point on separate sticky notes.
4. Students then share their responses with the members of their group. Allow time for students to adjust or add to their responses as they listen to and learn from one another.
5. Finally, determine the location in the room for each direction of the compass. Direct students to place their sticky notes at the appropriate location. Allow students to walk around to view other students' responses for each direction of the compass, taking note of similarities and key themes.
6. As a whole class, discuss the key themes and commonalities and possible conclusions.

**Table 5.2: Compass Points**

| E = EXCITING | W = WORRISOME | N = NEED TO KNOW | S = STANCE |
|---|---|---|---|
| What excites you about this idea or proposition? What are the positives? | What worries you about this idea or proposition? What are the disadvantages or negatives? | What else do you need to know or find out about this idea or proposition? What additional information would help you to decide? | What is your current stance or opinion on the idea or proposition? What suggestions do you have for moving forward with this idea? |

## APPLICATION

- This protocol is very versatile and can be used in many ways across all subject areas.

    - ❑ A character in a book might be confronted with making a choice, and students can use the protocol to consider the best options for the character.
    - ❑ Use the protocol to consider the pros, cons, and alternatives for a new classroom arrangement.
    - ❑ When introducing a new topic, teachers can use the protocol to activate prior knowledge and determine concerns students might have.
- The protocol can also be used for students to provide feedback to one another on proposals or potential research projects.
- When introducing a new initiative to teaching staff, I have used this protocol to elicit teachers' concerns and the support that they may need during the implementation process.

## TIPPING THE SCALES

*Tipping the scales* is a protocol adapted from Tactical Steps Education (n.d.b) and is useful for helping students to evaluate the extent to which their solution meets predetermined criteria. It requires them to analyze their solution to a problem by listing the pros and cons and then weighing them against the criteria for success. The criteria, for example, may be that the solution is cost effective, meets the needs of all stakeholders, is safe, and is practical.

### SETUP

| | |
|---|---|
| **Number of participants** | Groups of four to five |
| **Time needed** | Fifteen to twenty minutes |
| **Room arrangement** | Table groupings |
| **Materials** | Tipping the scales template |

### PROCESS

1. Provide each group of students with the template.
2. Have students list the pros and cons of their chosen or assigned solution on the template.
3. Using the predetermined criteria, students assign a score from one (weak) to three (strong) for each pro or con statement.
4. Have students add up the scores to determine the extent to which their solution meets the criteria.
5. Upon completion, have students consider if further information is required to create a more effective solution.

## APPLICATION

A template for completion is provided in figure 5.10. An alternative would be, rather than complete the template, to combine the strategy with the lineup technique. As each statement (advantage or disadvantage) is read, have students move to the left or right of the line—one step if the statement is weak, three if it is strong. Once all statements have been considered, have students look at their positions. Have the scales tipped for or against the solution?

| **Solution** | | | |
|---|---|---|---|
| **Advantages** | **Score** | **Disadvantages** | **Score** |
| | | | |
| **Total** | | **Total** | |

Source: Adapted from Tactical Steps Education, n.d.b.

**Figure 5.10: Tipping the scales template.**

# PROBLEM AND SOLUTION MAP

The *problem and solution map* adapted from Robert Marzano and Tammy Heflebower (2011) is not a protocol as such but a way of representing and recording the decision-making process once solutions have been generated. It is an effective way of guiding students through the problem-solving process as they identify goals, obstacles and constraints, and possible solutions. It may be used alongside other protocols where ideas have been generated, such as connect and solve (page 114), SCAMPER (page 110), circle of opportunity (page 140), and ideas in a box (page 116). The map may also be used alongside protocols where success criteria have been established or solutions have been identified, such as brainstorm and categorize (page 102) and the decision-making matrix (page 75).

## APPLICATION

If students are considering ways to raise money for volunteer firefighters, a completed map might resemble the one in figure 5.11 (page 146).

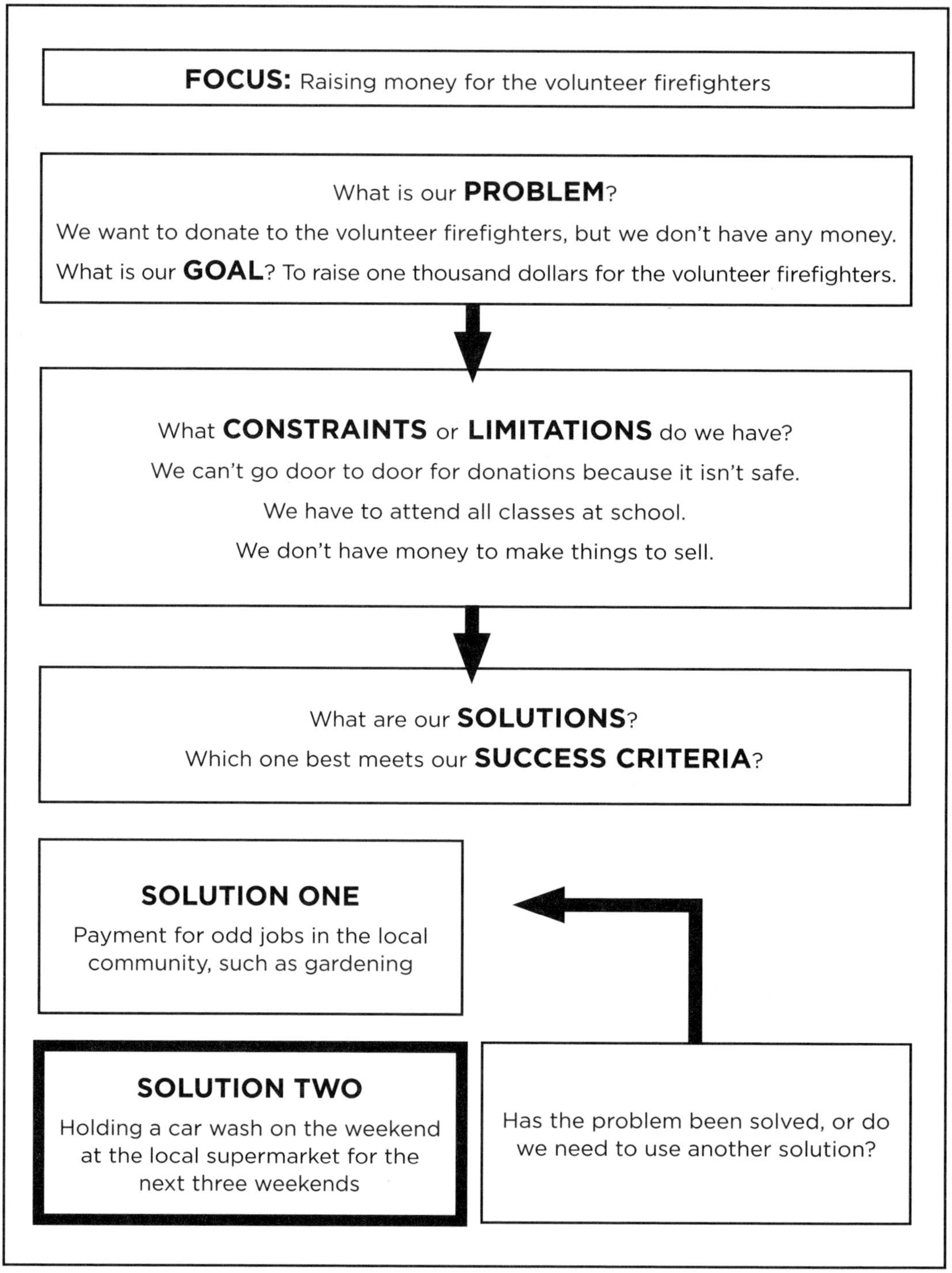

**FOCUS:** Raising money for the volunteer firefighters

What is our **PROBLEM**?

We want to donate to the volunteer firefighters, but we don't have any money.

What is our **GOAL**? To raise one thousand dollars for the volunteer firefighters.

What **CONSTRAINTS** or **LIMITATIONS** do we have?

We can't go door to door for donations because it isn't safe.

We have to attend all classes at school.

We don't have money to make things to sell.

What are our **SOLUTIONS**?

Which one best meets our **SUCCESS CRITERIA**?

**SOLUTION ONE**

Payment for odd jobs in the local community, such as gardening

**SOLUTION TWO**

Holding a car wash on the weekend at the local supermarket for the next three weekends

Has the problem been solved, or do we need to use another solution?

**Figure 5.11: Sample completed problem and solution map.**

## TAKE ACTION

Having considered possible solutions and then chosen a course of action, this next component requires students to plan how they will enact their solution (Beghetto, 2017; Roesler, 2016). In taking action, students ask questions, including:

- What is our first step?
- Who will be involved?
- What resources will we need?
- When will each step be completed?

## IMPACT GRID

The *impact grid* adapted from Gregory and Kuzmich (2007) is an excellent way of helping students prioritize solutions. Using the grid, students weigh the difficulties and potential benefits of their solutions. It can also be used to determine the best starting point.

### SETUP

| **Number of participants** | Groups of four to five |
|---|---|
| **Time needed** | Fifteen to twenty minutes |
| **Room arrangement** | Table groupings |
| **Materials** | Sticky notes<br>Grid template |

### PROCESS

1. Distribute the grid template to each group and explain the process.
2. Instruct students to write each solution or the solution steps on a sticky note.
3. Students discuss the ranking of the solution or steps in terms of impact. Once agreement has been reached, they place the sticky note along the impact line. Impact needs to be discussed in terms of the goal. For example, if the focus is on fundraising, will the solution or steps raise a great deal of money or a small amount?
4. Next, students discuss the rankings for difficulty in terms of resources, time, and people and move the sticky notes to the appropriate quadrant (as shown in figure 5.12, page 148). The solution or steps have now been ranked on impact and difficulty.
5. Each group then discusses the best solution or starting point.

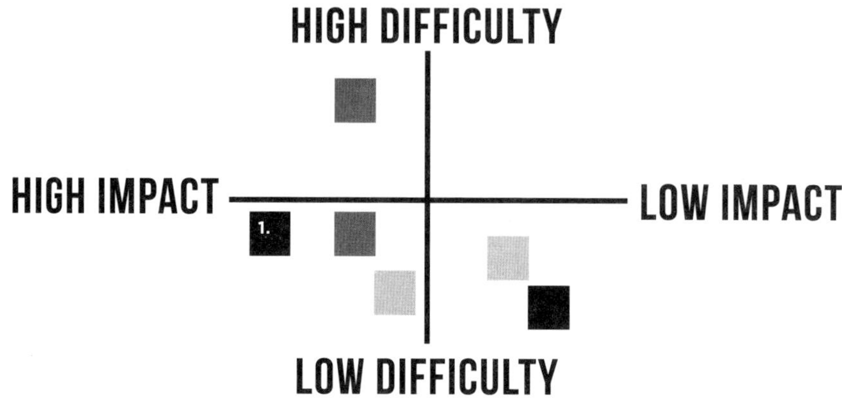


**Figure 5.12: Example of how an impact grid might look.**

### APPLICATION

This process is also a great strategy to use with staff to discuss the impact of various initiatives on student achievement and to determine the order of implementation.

## LOTUS BLOSSOM DIAGRAM

The *lotus blossom diagram* was originally developed by Yasuo Matsumura of Clover Management Research in Chiba City, Japan, and described in detail in Michael Michalko's (2006) book *Thinkertoys: A Handbook of Creative-Thinking Techniques*. It is an effective analytical tool for breaking down broad topics into components so that they can be prioritized for action. The diagram is named for its similarity to the petals of the lotus flower, and each new idea or component is "peeled back" one at a time to comprehensively explore a topic or issue. Although the technique is often used for idea generation, here it is used as a planning tool.

### SETUP

| | |
|---|---|
| **Number of participants** | Groups of four to five |
| **Time needed** | Fifteen to twenty minutes |
| **Room arrangement** | Table groupings |
| **Materials** | Lotus blossom diagram template |

### PROCESS

1. Distribute the lotus blossom diagram template (figure 5.13) to each group.
2. Instruct students to write their focus solution or idea in the center square of the grid. Next, students must identify up to eight major subtopics and write each one in the spaces around the center of the

grid marked A to H. (When using the diagram for solution planning, the eight major subtopics could include resources, people, and locations.)

3. Students then identify ideas around each subtopic and write them in the surrounding spaces marked one to eight.

| | | | | | | | | |
|---|---|---|---|---|---|---|---|---|
| 1 | 2 | 3 | 1 | 2 | 3 | 1 | 2 | 3 |
| 4 | A | 8 | 4 | B | 8 | 4 | C | 8 |
| 5 | 6 | 7 | 5 | 6 | 7 | 5 | 6 | 7 |
| 1 | 2 | 3 | 1 | 2 | 3 | 1 | 2 | 3 |
| 4 | D | 8 | 4 | Solution | 8 | 4 | E | 8 |
| 5 | 6 | 7 | 5 | 6 | 7 | 5 | 6 | 7 |
| 1 | 2 | 3 | 1 | 2 | 3 | 1 | 2 | 3 |
| 4 | F | 8 | 4 | G | 8 | 4 | H | 8 |
| 5 | 6 | 7 | 5 | 6 | 7 | 5 | 6 | 7 |

**Figure 5.13: Lotus blossom diagram template.**

## APPLICATION

In this partially completed example (figure 5.14, page 150), adapted from Primary Connections (2007), the diagram has been used to plan out a science investigation. Each subtopic indicates a variable. The grid is coded to show the variables that will stay the same (S), those that will change (C), and what will be measured (M) to create a fair test.

| | | | | | | | | |
|---|---|---|---|---|---|---|---|---|
| 1 | 2 | 3 | 1 wood | 2 carpet | 3 tiles | 1 | 2 | 3 |
| 4 | S Age of the ball | 8 | 4 grass | C Bounce surface | 8 sand | 4 | S Size of the ball | 8 |
| 5 | 6 | 7 | 5 gravel | 6 concrete | 7 metal | 5 | 6 | 7 |
| 1 | 2 | 3 | Age of the ball | Bounce surface | Size of the ball | 1 | 2 | 3 |
| 4 | S Type of the ball | 8 | Type of the ball | M How high can a ball bounce? | Drop height | 4 | S Drop height | 8 |
| 5 | 6 | 7 | Material of the ball | Push on the ball | Temper-ature of the ball | 5 | 6 | 7 |
| 1 | 2 | 3 | 1 | 2 | 3 | 1 | 2 | 3 |
| 4 | S Material of the ball | 8 | 4 | S Push on the ball | 8 | 4 | S Temper-ature of the ball | 8 |
| 5 | 6 | 7 | 5 | 6 | 7 | 5 | 6 | 7 |

**Figure 5.14: Sample partially completed lotus blossom diagram template.**

## PLANNING TEMPLATE

Although many planning tools are available, this planning template (figure 5.15) adapted from Gregory and Kuzmich (2007) is ideal for helping students document the order and priority of their action steps.

| What is our goal? | | |
|---|---|---|
| What are our tasks? | What are our steps? | Who will do this and when? |
| Task 1: | Action 1: | |
| | Action 2: | |
| | Action 3: | |
| Task 2: | Action 1: | |
| | Action 2: | |
| | Action 3: | |

Source: Adapted from Gregory & Kuzmich, 2007.

**Figure 5.15: Planning template.**

# EVALUATE

This component requires students to determine the extent to which their goals have been met and to monitor their progress (Antonenko et al., 2014; Beghetto, 2017; Roesler, 2016). This aspect of problem solving is an ongoing process as students continually monitor their established goals and the revisions that may need to be made along the way (Marzano & Heflebower, 2011). A critical aspect of this component is willingness to abandon a solution that is not working well (Marzano & Heflebower, 2011). Rather than using specific thinking protocols, students need to be encouraged to ask the following questions upon completion of their task.

- Did we solve the problem?
- What could we do differently?
- What did we learn in the process?
- Could this solution be used elsewhere?

Questions relating to how the students worked as a group can also be posed to evaluate their performance.

- How well did we work as a group?
- Did we listen to one another's ideas?
- What went well?
- Did each person contribute to the solution?
- What can we do better next time?
- What positive steps did we take to overcome any difficulties that we experienced?

# CONCLUSION

Problem solving can no longer be viewed as the domain of the traditional mathematics classroom—where problem-solving approaches are taught, and students are given problems to solve using those same approaches to find the correct answer. Wormeli (2009) claims that metaphors need to be busted out of the solitary confinement of English classes because their usefulness is much broader, going way beyond the scope of the English classroom application. I would argue equally that problem solving needs to be busted out of the mathematics classroom and broadened so that students are not simply exposed to well-defined, well-structured problems with only one answer. Rather, our students need to be exposed more often to problem-solving opportunities where the problems are messy, ill structured, and ill defined with multiple solutions and possibilities. These are the types of problems that they face in everyday life and will face in their lives in the future. As Sternberg (2001) states, "If problem-solving is taught well, students will not view these as special skills to take out of a dusty closet for special purposes, but rather as skills to hone and use on a daily basis" (p. 454). We need to equip our students to be problem finders and problem solvers so that they can successfully navigate the challenges that they will face now and in the future.

# CHAPTER 6

# ETHICAL THINKING

***Today I shall behave, as if this is the day I will be remembered.***

***—Dr. Seuss***

## RESEARCH AND THEORY

Ethical thinking positions thinking as more than the mere accumulation of knowledge (Panissal, 2017). It adds another dimension to thinking, drawing on the skills and dispositions of critical thinking, creative thinking, and problem solving by asking critical questions.

- We have this idea, but is it the right thing to do?
- Who will it affect?
- If this solution is implemented, how will others feel?
- What will happen if we don't act?
- Is this a problem to solve?
- Is it the right problem to solve?
- Whose problem is it?

Ethical thinking involves the ability to value, choose, and actively participate in society with a concern for the common good (Lipman, 2003; Panissal, 2017). Thinking without values, de Bono (2009) maintains, is meaningless and achieves nothing. However, he also warns that values without thinking are dangerous—resulting in persecution and the belief that if someone has different values, then that person must be wrong. This type of thinking has had dire consequences throughout history. Berenice Fisher and Joan Tronto (1990) assert that ethical thinking includes everything that we do to maintain, perpetuate, and repair our world to live in it as well as we can. The problem we face is that at times of rapid change, determining what is ethical is not always easy (Gardner, 2010). Hence the need for its focus and explicit instruction. As Douglas Fisher and Nancy Frey (2017) point out, "Hope isn't a plan" (p. 83). Hoping that students will engage in ethical thinking now and in the future isn't enough. We need intentional and targeted instruction.

Words typically associated with ethical thinking include *tolerance*, *respect*, *empathy*, *responsibility*, *care*, *mindfulness*, and *personal morality* (Gardner, 2006; Lipman, 2003; Rowan, Gauld, Cole-Adams, & Connolly, 2007). However, one of the problems that arises when discussing ethical thinking is the subjective nature of some of these commonly used terms (Rowan et al., 2007). There are multiple meanings and different expectations in the ways that people might see each value enacted (Rowan et al., 2007). For example, a student keeping eye contact when speaking to an adult might be viewed as a sign of respect in one culture but considered to be a display of disrespect in another. Further, some psychologists believe that aspects of ethical thinking, such as the ability to listen to others, empathize with them, and understand their points of view, are some of the highest forms of intelligence (Costa, 2001a). All of this requires high levels of listening, and yet Costa (2001a) maintains that listening is one of the least-taught skills in schools. The research of Christine Edwards-Groves and Christina Davidson (2017) echoes Costa's concerns. They propose that the explicit teaching of empathetic listening has the potential to develop students' logical-thinking abilities and capacities for persuading, arguing, and posing questions for further investigation (Edwards-Groves & Davidson, 2017).

Ethical thinking requires mindfulness. *Mindfulness* is defined as a heightened sense of awareness and conscious control over one's thoughts and behavior relative to a situation (Scott & Marzano, 2014). It requires the ability to be mindful of both what is occurring inside us and what is happening outside us. When being mindful of what is occurring inside, a person might ask the following questions:

- ***How am I interpreting this event?***
- ***Does this interpretation help serve an important goal or an important principle in my life?***
- ***If not, what is a more useful interpretation? (Marzano & Marzano, 2010, p. 356)***

Mindfulness outside of us occurs through questions such as:

- ***Right now, who or what are my actions affecting?***
- ***Are my actions affecting my environment in a positive or negative way?***
- ***If my actions are having a negative effect, what should I stop doing or what should I start doing? (Scott & Marzano, 2014, p. 142)***

Both sets of questions help students to consider how their actions are affecting others. Darrell Scott and Robert Marzano (2014) report that prior to being exposed to questions of this type, students had not been aware of the potential negative impact of their actions on others.

A discussion of mindfulness in relation to ethical thinking must recognize the role of emotions. Emotions such as anger, fear, and jealousy often lead people to lose control and behave in ways that they normally shouldn't or wouldn't. It is not that the presence of emotion is negative; indeed, it is emotion that moves us to action—both positive and negative. Thought and emotion are inextricably connected: "thought without emotion is dormant; emotion without thought is blind" (Swartz, 2001, p. 164). Therefore, Robert J. Swartz (2001) proposes that we need to consider two fundamental tenets. First, as human beings, we have emotions, they have a function, and we should accept them. Second, we need thought to reflect on what we should do based on the emotions we feel. Habits of mind can be developed early, and harder habits, such as reflecting on our emotions in a process of thinking and reasoning, will not become habits if delayed (Swartz, 2001). And where else can students learn to develop these habits in a sustained way other than in school?

# THE ROLE OF SCHOOL

The building blocks for developing ethical thinking are formed in childhood and are clearly identifiable—they are the words and actions of respected elders at home, at school, and in the community (Gardner, 2010). Understandably, Gardner (2010) points out that when one is part of an ethical environment, the development of an ethical mind is much easier. Although ethical orientation begins at home, young people spend more time in school than in any other institution. At school, they are surrounded by schoolmates more than by their siblings and in the presence of teachers more than in the company of their parents. Consequently, formal education plays a key role in determining whether students will engage in active citizenship and in taking an ethical stance (Gardner, 2006, 2010). The role of the teacher in this process is paramount since "teachers serve as crucial models" (Gardner, 2006, p. 141). When students see adults reflecting on their decisions and explicitly citing moral concerns, they witness ethical thinking in action. In this way, teaching ethical thinking is constant and ongoing. It doesn't just happen in a lesson period labeled *ethical thinking*.

We have long agreed on the importance of highlighting for students clear learning goals and why what they are learning is important. But the teaching of ethical thinking requires an additional step of showing students how this knowledge can be put to constructive uses, such as improving quality of life across the world. An understanding of the world and knowledge is also necessary to be able to take a stand when knowledge (or faulty logic) is being used in destructive ways (Gardner, 2006). However, unless ethical thinking is embodied in action, it remains abstract (Berman, 2001). When students can observe the impact of their actions, they experience the power and quality of their thinking (Berman, 2001). We need to educate students that they really do matter for a sustainable society (Panissal, 2017).

Providing opportunities for students to contribute and have influence not only improves the quality of their thinking but also builds self-esteem and a sense of connection with the world around them. Altruistic behavior such as this was identified by Maslow (1954) as part of the hierarchy of needs—the most basic needs being physiological (sleep, food, and water), followed by security (safety, health, and financial security), belongingness, esteem, and, finally, self-actualization. Motivation and inspiration occur, according to Marzano (2017), when students have opportunities to be self-actualized and connected to something greater than self. *Self-actualization* means that students feel that they are becoming closer to the type of person they want to be in the future (Marzano, 2017). *Connection to something greater than self* means that students feel that they are part of something important (Marzano, 2017). Working in this way requires students to:

- ***Set long-term goals and identify steps they must take to accomplish them***
- ***Engage with community members in meaningful ways***
- ***Work on projects of their own design that are meaningful to them (Marzano, 2017, p. 76)***

When engaging students with altruistic or personal projects, David Sobel (1999) indicates that acting locally by focusing on local problems is crucial for students. He warns that if teachers only focus on large-scale issues such as climate change and global warming, students become afraid of their natural world—something Sobel (1999) termed *ecophobia*. Although Sobel was speaking in the 20th century, his warning is even more relevant in the 21st century, with the advent of social media and sensationalized news reports. It is too easy for students to imagine a bleak future in which they have little or no impact (Lowenstein & Smith, 2017). Acclaimed education futurist Tony Ryan (2018) concurs, arguing that we constantly overwhelm students with how difficult the world is likely to be rather than acknowledge that although the future might be a complex and unpredictable place, it doesn't mean that we can't positively influence what will occur. It's time for a change in focus. "Let's dump the scare campaigns that leave our next generation feeling helpless, and instead show them how their choices today can create an inspiring future" (Ryan, 2018, p. xviii).

Ethical thinking cannot occur without collaboration and inquiry. It requires authentic dialogue, respect for each other, trust, and an ability to communicate effectively (Johnson & Johnson, 2017; Panissal, 2017). Through such dialogue, students can discover the values of others and consider what other people care about. Importantly, this helps students move beyond the limitations of their own experiences and consider the viewpoints and perspectives of others (Berman,

2001; Johnson & Johnson, 2017). Contemplating the perspectives of others compels us to tolerate ambiguity and be open to change as we consider that our answer may not be right. Through such openness, students can evaluate and act during situations of social conflict with compassion and insight (Berman, 2001). As interdependence develops, students begin to place the interests of the group above their own and draw on the communal resources to contribute to a common good (Costa & Garmston, 2001). When creating opportunities for collaboration and dialogue, remember that whenever individuals come together to work as a group, responsible interaction is essential (Marzano & Heflebower, 2011). Parameters and conditions such as those outlined in chapter 2 (page 27) must be in place to ensure all voices are heard and respected.

# THINKING PROTOCOLS

Since ethical thinking draws on the skills of critical and creative thinking and problem solving, many of the protocols in previous chapters can be used to support the development of ethical thinking. For example, if criteria such as inclusivity and fairness are added to the decision-making matrix (page 75), students can weigh the potential impact their choices might have on others. Similarly, the how I see it protocol (page 76) can help students consider differing perspectives and viewpoints. The following protocols can also be implemented to assist students to express their opinions, be mindful of the impact of emotions, deal with conflict, and consider consequences.

# CLASS MEETINGS

Jonathan C. Erwin (2004) recommends the class meeting format as "one of the most effective practices for allowing students to express their thoughts, feelings, and opinions and to be listened to by both the teacher and the other students" (p. 110).

## SETUP

| | |
|---|---|
| **Number of participants** | Whole class |
| **Time needed** | The length of the meeting should vary depending on the age of the students. The general rule of thumb recommended by Erwin (2004) is age of the students multiplied by two. |
| **Room arrangement** | Table groupings |
| **Materials** | None required |

## PROCESS

1. Determine a topic for the class meeting. This might be a problem to be solved or an issue that has arisen.
2. Set up the following guidelines prior to each class meeting.
   - ❑ The person speaking must keep to the here and now rather than bring up a topic from the past.
   - ❑ Only one person can speak at a time.
   - ❑ The person speaking must use *I* statements ("I would like . . ." or "I believe . . ." rather than "There should be . . ." or "They say . . .").
   - ❑ Everyone must focus on the person speaking—no other activity should be taking place.
   - ❑ Everyone can participate.
   - ❑ There should be no put-downs, either verbal or nonverbal.

## APPLICATION

A problem-solving meeting according to Erwin (2004) might take the following format.

1. **State the problem and define any terms:** A student who believes the class is too noisy may raise the issue by saying, "I think there is too much noise in the classroom when we are working in groups, and I think this is a problem because some people find it hard to hear and concentrate."
2. **Describe the desired state:** What is the goal? The student might say, "I think that when we are working in groups, only one person should be speaking at a time, and that person should speak only loudly enough for the people in the group to hear."
3. **Describe the present state:** The student might say, "Although we have created a norm for our group work stating that only one person should speak at a time, people are not sticking to it."
4. **Describe the current behavior:** The student might say, "Since more than one person is speaking at a time, people raise their voices to be heard. Nothing is being done to stop the noisiness."
5. **Evaluate the current behavior:** Is the current behavior accomplishing the goal? Why or why not? The student might say, "Unless we commit to our group norms and listen respectfully to one another, nothing is going to change."
6. **Brainstorm possible plans:** What can be done to accomplish the goal? For example, one student might suggest that a person be nominated in each group to remind the group of the norms during group work and monitor how well the group sticks to the norm of respectful listening. Another student might suggest that the norms for group work need to

be reviewed because nothing has been written about how loudly people should speak.

7. **Make a plan:** Students rate the proposed plans in terms of how likely they are to succeed and then choose one to implement.

# REACTION REFLECTION

As previously mentioned, ethical thinking requires a level of mindfulness. Johnson and Johnson (2017) propose that we usually overlearn the strategies that we use to make decisions and deal with conflict and that these behaviors operate as automatic habit patterns. They are learned behaviors, so they can be changed (Johnson & Johnson, 2017). This protocol helps students to reflect on the strategies they use.

When we engage in a controversy, we should take two concerns into account: (1) reaching a decision that combines sound reasoning and information from all points of view and (2) maintaining an effective relationship with each group member (Johnson & Johnson, 2017). Based on how important the goal of making the best possible decision is to the group members and how important their relationships with each other are to them, Johnson and Johnson (2017) created a continuum with five basic strategies that are used to make decisions. They assigned animals and behaviors to each. Figure 6.1 (page 160) is an adaptation of Johnson and Johnson's (2017) original work adjusted for student use.

## SETUP

| | |
|---|---|
| **Number of participants** | Small groups |
| **Time needed** | Five to ten minutes |
| **Room arrangement** | Table groupings |
| **Materials** | Five strategies template<br>Reflection logs |

## PROCESS

1. Introduce the five strategies to students. Adjust the wording depending on the age of the students.
2. After students have been involved in group discussions or a decision-making process, have them consider which of the five strategies they used most of the time during the process.
3. This may be recorded in a reflection log.

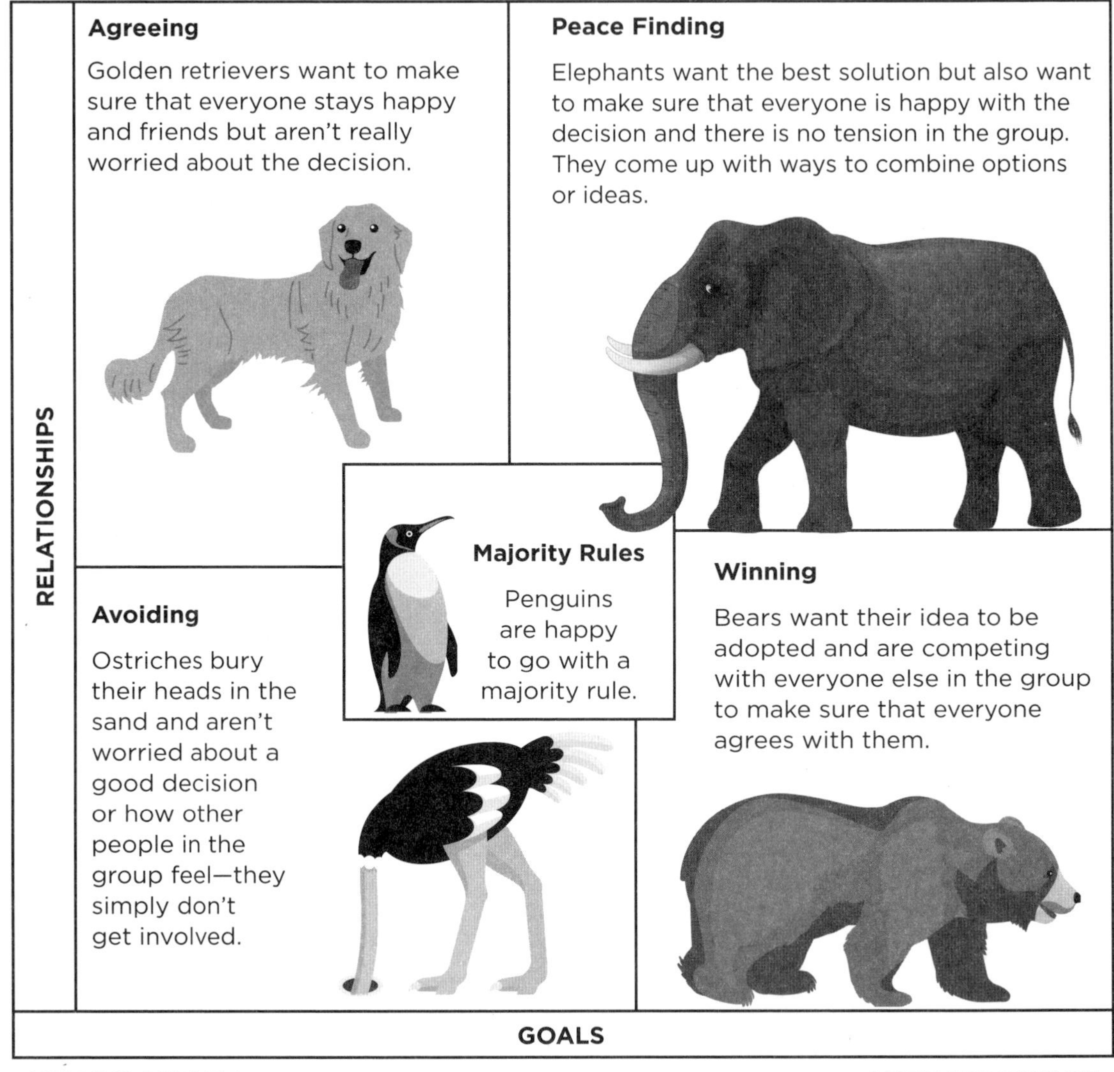


Source: Adapted from Johnson & Johnson, 2017.

**Figure 6.1: Five strategies for making decisions.**

## APPLICATION

- As a group, have students discuss the strategies that were used by members of the group and why problems may have arisen (for example, there were too many bears, with everyone wanting to win).

- Have individual students create goals for the next time they are involved in group work, such as aiming to be more like elephants, combining ideas so that everyone is happy.
- After each group interaction, have students reflect on their goals and behaviors.

## THINKING SKILLFULLY ABOUT EMOTIONS

Although not a protocol set out in the same way as previous routines, the following questions were developed by Swartz (2001) to help students be mindful of the impact of emotions—either someone else's or their own:

- ***What is the emotion that the person is experiencing? To what degree is the person experiencing this emotion?***
- ***What is the emotion about?***
- ***Is what the person thinks the emotion is about accurate? What information is there for and against this belief? What does this information show about the accuracy of the belief?***
- ***If accurate, does the belief justify the person's emotion?***
- ***What is the best thing for the person to do given that they are experiencing that emotion on that occasion? What options are there? What are the consequences of these options and which are pros and cons? Which option is best in light of the consequences? (p. 167)***

If the student is self-reflecting, the questions are changed to the first person. For younger students, the questions would be simplified and the number of questions reduced.

## RIPPLE EFFECT

After a decision has been made or while options are being considered, this protocol can be used for students to consider the short-, medium-, and long-term consequences of their decisions. They may also begin to consider any unintended consequences.

### SETUP

| | |
|---|---|
| **Number of participants** | Small groups |
| **Time needed** | Twenty to thirty minutes |
| **Room arrangement** | Table groupings |
| **Materials** | Ripple effect template |

## PROCESS

1. Distribute the ripple effect template to each group.
2. Have the groups consider and record the short-, medium-, and long-term consequences of their decisions or options.
3. Upon completion, have groups discuss any unintended consequences and their potential impact. If necessary, students may take time to review their original proposal or decision.

## APPLICATION

Use the template in figure 6.2 when implementing the ripple effect protocol in your classroom.

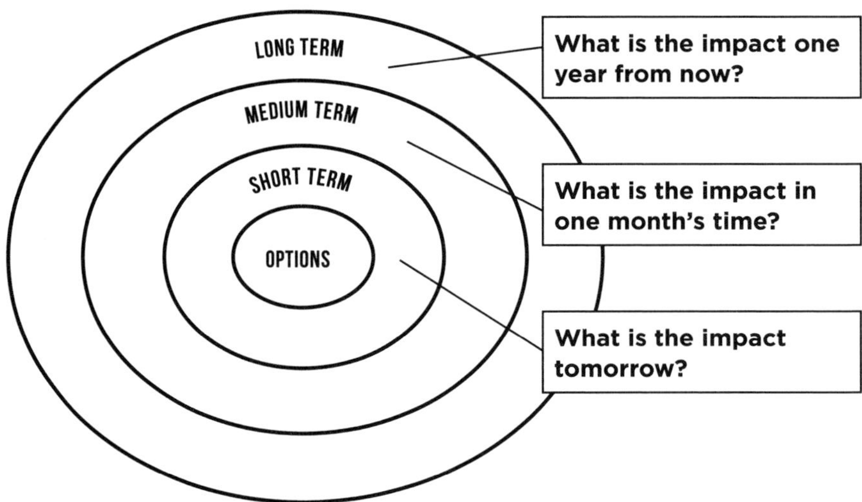


**Figure 6.2: Ripple effect template.**

# TO REJECT OR REVAMP

An aspect of ethical thinking is considering differing perspectives and being mindful of how others may feel. This protocol takes common quotes and asks students to reflect on the relevance of the quotes in the current context.

## SETUP

| | |
|---|---|
| **Number of participants** | Small groups |
| **Time needed** | Fifteen to twenty minutes |
| **Room arrangement** | Table groupings |
| **Materials** | Common quotes<br>Question prompts |

## PROCESS

1. Provide each group with a quote. Groups may each have a different quote or discuss the same quote.
2. Have each group discuss the meaning of the quote. If possible, have students consider the context in which the quote was initiated. For example, "Do unto others as you would have them do unto you" is often considered to be the golden rule, with a historical background linked to many religions.
3. Provide the groups with question prompts such as:
   - ❏ Is this still true today?
   - ❏ Is this important for everyone?
   - ❏ Could there be unintended consequences?
   - ❏ Does this quote include a form of bias or exclude people?
4. Have the groups decide whether their quote is still relevant and whether it should be rejected entirely or revamped for today's society.

## APPLICATION

While discussing the golden rule, a group of students reflected that the quote needed to be revamped. With insight, they discussed the notion that just because they like to be treated in a particular way, that doesn't mean that everyone would want to be treated that same way. They mentioned that although they like to be asked questions, other people might not like that and even consider it intrusive and an invasion of privacy. For example, for some First Australians, direct questioning is rude. Rather than ask about someone's family directly, a preferred approach is to share something about your own family, and then the person listening may also share something if he or she wishes. The students' revamped quote was "treat other people as they would like to be treated." Other possible quotes for discussion might include the following.

- "An eye for an eye."
- "Too many cooks spoil the broth."
- "It takes a village to raise a child."
- "When the going gets tough, the tough get going."
- "No one can make you feel inferior without your consent" (Eleanor Roosevelt; Goodreads, n.d.a).
- "We must build dikes of courage to hold back the flood of fear" (Martin Luther King Jr.; Goodreads, n.d.c).
- "I used to think anyone doing anything weird was weird. Now I know that it is the people that call others weird that are weird" (Paul McCartney; Goodreads, n.d.d).
- "You cannot lead from the crowd" (Margaret Thatcher; BrainyQuote, n.d.a).

- "Change your thoughts and you change your world" (Norman Vincent Peale; BrainyQuote, n.d.b).
- "It's not whether you get knocked down; it's whether you get up" (Vince Lombardi; BrainyQuote, n.d.c).

# CIRCLES OF RESPONSIBILITY

Associated with ethical thinking is the notion of taking responsibility and being accountable for one's own actions. The *circles of responsibility* protocol is adapted from a process used by Leonie Rowan, Judy Gauld, Jennet Cole-Adams, and Andrew Connolly (2007) to help students reflect on the responsibilities they have in different facets of their lives. At a deeper level, the process can be used to examine how individual responsibilities differ depending on the roles and jobs people have within society.

## SETUP

| | |
|---|---|
| **Number of participants** | Individuals, then whole class |
| **Time needed** | Twenty to thirty minutes |
| **Room arrangement** | Table groupings |
| **Materials** | Circles of responsibility template<br>Sticky notes |

## PROCESS

1. Review the term *responsibility* with students.
2. Have students reflect on their own responsibilities by considering each layer of the concentric circles of the template (figure 6.3).
3. Ask students to record each responsibility on a sticky note and then place the sticky note on the appropriate layer of the template.
4. As a whole class, have students examine and discuss the different responsibilities that students have identified and contributed.

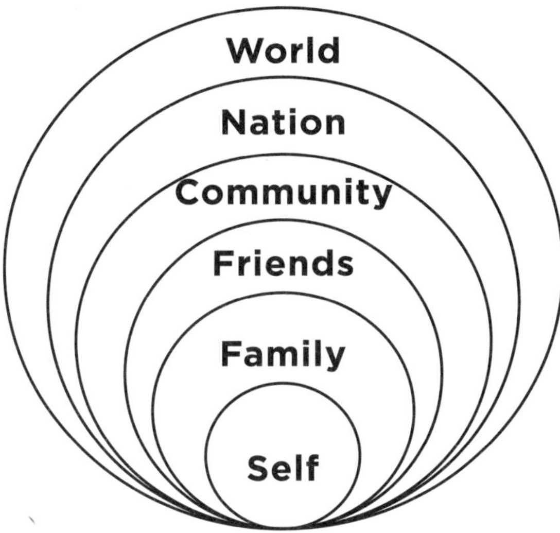


**Figure 6.3: Circles of responsibility template.**

## APPLICATION

To extend students' thinking further, discuss with students how responsibilities differ from person to person. Use the circles of responsibility template for students to explore the responsibilities of a range of people in their community. The list might include roles such as the principal, parents, the president, and emergency service personnel.

# CONCLUSION

It seems fitting that a book that began with questioning the role of school and whether schools are needed concludes with a call to action. A call to go beyond hoping that students will develop empathy, tolerance, and respect. A call to instead actively model and explicitly teach these behaviors. A call to help our students become hopeful and optimistic about the future rather than fearful and despondent or even apathetic. A call to empower students by showing them that they can make a difference and have a positive impact on the world around them. A call for each of us to embrace this educational responsibility at all levels of the education system—to have a true education revolution.

> ***Unless someone like you cares a whole awful lot, nothing is going to get better. It's not.***
>
> ***—Dr. Seuss***

# REFERENCES AND RESOURCES


Alexander, S. (2008). *Kitchen garden cooking for kids*. Sydney, Australia: Penguin Australia.

Antonenko, P. D., Jahanzad, F., & Greenwood, C. (2014). Fostering collaborative problem solving and 21st century skills using the DEEPER scaffolding framework. *Journal of College Science Teaching, 43*(6), 78–87.

Australian Curriculum, Assessment and Reporting Authority. (2018a). *Critical and creative thinking*. Accessed at www.australiancurriculum.edu.au/f-10-curriculum/general-capabilities/critical-and-creative-thinking on September 22, 2020.

Australian Curriculum, Assessment and Reporting Authority. (2018b). *Personal and social capability*. Accessed at www.australiancurriculum.edu.au/f-10-curriculum/general-capabilities/personal-and-social-capability on September 22, 2020.

Azzam, A. M. (2009). Why creativity now? A conversation with Sir Ken Robinson. *Educational Leadership, 67*(1), 22–26.

Bacon, F. (1625). *The essays or counsels, civil and moral, of Francis Ld. Verulam Viscount St. Albans*. Accessed at http://www.authorama.com/book/essays-of-francis-bacon.html on September 22, 2020.

Baker, L. (2010). Metacognition. In P. Peterson, E. Baker, & B. McGaw (Eds.), *International encyclopedia of education* (Vol. 3, pp. 204–210). Amsterdam, Netherlands: Elsevier Science. Accessed at https://doi.org/10.1016/B978-0-08-044894-7.00484-X on September 22, 2020.

Baker, L., & Cerro, L. (2000). Assessing metacognition in children and adults. In G. Schraw & J. C. Impara (Eds.), *Issues in the measurement of metacognition* (pp. 99–145). Lincoln, NE: Buros Institute of Mental Measurements.

Bandura, A. (1993). Perceived self-efficacy in cognitive development and functioning. *Educational Psychologist, 28*(2), 117–148. Accessed at https://doi.org/10.1207/s15326985ep2802_3 on September 22, 2020.

Bandura, A. (1994). Self-efficacy. In V. S. Ramachandran (Ed.), *Encyclopedia of human behavior* (Vol. 4, pp. 71–81). San Diego, CA: Academic Press.

Bandura, A. (1995). Exercise of personal and collective efficacy in changing societies. In A. Bandura (Ed.), *Self-efficacy in changing societies* (pp. 1–45). New York: Cambridge University Press.

Bauer, I. M., & Baumeister, R. F. (2011). Self-regulatory strength. In K. D. Vohs & R. F. Baumeister (Eds.), *Handbook of self-regulation: Research, theory, and applications* (2nd ed., pp. 64–82). New York: Guilford Press.

Beghetto, R. A. (2017). Inviting uncertainty into the classroom. *Educational Leadership, 75*(2), 20–25.

Bellanca, J. A., Fogarty, R. J., & Pete, B. M. (2020). *How to teach thinking skills: 7 key student proficiencies for college and career readiness* (2nd ed.). Bloomington, IN: Solution Tree Press.

Bennett, N., & Cass, A. (1989). The effects of group composition on group interactive processes and pupil understanding. *British Educational Research Journal, 15*(1), 19–32.

Bennion, L. L. (1959). *Religion and the pursuit of truth*. Salt Lake City, UT: Deseret Book.

Bereiter, C., & Scardamalia, M. (1987). *The psychology of written composition*. Mahwah, NJ: Lawrence Erlbaum Associates.

Berger, R. (2017, June 23). *Sir Ken Robinson: Finding market pressures to innovate education*. Accessed at https://www.forbes.com/sites/rodberger/2017/06/23/sir-ken-robinson-finding-market-pressures-to-innovate-education/#27ab1d851e77 on October 26, 2020.

Berman, S. (2001). Thinking in context: Teaching for open-mindedness and critical understanding. In A. L. Costa (Ed.), *Developing minds: A resource book for teaching thinking* (3rd ed., pp. 11–17). Alexandria, VA: Association for Supervision and Curriculum Development.

Beyer, B. K. (1988). *Developing a thinking skills program*. Boston: Allyn & Bacon.

Beyer, B. K. (2001a). Infusing thinking in history and the social sciences. In A. L. Costa (Ed.), *Developing minds: A resource book for teaching thinking* (3rd ed., pp. 317–325). Alexandria, VA: Association for Supervision and Curriculum Development.

Beyer, B. K. (2001b). Teaching thinking skills—defining the problem. In A. L. Costa (Ed.), *Developing minds: A resource book for teaching thinking* (3rd ed., pp. 35–40). Alexandria, VA: Association for Supervision and Curriculum Development.

Blabey, A. (2009). *Sunday Chutney*. Asheville, NC: Front Street.

Boaler, J. (2015). *Mathematical mindsets: Unleashing students' potential through creative math, inspiring messages and innovative teaching*. San Francisco: Jossey-Bass.

Bowkett, S. (2007). *100+ ideas for teaching thinking skills* (2nd ed.). London: Continuum.

BrainyQuote. (n.d.a). *Margaret Thatcher quotes*. Accessed at https://www.brainyquote.com/quotes/margaret_thatcher_166936 on October 26, 2020.

BrainyQuote. (n.d.b). *Norman Vincent Peale quotes*. Accessed at https://www.brainyquote.com/quotes/norman_vincent_peale_130593 on October 26, 2020.

BrainyQuote. (n.d.c). *Vince Lombardi quotes*. Accessed at https://www.brainyquote.com/quotes/vince_lombardi_121925 on October 26, 2020.

Brookhart, S. M. (2011). *How to assess higher-order thinking skills in your classroom*. Alexandria, VA: Association for Supervision and Curriculum Development.

Browning, R. (1835). *Paracelsus: Part I—Paracelsus aspires*. Accessed at https://allpoetry.com/Paracelsus:-Part-I:-Paracelsus-Aspires on October 23, 2020.

Bruce, M., & Robinson, G. (2002). The effectiveness of a metacognitive approach to teaching word identification skills to upper primary poor readers. *Special Education Perspectives, 11*(1), 3–30.

Bruer, J. T. (1994). Classroom problems, school culture, and cognitive research. In K. McGilly (Ed.), *Classroom lessons: Integrating cognitive theory and classroom practice* (pp. 273–290). Cambridge, MA: MIT Press.

Bruner, J. S. (1986). *Actual minds, possible worlds*. Cambridge, MA: Harvard University Press.

Carver, C. S., Scheier, M. F., & Fulford, D. (2008). Self-regulatory processes, stress, and coping. In O. P. John, R. W. Robins, & L. A. Pervin (Eds.), *Handbook of personality: Theory and research* (3rd ed., pp. 725–742). New York: Guilford Press.

Cazden, C. B. (2001). *Classroom discourse: The language of teaching and learning* (2nd ed.). Portsmouth, NH: Heinemann.

Centers for Disease Control and Prevention. (n.d.). *Motor vehicle safety*. Accessed at https://www.cdc.gov/motorvehiclesafety/teen_drivers/teendrivers_factsheet.html on October 26, 2020.

City, E. A. (2014). Talking to learn. *Educational Leadership, 72*(3), 10–16.

CoRT Thinking. (2019a). *ADI: Agreement, disagreement, irrelevant*. Accessed at http://www.cortthinking.com/cort/3/agreement-disagreement-irrelevant on September 22, 2020.

CoRT Thinking. (2019b). *CAF: The factors involved*. Accessed at http://www.cortthinking.com/cort/1/caf-consider-all-factors-cort-1-lesson-2 on September 22, 2020.

Costa, A. L. (2001a). Habits of mind. In A. L. Costa (Ed.), *Developing minds: A resource book for teaching thinking* (3rd ed., pp. 80–86). Alexandria, VA: Association for Supervision and Curriculum Development.

Costa, A. L. (2001b). Mediating the metacognitive. In A. L. Costa (Ed.), *Developing minds: A resource book for teaching thinking* (3rd ed., pp. 408–413). Alexandria, VA: Association for Supervision and Curriculum Development.

Costa, A. L. (2001c). The need to teach thinking: Introduction. In A. L. Costa (Ed.), *Developing minds: A resource book for teaching thinking* (3rd ed., p. 2). Alexandria, VA: Association for Supervision and Curriculum Development.

Costa, A. L., & Garmston, R. J. (2001). Five human passions: The origins of effective thinking. In A. L. Costa (Ed.), *Developing minds: A resource book for teaching thinking* (3rd ed., pp. 18–22). Alexandria, VA: Association for Supervision and Curriculum Development.

Costa, A. L., & O'Leary, P. W. (2013). Teaching the dispositions of interdependent thought. In A. L. Costa & P. W. O'Leary (Eds.), *The power of the social brain: Teaching, learning, and interdependent thinking* (pp. 176–199). New York: Teachers College Press.

Craft, A. (2013). Childhood, possibility thinking and wise, humanising educational futures. *International Journal of Educational Research, 61*, 126–134. Accessed at https://doi.org/10.1016/j.ijer.2013.02.005 on September 22, 2020.

Craft, A., & Chappell, K. (2014). Possibility thinking and social change in primary schools. *Education 3–13: International Journal of Primary, Elementary and Early Years Education, 44*(4), 407–425. Accessed at https://doi.org/10.1080/03004279.2014.961947 on September 22, 2020.

Craft, A., Cremin, T., Burnard, P., Dragovic, T., & Chappell, K. (2012). Possibility thinking: Culminative studies of an evidence-based concept driving creativity? *Education 3–13: International Journal of Primary, Elementary and Early Years Education, 41*(5), 538–556. Accessed at http://dx.doi.org/10.1080/03004279.2012.656671 on September 22, 2020.

Cramond, B. (2001). Interview with E. Paul Torrance on creativity in the last and next millennia. *Journal of Secondary Gifted Education, 12*(3), 116–120. Accessed at https://doi.org/10.4219/jsge-2001-664 on September 22, 2020.

Crawford, M. B. (2009). *Shop class as soulcraft: An inquiry into the value of work*. New York: Penguin.

Csikszentmihalyi, M. (1996). *Creativity: Flow and the psychology of discovery and invention*. New York: HarperCollins.

Darling-Hammond, L., Barron, B., Pearson, P. D., Schoenfeld, A. H., Stage, E. K., Zimmerman, T. D., et al. (2008). *Powerful learning: What we know about teaching for understanding*. San Francisco: Jossey-Bass.

Davis, G. A. (1989). Testing for creative potential. *Contemporary Educational Psychology, 14*(3), 257–274. Accessed at https://doi.org/10.1016/0361-476X(89)90014-3 on September 22, 2020.

Dean, C. B., Hubbell, E. R., Pitler, H., & Stone, B. J. (2012). *Classroom instruction that works: Research-based strategies for increasing student achievement* (2nd ed.). Alexandria, VA: Association for Supervision and Curriculum Development.

de Bono, E. (2004). *How to have a beautiful mind*. London: Vermilion.

de Bono, E. (2007). *How to have creative ideas: 62 exercises to develop the mind*. London: Vermilion.

de Bono, E. (2009). *Think! Before it's too late*. London: Vermilion.

Derewianka, B. (2018). Creating dialogic contexts for learning. In P. Jones, A. Simpson, & A. Thwaite (Eds.), *Talking the talk: Snapshots from Australian classrooms* (pp. 7–18). Newtown, Australia: Primary English Teaching Association Australia.

Dinham, S. (2016). *Leading learning and teaching*. Melbourne, Australia: Australian Council for Educational Research Press.

Drapeau, P. (2014). *Sparking student creativity: Practical ways to promote innovative thinking and problem solving*. Alexandria, VA: Association for Supervision and Curriculum Development.

Dr. Seuss, Prelutsky, J., & Smith, L. (1998). *Hooray for Diffendoofer Day!* New York: Scholastic.

Duckworth, E. (1964). Piaget rediscovered. *The Arithmetic Teacher, 11*(7), 496–499.

Dweck, C. S. (2000). *Self-theories: Their role in motivation, personality, and development*. Philadelphia: Psychology Press.

Dweck, C. S. (2007). *Mindset: The new psychology of success*. New York: Ballantine Books.

Easton, L. B. (2009). *Protocols for professional learning*. Alexandria, VA: Association for Supervision and Curriculum Development.

Eberle, R. F. (1972). Developing imagination through scamper. *Journal of Creative Behavior, 6*(3), 199–203. Accessed at https://doi.org/10.1002/j.2162-6057.1972.tb00929.x on September 22, 2020.

Edwards-Groves, C., & Davidson, C. (2017). *Becoming a meaning maker: Talk and interaction in the dialogic classroom*. Sydney, Australia: Primary English Teaching Association Australia.

Elementary and Secondary Education Act of 1965, Pub. L. No. 89-10, 20 U.S.C. § 6301 (1965). Accessed at https://www2.ed.gov/about/offices/list/oii/nonpublic/eseareauth.pdf on November 16, 2020.

Ennis, R. H. (2001). Goals for a critical thinking curriculum and its assessment. In A. L. Costa (Ed.), *Developing minds: A resource book for teaching thinking* (3rd ed., pp. 44–46). Alexandria, VA: Association for Supervision and Curriculum Development.

Erikson, E. H. (1959). *Identity and the life cycle*. New York: Norton.

Erwin, J. C. (2004). *The classroom of choice: Giving students what they need and getting what you want*. Alexandria, VA: Association for Supervision and Curriculum Development.

Every Student Succeeds Act of 2015, Pub. L. No. 114-95, 20 U.S.C. § 1177 (2015). Accessed at https://www.congress.gov/bill/114th-congress/senate-bill/1177 on November 16, 2020.

Evidence for Learning. (n.d.). *The teaching and learning toolkit*. Accessed at http://evidenceforlearning.org.au/the-toolkit on September 22, 2020.

Fettig, A., Schultz, T. R., & Ostrosky, M. M. (2016). Storybooks and beyond: Teaching problem solving skills in early childhood classrooms. *Young Exceptional Children, 19*(3), 18–31. Accessed at https://doi.org/10.1177/1096250615576803 on September 22, 2020.

Fields, A. M. (2006). Ill-structured problems and the reference consultation: The librarian's role in developing student expertise. *Reference Services Review, 34*(3), 405–420. Accessed at https://doi.org/10.1108/00907320610701554 on September 22, 2020.

Fisher, B., & Tronto, J. (1990). Toward a feminist theory of caring. In E. K. Abel & M. K. Nelson (Eds.), *Circles of care: Work and identity in women's lives* (pp. 35–54). Albany, NY: State University of New York Press.

Fisher, D., & Frey, N. (2017). Apprenticing students into a way of thinking. *Educational Leadership, 75*(2), 83–84.

Fisher, R. (2003). *Teaching thinking: Philosophical enquiry in the classroom* (2nd ed.). London: Continuum.

Fisher, R. (2013). *Teaching thinking: Philosophical enquiry in the classroom* (4th ed.). London: Bloomsbury.

Fleming, S. M., & Frith, C. D. (Eds.). (2014). *The cognitive neuroscience of metacognition*. New York: Springer.

Flynn, M. (2017). From answer-getters to problem solvers. *Educational Leadership, 75*(2), 26–31.

Foundation for Young Australians. (2016). *The new basics: Big data reveals the skills young people need for the New Work Order*. Accessed at https://www.fya.org.au/wp-content/uploads/2016/04/The-New-Basics_Update_Web.pdf on September 22, 2020.

Frey, N., Fisher, D., & Everlove, S. (2009). *Productive group work: How to engage students, build teamwork, and promote understanding*. Alexandria, VA: Association for Supervision and Curriculum Development.

Gardner, H. (2006). *Five minds for the future*. Cambridge, MA: Harvard Business School Press.

Gardner, H. (2010). Five minds for the future. In J. A. Bellanca & R. Brandt (Eds.), *21st century skills: Rethinking how students learn* (pp. 9–31). Bloomington, IN: Solution Tree Press.

Gaskill, P. J., & Hoy, A. W. (2002). Self-efficacy and self-regulated learning: The dynamic duo in school performance. In J. Aronson (Ed.), *Improving academic achievement: Impact of psychological factors on education* (pp. 185–208). San Diego, CA: Academic Press.

Glasser, W. (1998). *Choice theory: A new psychology of personal freedom*. New York: HarperCollins.

Goodreads. (n.d.a). *Eleanor Roosevelt quotes*. Accessed at https://www.goodreads.com/quotes/11035-no-one-can-make-you-feel-inferior-without-your-consent on October 26, 2020.

Goodreads. (n.d.b). *Leo Tolstoy quotes*. Accessed at https://www.goodreads.com/quotes/489051-all-we-can-know-is-that-we-know-nothing-and on October 26, 2020

Goodreads. (n.d.c). *Martin Luther King Jr. quotes*. Accessed at https://www.goodreads.com/quotes/686570-we-must-constantly-build-dykes-of-courage-to-hold-back on October 26, 2020.

Goodreads. (n.d.d). *Paul McCartney quotes*. Accessed at https://www.goodreads.com/quotes/124381-i-used-to-think-anyone-doing-anything-weird-was-weird on October 26, 2020.

Goodwin, B. (2017). Helping students develop schemas. *Educational Leadership, 75*(2), 81–82.

Greene, K., Heyck-Williams, J., & Gray, E. T. (2017). Problem solving in practice. *Educational Leadership, 75*(2), 44–48.

Gregory, G., & Kaufeldt, M. (2015). *The motivated brain: Improving student attention, engagement, and perseverance*. Alexandria, VA: Association for Supervision and Curriculum Development.

Gregory, G., & Kuzmich, L. (2007). *Teacher teams that get results: 61 strategies for sustaining and renewing professional learning communities*. Thousand Oaks, CA: Corwin Press.

Guthrie, J. T., Wigfield, A., & VonSecker, C. (2000). Effects of integrated instruction on motivation and strategy use in reading. *Journal of Educational Psychology, 92*(2), 331–341. Accessed at https://doi.org/10.1037/0022-0663.92.2.331 on September 22, 2020.

Hajhosseiny, M. (2012). The effect of dialogic teaching on students' critical thinking disposition. *Procedia—Social and Behavioral Sciences, 69*, 1358–1368. Accessed at https://doi.org/10.1016/j.sbspro.2012.12.073 on September 22, 2020.

Hallahan, K. (1999). Seven models of framing: Implications for public relations. *Journal of Public Relations Research, 11*(3), 205–242. Accessed at https://doi.org/10.1207/s1532754xjprr1103_02 on September 22, 2020.

Hargreaves, A. (2010). Leadership, change, and beyond the 21st century skills agenda. In J. A. Bellanca & R. Brandt (Eds.), *21st century skills: Rethinking how students learn* (pp. 327–348). Bloomington, IN: Solution Tree Press.

Harvey, S., & Goudvis, A. (2007). *Strategies that work: Teaching comprehension for understanding and engagement* (2nd ed.). Portland, ME: Stenhouse.

Harvey, S., & Goudvis, A. (2017). *Strategies that work: Teaching comprehension for understanding, engagement, and building knowledge* (3rd ed.). Portland, ME: Stenhouse.

Heflebower, T., Hoegh, J. K., & Warrick, P. B. (2014). *A school leader's guide to standards-based grading*. Bloomington, IN: Marzano Resources.

Heflebower, T., Hoegh, J. K., Warrick, P. B., & Flygare, J. (2019). *A teacher's guide to standards-based learning*. Bloomington, IN: Marzano Resources.

Henderson, M., Presbury, J., & Torrance, E. P. (1983). *Manifesto for children*. Athens, GA: Torrance Center for Creativity and Talent Development.

Higgins, S., Hall, E., Baumfield, V., & Moseley, D. (2005). *A meta-analysis of the impact of the implementation of thinking skills approaches on pupils*. London: EPPI-Centre, Social Science Research Unit, Institute of Education, University of London. Accessed at https://eppi.ioe.ac.uk/cms/Portals/0/PDF%20reviews%20and%20summaries/t_s_rv2.pdf?ver=2006-03-02-125128-393 on September 22, 2020.

Holyoak, K. J., & Morrison, R. G. (Eds.). (2005). *The Cambridge handbook of thinking and reasoning*. New York: Cambridge University Press.

Hulse-Killacky, D., Killacky, J., & Donigian, J. (2001). *Making task groups work in your world*. Upper Saddle River, NJ: Prentice Hall.

Ishikawa, K. (1990). *Introduction to quality control*. Tokyo, Japan: 3A Corporation.

Jinks, J., & Lorsbach, A. (2003). Introduction: Motivation and self-efficacy belief. *Reading and Writing Quarterly, 19*(2), 113–118. Accessed at https://doi.org/10.1080/10573560308218 on September 22, 2020.

Jinks, J., & Morgan, V. (1999). Children's perceived academic self-efficacy: An inventory scale. *The Clearing House: A Journal of Educational Strategies, Issues and Ideas, 72*(4), 224–230. Accessed at https://doi.org/10.1080/00098659909599398 on September 22, 2020.

Johnson, D. W., & Johnson, F. P. (2017). *Joining together: Group theory and group skills* (12th ed.). New York: Pearson.

Johnson, S., & Siegel, H. (2010). *Teaching thinking skills* (2nd ed.). London: Continuum.

Joseph, G. E., & Strain, P. S. (2010). Teaching young children interpersonal problem-solving skills. *Young Exceptional Children, 13*(3), 28–40. Accessed at https://doi.org/10.1177/1096250610365144 on September 22, 2020.

Judkins, R. (2015). *The art of creative thinking*. London: Sceptre.

Kagan, S., & Kagan, M. (2009). *Kagan cooperative learning*. San Clemente, CA: Kagan Publishing.

Kay, K. (2010). 21st century skills: Why they matter, what they are, and how we get there. In J. A. Bellanca & R. Brandt (Eds.), *21st century skills: Rethinking how students learn* (pp. xiii–xxxi). Bloomington, IN: Solution Tree Press.

Lassig, C. J. (2012). *Perceiving and pursuing novelty: A grounded theory of adolescent creativity*. Unpublished doctoral dissertation, Queensland University of Technology, Brisbane, Australia. Accessed at https://eprints.qut.edu.au/50661/1/Carly_Lassig_Thesis.pdf on September 22, 2020.

Linnenbrink, E. A., & Pintrich, P. R. (2002). Motivation as an enabler for academic success. *School Psychology Review*, *31*(3), 313–327. Accessed at https://doi.org/10.1080/02796015.2002.12086158 on September 22, 2020.

Linnenbrink, E. A., & Pintrich, P. R. (2003). The role of self-efficacy beliefs in student engagement and learning in the classroom. *Reading and Writing Quarterly*, *19*(2), 119–137. Accessed at https://doi.org/10.1080/10573560308223 on September 22, 2020.

Lipman, M. (2003). *Thinking in education* (2nd ed.). New York: Cambridge University Press.

Lipton, L., & Wellman, B. (2016). *Groups at work: Strategies and structures for professional learning*. Arlington, MA: MiraVia.

Lowenstein, E., & Smith, G. (2017). Making a world of difference by looking locally. *Educational Leadership*, *75*(2), 50–56.

Lucas, B., & Spencer, E. (2017). *Teaching creative thinking: Developing learners who generate ideas and can think critically*. Carmarthen, United Kingdom: Crown House Publishing.

Lyman, F. (1981). The responsive classroom discussion: The inclusion of *all* students. In A. S. Anderson (Ed.), *Mainstreaming digest: A collection of faculty and student papers* (pp. 109–113). College Park, MD: University of Maryland.

Margolis, H., & McCabe, P. P. (2003). Self-efficacy: A key to improving the motivation of struggling learners. *Preventing School Failure*, *47*(4), 162–169. Accessed at https://doi.org/10.1080/10459880309603362 on September 22, 2020.

Margolis, H., & McCabe, P. P. (2006). Improving self-efficacy and motivation: What to do, what to say. *Intervention in School and Clinic*, *41*(4), 218–227. Accessed at https://doi.org/10.1177/10534512060410040401 on September 22, 2020.

Marzano, R. J. (1998). *A theory-based meta-analysis of research on instruction*. Aurora, CO: Mid-continent Regional Educational Laboratory.

Marzano, R. J. (2006). *Classroom assessment and grading that work*. Alexandria, VA: Association for Supervision and Curriculum Development.

Marzano, R. J. (2007). *The art and science of teaching: A comprehensive framework for effective instruction*. Alexandria, VA: Association for Supervision and Curriculum Development.

Marzano, R. J. (2009). *Designing and teaching learning goals and objectives*. Bloomington, IN: Marzano Resources.

Marzano, R. J. (2017). *The new art and science of teaching*. Bloomington, IN: Solution Tree Press.

Marzano, R. J. (2019). *The handbook for the new art and science of teaching*. Bloomington, IN: Solution Tree Press.

Marzano, R. J., Gaddy, B., & Dean, C. (2000). *What works in classroom instruction*. Aurora, CO: Mid-continent Regional Educational Laboratory.

Marzano, R. J., & Haystead, M. W. (2008). *Making standards useful in the classroom*. Alexandria, VA: Association for Supervision and Curriculum Development.

Marzano, R. J., & Heflebower, T. (2011). *Teaching and assessing 21st century skills*. Bloomington, IN: Marzano Resources.

Marzano, R. J., & Kendall, J. S. (2007). *The new taxonomy of educational objectives* (2nd ed.). Thousand Oaks, CA: Corwin Press.

Marzano, R. J., & Marzano, J. S. (2010). The inner game of teaching. In R. J. Marzano (Ed.), *On excellence in teaching* (pp. 345–367). Bloomington, IN: Solution Tree Press.

Marzano, R. J., Pickering, D. J., & Pollock, J. E. (2001). *Classroom instruction that works: Research-based strategies for increasing student achievement*. Alexandria, VA: Association for Supervision and Curriculum Development.

Marzano Resources. (2016). *Marzano compendium of instructional strategies*. Bloomington, IN: Author.

Maslow, A. H. (1954). *Motivation and personality*. New York: Harper & Row.

May, R. (1953). *Man's search for himself*. New York: W. W. Norton.

May, R. (2009). *Man's search for himself*. New York: W. W. Norton.

McKinsey Global Institute. (2019, July). *The future of work in America: People and places, today and tomorrow*. New York: McKinsey & Company. Accessed at https://www.mckinsey.com/-/media/mckinsey/industries/public%20and%20social%20sector/our%20insights/future%20of%20organizations/the%20future%20of%20work%20in%20america%20people%20and%20places%20today%20and%20tomorrow/the-future-of-work-in-america-full-report.pdf on October 28, 2020.

McTighe, J. (2019). *Mapping an understanding-based curriculum for 21st century learning* [Slideware presentation]. Accessed at https://jaymctighe.com/wp-content/uploads/2019/08/Jays-PP-SLides---Mapping-a-UbD-Curriculum-MCIU-8.15.19.pdf on September 22, 2020.

Meyer, K. (2014). Making meaning in mathematics problem-solving using the reciprocal teaching approach. *Literacy Learning: The Middle Years*, *22*(2), 7–14.

Michalko, M. (2006). *Thinkertoys: A handbook of creative-thinking techniques*. Berkeley, CA: Ten Speed Press.

Ministerial Council on Education, Employment, Training and Youth Affairs. (2008). *Melbourne declaration on educational goals for young Australians*. Accessed at http://www.curriculum.edu.au/verve/_resources/National_Declaration_on_the_Educational_Goals_for_Young_Australians.pdf on September 22, 2020.

Ministerial Council on Education, Employment, Training and Youth Affairs. (2019). *Alice Springs (Mparntwe) education declaration*. Accessed at https://uploadstorage.blob.core.windows.net/public-assets/education-au/melbdec/ED19-0230%20-%20SCH%20-%20Alice%20Springs%20(Mparntwe)%20Education%20Declaration_ACC.pdf on September 22, 2020.

Moon, J. (2008). *Critical thinking: An exploration of theory and practice*. New York: Routledge.

Naiditch, F. (2017). Understanding critical thinking: What is it? Can we teach it? How do we learn it? In F. Naiditch (Ed.), *Developing critical thinking: From theory to classroom practice* (pp. 1–10). Lanham, MD: Rowman & Littlefield.

National Association of Colleges and Employers. (2020, January 16). *The top attributes employers want to see on resumes* [Press release]. Accessed at https://www.naceweb.org/about-us/press/2020/the-top-attributes-employers-want-to-see-on-resumes on October 28, 2020.

National Governors Association Center for Best Practices & Council of Chief State School Officers. (2010a). *Common Core State Standards for English language arts and literacy in history/social studies, science, and technical subjects*. Washington, DC: Authors. Accessed at www.corestandards.org/assets/CCSSI_ELA%20Standards.pdf on October 27, 2020.

National Governors Association Center for Best Practices & Council of Chief State School Officers. (2010b). *Common Core State Standards for mathematics*. Washington, DC: Authors. Accessed at www.corestandards.org/assets/CCSSI_Math%20Standards.pdf on October 27, 2020.

National Research Council. (2000). *How people learn: Brain, mind, experience, and school*. Washington, DC: National Academies Press.

NGSS Lead States. (2013). *Next Generation Science Standards: For states, by states*. Washington, DC: National Academies Press.

Nielsen, O. (2015). *Gert Biesta: What really matters in education* [Video file]. Accessed at https://www.youtube.com/watch?v=CLcphZTGejc on September 22, 2020.

Ohno, T. (1988). *Toyota production system: Beyond large-scale production*. Portland, OR: Productivity Press.

Organisation for Economic Co-operation and Development. (2012). *Better skills, better jobs, better lives: A strategic approach to skills policies*. Accessed at http://dx.doi.org/10.1787/9789264177338-en on September 22, 2020.

Ostroff, W. L. (2016). *Cultivating curiosity in K–12 classrooms: How to promote and sustain deep learning*. Alexandria, VA: Association for Supervision and Curriculum Development.

Ozturk, N. (2017). Assessing metacognition: Theory and practices. *International Journal of Assessment Tools in Education*, *4*(2), 134–148.

Paivio, A. (2014). Intelligence, dual coding theory, and the brain. *Intelligence, 47*, 141–158. Accessed at https://doi.org/10.1016/j.intell.2014.09.002 on September 22, 2020.

Pajares, F., & Schunk, D. H. (2002). Self and self-belief in psychology and education: A historical perspective. In J. Aronson (Ed.), *Improving academic achievement: Impact of psychological factors on education* (pp. 3–21). San Diego, CA: Academic Press.

Palincsar, A. S., & Brown, A. L. (1984). Reciprocal teaching of comprehension-fostering and comprehension-monitoring activities. *Cognition and Instruction, 1*(2), 117–175.

Palmer, E. (2014). *Teaching the core skills of listening and speaking*. Alexandria, VA: Association for Supervision and Curriculum Development.

Panissal, N. (2017). Citizenship education in nanotechnologies as a means of developing ethical thinking among students. *Sisyphus—Journal of Education, 5*(2), 138–154. Accessed at https://doi.org/10.25749/sis.11842 on September 22, 2020.

Partnership for 21st Century Learning. (2015). *P21 framework definitions*. Hilliard, OH: Battelle for Kids. Accessed at http://static.battelleforkids.org/documents/p21/P21_Framework_Definitions_New_Logo_2015_9pgs.pdf on October 26, 2020.

Partnership for 21st Century Learning. (2019). *Framework for 21st century learning*. Hilliard, OH: Battelle for Kids. Accessed at http://static.battelleforkids.org/documents/p21/P21_Framework_Brief.pdf on October 26, 2020.

Paul, R. (2001). Dialogical and dialectical thinking. In A. L. Costa (Ed.), *Developing minds: A resource book for teaching thinking* (3rd ed., pp. 427–436). Alexandria, VA: Association for Supervision and Curriculum Development.

Paul, R., & Elder, L. (2008). *The miniature guide to critical thinking: Concepts and tools*. Tomales, CA: Foundation for Critical Thinking. Accessed at https://www.criticalthinking.org/files/Concepts_Tools.pdf on September 23, 2020.

Piaget, J. (1973). *Main trends in psychology*. New York: Harper & Row.

Piirto, J. (2004). *Understanding creativity*. Goshen, KY: Great Potential Press.

Pinker, S. (2007). *The stuff of thought: Language as a window into human nature*. New York: Viking.

Pintrich, P. R. (2002). The role of metacognitive knowledge in learning, teaching, and assessing. *Theory Into Practice, 41*(4), 219–225. Accessed at https://doi.org/10.1207/s15430421tip4104_3 on September 22, 2020.

Primary Connections. (2007). *Making connections: Facilitation tools and techniques*. Workshop presentation at the Australian Academy of Science, Canberra, Australia.

Project Zero. (n.d.a). *Circle of viewpoints*. Accessed at https://pz.harvard.edu/resources/circle-of-viewpoints on October 14, 2020.

Project Zero. (n.d.b). *Colour, symbol, image*. Accessed at https://pz.harvard.edu/resources/color-symbol-image on October 14, 2020.

Project Zero. (n.d.c). *Compass points*. Accessed at http://www.pz.harvard.edu/resources/compass-points on October 14, 2020.

Project Zero. (n.d.d). *Headlines*. Accessed at https://pz.harvard.edu/resources/headlines on October 14, 2020.

Project Zero. (n.d.e). *True for who?* Accessed at https://pz.harvard.edu/resources/true-for-who on October 14, 2020.

Project Zero. (n.d.f). *What makes you say that?* Accessed at https://pz.harvard.edu/resources/what-makes-you-say-that on October 14, 2020.

Puccio, G. J., & Murdock, M. C. (2001). Creative thinking: An essential life skill. In A. L. Costa (Ed.), *Developing minds: A resource book for teaching thinking* (3rd ed., pp. 67–71). Alexandria, VA: Association for Supervision and Curriculum Development.

ReadWriteThink. (2005). *Writing habits journal questions*. Accessed at http://www.readwritethink.org/files/resources/lesson_images/lesson905/WritingHabits.pdf on September 22, 2020.

Reilly, Y., Parsons, J., & Bortolot, E. (2009). *Reciprocal teaching in mathematics*. Paper presented at the Mathematics: Of Prime Importance Conference, La Trobe University, Melbourne, Australia.

Risemberg, R., & Zimmerman, B. J. (1992). Self-regulated learning in gifted students. *Roeper Review, 15*(2), 98–101. Accessed at https://doi.org/10.1080/02783199209553476 on September 22, 2020.

Ritchey, T. (1998, January). *Fritz Zwicky, "morphologie" and policy analysis*. Conference session at the sixteenth Euro Conference on Operational Analysis, Brussels, Belgium.

Rochester Community Schools. (n.d.). *Headlines: A routine for capturing core ideas*. Accessed at http://www.rcsthinkfromthemiddle.com/headlines.html on September 22, 2020.

Roesler, R. A. (2016). Toward solving the problem of problem solving: An analysis framework. *Journal of Music Teacher Education, 26*(1), 28–42. Accessed at https://doi.org/10.1177/1057083715602124 on September 22, 2020.

Rowan, L., Gauld, J., Cole-Adams, J., & Connolly, A. (2007). *Teaching values*. Sydney, Australia: Primary English Teaching Association Australia.

Roy, P. A. (2013). We instead of me: The teacher's role in engendering interdependent student thinking. In A. L. Costa & P. W. O'Leary (Eds.), *The power of the social brain: Teaching, learning, and interdependent thinking* (pp. 129–139). New York: Teachers College Press.

Rubin, D. L. (1988). Introduction: Four dimensions of social construction in written communication. In B. A. Rafoth & D. L. Rubin (Eds.), *The social construction of written communication* (pp. 1–33). Norwood, NJ: Ablex.

Ryan, T. (2018). *The next generation: Preparing today's kids for an extraordinary future*. Brisbane, Australia: John Wiley & Sons.

Ryan, T. (2019). *Thinkers keys cards*. Accessed at http://tonyryan.com.au/download/TKBook.pdf on September 22, 2020.

Salend, S. J. (2011). *Creating inclusive classrooms: Effective and reflective practices* (7th ed.). Upper Saddle River, NJ: Merrill.

Sawyer, R. K. (2006). Educating for innovation. *Thinking Skills and Creativity, 1*(1), 41–48. Accessed at http://dx.doi.org/10.1016/j.tsc.2005.08.001 on September 22, 2020.

Schawbel, D. (2013, June 5). *Sir Ken Robinson: How to discover your true talents*. Accessed at https://www.forbes.com/sites/danschawbel/2013/06/05/sir-ken-robinson-how-to-discover-your-true-talents/#5283070e2553 on September 22, 2020.

Schunk, D. H. (2001). Social cognitive theory and self-regulated learning. In B. J. Zimmerman & D. H. Schunk (Eds.), *Self-regulated learning and academic achievement: Theoretical perspectives* (2nd ed., pp. 125–151). Mahwah, NJ: Lawrence Erlbaum Associates.

Schunk, D. H. (2003). Self-efficacy for reading and writing: Influence of modeling, goal setting, and self-evaluation. *Reading and Writing Quarterly, 19*(2), 159–172. Accessed at https://doi.org/10.1080/10573560308219 on September 22, 2020.

Schunk, D. H. (2012). *Learning theories: An educational perspective* (6th ed.). Boston: Pearson.

Schunk, D. H., & Rice, J. M. (1991). Learning goals and progress feedback during reading comprehension instruction. *Journal of Reading Behavior, 23*(3), 351–364.

Schunk, D. H., & Rice, J. M. (1992). *Influence of reading comprehension strategy information on children's self-efficacy and skills*. Paper presented at the annual meeting of the American Educational Research Association, San Francisco, California.

Schunk, D. H., & Swartz, C. W. (1993). Writing strategy instruction with gifted students: Effects of goals and feedback on self-efficacy and skills. *Roeper Review, 15*(4), 225–231.

Scott, D., & Marzano, R. J. (2014). *Awaken the learner: Finding the source of effective education*. Bloomington, IN: Marzano Resources.

Sedova, K., Salamounova, Z., & Svaricek, R. (2014). Troubles with dialogic teaching. *Learning, Culture and Social Interaction, 3*(4), 274–285. Accessed at https://doi.org/10.1016/j.lcsi.2014.04.001 on September 22, 2020.

Seeley, C. L. (2017). Turning teaching upside down. *Educational Leadership, 75*(2), 32–36.

Shaughnessy, M. F. (1998). An interview with E. Paul Torrance: About creativity. *Educational Psychology Review, 10*(4), 441–452. Accessed at https://doi.org/10.1023/A:1022849603713 on September 22, 2020.

Silberman, M. (1999). *101 ways to make meetings active: Surefire ideas to engage your group*. San Francisco: Jossey-Bass.

Simon, H. A., Dantzig, G. B., Hogarth, R., Plott, C. R., Raiffa, H., Schelling, T. C., et al. (1986). Report of the research briefing panel on decision making and problem solving. In National Academy of Sciences, National Academy of Engineering, & Institute of Medicine (Eds.), *Research briefings 1986* (pp. 17–36). Washington, DC: National Academies Press. Accessed at https://doi.org/10.17226/911 on September 22, 2020.

Sobel, D. (1999). *Beyond ecophobia: Reclaiming the heart in nature education* (2nd ed.). Great Barrington, MA: Orion Society.

Sorman-Nilsson, A. (2009). *Thinque funky: Upgrade your thinking*. Sydney, Australia: Thinque Publishing.

Sousa, D. A. (2001). *How the brain learns* (2nd ed.). Thousand Oaks, CA: Corwin Press.

Sousa, D. A. (2011). *How the brain learns* (4th ed.). Thousand Oaks, CA: Corwin Press.

Sousa, D. A. (2017). *How the brain learns* (5th ed.). Thousand Oaks, CA: Corwin Press.

Spencer, J. (2017). Think inside the box. *Educational Leadership, 75*(2), 39–42.

Stahl, R. J. (1985). *Cognitive information processes and processing within a uniprocess superstructure/microstructure framework: A practical information-based model*. Unpublished manuscript.

Sternberg, R. J. (2001). Teaching problem solving as a way of life. In A. L. Costa (Ed.), *Developing minds: A resource book for teaching thinking* (3rd ed., pp. 451–454). Alexandria, VA: Association for Supervision and Curriculum Development.

Sternberg, R. J. (2007). Creativity as a habit. In A. Tan (Ed.), *Creativity: A handbook for teachers* (pp. 3–25). Singapore: World Scientific.

Sternberg, R. J., & Grigorenko, E. L. (2016). *Teaching for successful intelligence to increase learning and achievement* (2nd ed.). New York: Skyhorse.

Sternberg, R. J., Jarvin, L., & Grigorenko, E. L. (2011). *Explorations in giftedness*. New York: Cambridge University Press.

Swartz, R. J. (2001). In the grips of emotion. In A. L. Costa (Ed.), *Developing minds: A resource book for teaching thinking* (3rd ed., pp. 164–169). Alexandria, VA: Association for Supervision and Curriculum Development.

Swartz, R. J., Costa, A. L., Beyer, B. K., Reagan, R., & Kallick, B. (2007). *Thinking-based learning: Activating students' potential*. Norwood, MA: Christopher-Gordon.

Swartz, R. J., & McGuiness, C. (2014). *Developing and assessing thinking skills: Final report part 1, literature review and evaluation framework*. Accessed at https://doi.org/10.13140/RG.2.1.4917.6163 on September 22, 2020.

Tactical Steps Education. (n.d.a). *Looking outside the box: Encouraging creative thinking course book*. Richmond, United Kingdom: Author.

Tactical Steps Education. (n.d.b). *Thinking: Why is it so? Stimulating critical thinking course book*. Richmond, United Kingdom: Author.

Taibbi, C., & Iseminger, B. (2015). *Cultivating classroom conversation: Strategies and activities that build student dialogue into standards-based lessons*. Marion, IL: Pieces of Learning.

Tishman, S., & Clapp, E. P. (2017). Building students' sense of agency. *Educational Leadership, 75*(2), 58–65.

Toffler, A. (1970). *Future shock*. New York: Bantam Books.

Tomlinson, C. A. (2017). Catalysts for creativity. *Educational Leadership, 75*(2), 91–92.

Toner, P. (2011). *Workforce skills and innovation: An overview of major themes in the literature*. Paris: Organisation for Economic Co-operation and Development. Accessed at https://www.oecd.org/innovation/inno/46970941.pdf on September 22, 2020.

Torrance, E. P. (1974). *Norms and technical manual for the Torrance Tests of Creative Thinking*. Bensenville, IL: Scholastic Testing.

Treffinger, D. J., & Isaksen, S. G. (2001). Teaching for creative learning and problem solving. In A. L. Costa (Ed.), *Developing minds: A resource book for teaching thinking* (3rd ed., pp. 442–445). Alexandria, VA: Association for Supervision and Curriculum Development.

U.S. Department of Education. (n.d.). *Every Student Succeeds Act (ESSA)*. Accessed at https://www.ed.gov/essa?src=rn on October 28, 2020.

VanGundy, A. B. (2005). *101 activities for teaching creativity and problem solving*. Hoboken, NJ: Pfeiffer.

Walker, B. J. (2003). The cultivation of student self-efficacy in reading and writing. *Reading and Writing Quarterly*, *19*(2), 173–187. Accessed at https://doi.org/10.1080/10573560308217 on September 22, 2020.

Walsh, J. A., & Sattes, B. D. (2011). *Thinking through quality questioning: Deepening student engagement*. Thousand Oaks, CA: Corwin Press.

Walsh, J. A., & Sattes, B. D. (2015). *Questioning for classroom discussion: Purposeful speaking, engaged listening, deep thinking*. Alexandria, VA: Association for Supervision and Curriculum Development.

Wegerif, R. (2017, September 30). *A dialogic approach to teaching thinking*. Accessed at https://www.rupertwegerif.name/blog/a-dialogic-approach-to-teaching-thinking on September 22, 2020.

Westwood, P. S. (2016). *Numeracy and learning difficulties: Approaches to teaching and assessment*. New York: David Fulton.

Wiederhold, C. (1991). *Cooperative learning and higher-level thinking: The question matrix*. San Clemente, CA: Kagan Cooperative Learning.

Willingham, D. T. (2008). Critical thinking: Why is it so hard to teach? *Arts Education Policy Review*, *109*(4), 21–32. Accessed at https://doi.org/10.3200/AEPR.109.4.21-32 on September 22, 2020.

Wills, J. (2012). *The self-efficacy of gifted students with a reading disability: The impact of lived experience*. Unpublished doctoral dissertation, Queensland University of Technology, Brisbane, Australia. Accessed at http://eprints.qut.edu.au/64452/1/Janelle_Wills_Thesis.pdf on September 22, 2020.

Wills, J. (2018, August). *Optimising listening conditions and classroom communications in collaborative learning environments: "Activate" technology case study*. Accessed at https://www.hearandlearn.com.au/wp-content/uploads/pdf/Hear-and-Learn-Janelle-Wills-Activate-Case-Study-Report.pdf on September 22, 2020.

Winsler, A., Fernyhough, C., & Montero, I. (2009). *Private speech, executive functioning, and the development of verbal self-regulation*. New York: Cambridge University Press.

World Wildlife Fund. (n.d.). *Plains bison*. Accessed at https://www.worldwildlife.org/species/plains-bison on October 26, 2020.

Wormeli, R. (2009). *Metaphors and analogies: Power tools for teaching any subject*. Portland, ME: Stenhouse.

Wormeli, R., & Stafford, D. (2018). *Summarization in any subject: 60 innovative, tech-infused strategies for deeper student learning* (2nd ed.). Alexandria, VA: Association for Supervision and Curriculum Development.

Zimmerman, B. J. (2002). Becoming a self-regulated learner: An overview. *Theory Into Practice*, *41*(2), 64–70. Accessed at https://doi.org/10.1207/s15430421tip4102_2 on September 22, 2020.

# INDEX

# D



# E

# F



# G

## H



## I



## J



## K



## L



## M

# U



# V



# W



# Y



# Z

**Metacognition**
***Robin J. Fogarty and Brian M. Pete***
Empower your students to become mindful, reflective, and proficient thinkers and problem solvers. In Metacognition, authors Robin J. Fogarty and Brian M. Pete provide a practical framework to nurture these essential skills in every learner.
**BKB008**

**The Agile Learner**
***James Anderson***
Empower your students to become confident learners in a world of constant change. In The Agile Learner, author James Anderson draws from ample research to detail the dispositions, skills, and behaviors every student needs for lifelong success.
**BKB011**

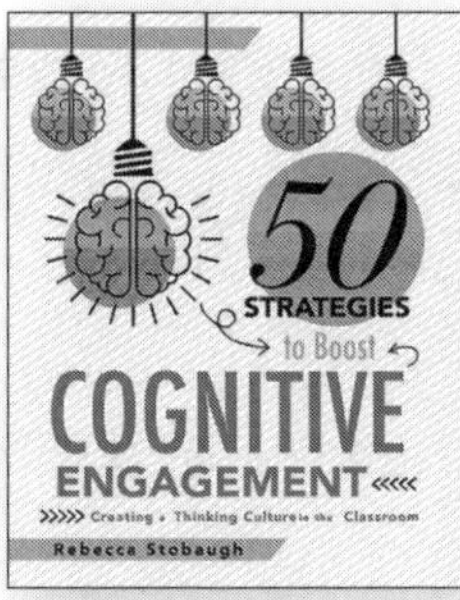


**Fifty Strategies to Boost Cognitive Engagement**
***Rebecca Stobaugh***
Transform your classroom from one of passive knowledge consumption to one of active engagement. In this well-researched book, Rebecca Stobaugh shares 50 strategies for building a thinking culture that emphasizes essential 21st century skills—from critical thinking and problem-solving to teamwork and creativity.
**BKF894**

**Problems-First Learning**
***Ted McCain***
Discover a compelling alternative to traditional teaching practices: the problems-first instructional method. Using this method, you will fully engage students by first introducing a problem and then empowering learners to solve it using creativity, collaboration, and other essential skills.
**BKF944**

Solution Tree | Press 

Visit SolutionTree.com or call 800.733.6786 to order.